D0891471

LOOKING AT AMERICA

LOOKING AT AMERICA

BY

BERNARD DRACHMAN

Essay Index Reprint Series

originally published by

G. P. PUTNAM'S SONS

 BOOKS FOR LIBRARIES PRESS
FREEPORT, NEW YORK

First Published 1934
Reprinted 1970

STANDARD BOOK NUMBER:
8369-1499-6

LIBRARY OF CONGRESS CATALOG CARD NUMBER:
76-107696

PRINTED IN THE UNITED STATES OF AMERICA

To
H. L. D.
A Loving and Understanding Companion
My Wife

CONTENTS

CONTENTS

FOREWORD

AMERICA, by which term in this treatise is mainly to be understood the United States of North America, is today unquestionably the greatest nation and the mightiest power in the world. This statement, the correctness of which is not and cannot be affected by the economic depression prevailing since 1929 which is, by its very nature, a temporary condition, is not the mere boastful utterance of one whose good fortune it is to be a native of this most favored portion of the earth but is a simple conclusion drawn from an impartial examination of the facts. In mere consideration of population or territorial extent there are nations which surpass the United States. In number of inhabitants it occupies the fourth, in territorial extent the third place among the nations of the world.

But its vast wealth, produced by the wonderful industrial and commercial activity and inventive talent of its citizens and its tremendous physical power, the result of their virile and courageous character, easily give it economic and political, that is, the real preëminence among the nations of earth. But whoever would say that all is well with America would be very grossly in error. In common with all other human organizations the American nation has its problems to solve, upon the correct solution of which the ultimate happiness and well being of its people depend. Because of the outstanding greatness of America the correct solution of these problems is of exceptional importance, not only to itself but to all the world.

Most of these problems have been considered singly or individually many times by many thinkers and writers and from many varying points of view. But there is not, as far as the present writer is aware, any comprehensive treatise which considers them from a broad and general viewpoint,

9

which deals with them as a totality, as constituent parts or elements of the great, all-embracing problem or question "What is America? What should it be? What steps or actions are called for in order to make America conform to its principles and ideals, to cause it to be true to itself?" And yet such a broad and comprehensive survey of all the conditions and principles which enter into the making of America as a political, economic and cultural unit is a vital necessity of true Americanism. The subjects of a monarchy or dictatorship can get along very well without any particular knowledge of the governmental system under which they live. Their thinking is done for them by others, all they need do is to pay and to obey. Not so the citizens of a free republic such as America. Every American needs to know the nature and the character of the nation into which he has been born or adopted, the varied possibilities inherent in this vast and blessed continent, the desires and hopes which lived in the minds of the founders of the Republic and the ideals which their descendants and successors should strive to attain, in order to perform intelligently his part in shaping the future of this exceptionally important segment of humanity. This knowledge and understanding are essential and indispensable to the making of a full and completely competent American citizen. Without them he is but a torso, a mutilated fragment of citizenship.

It is because so many Americans are lacking in this broad understanding of their own nation, because they regard matters which are of the deepest concern to the entire people, from the narrow and restricted viewpoints of the ideas, beliefs, prejudices and interests of particular groups, classes or sections that so much improper and mischievous legislation is constantly enacted and that such misunderstandings and antagonisms exist between various elements of the nation although the fact that they are all Americans should unite them on all fundamental questions of national significance.

It will be the effort of this work to give this comprehensive view of America, to study it as a whole and to seek a solution of the individual problems not merely from the

viewpoint of their individual importance but from that of
their importance as constituent factors of the entire great
edifice of Americanism. In this effort the writer will strive
to be governed and influenced by no narrow considerations
of the views or interests of any one group of Americans, as
little by those of his own particular group as by those of
any other, but only by that which is in the truest and most
universal sense American and in most genuine harmony
with the principles of historical and ideal Americanism and
promotive, as he sees it, of the welfare of the American
nation as a whole.

In concluding this foreword attention is called to two
matters the understanding of which is essential to a proper
concept of the scope of this work. First, the writer has
made no attempt to deal with all the problems which
America is called upon to solve. That would be a task
beyond the powers of any one man and would require a
library for its adequate fulfillment rather than one book.
The problems with which this book deals are those which
have to do with the nature and essence of Americanism,
through the solution of which in one way or another the
character of the nation is influenced. It does not concern
itself with those numerous questions of policy or legislation
which have no special American implication but are common to practically all civilized nations. Second, the writer
makes no pretense to absolute knowledge and does not claim
that the solutions which he has suggested are guaranteed
fully adequate and conclusive and the best that can be proposed. He does claim that he has read considerably and
reflected earnestly upon these questions, so profoundly important to his beloved native land, and that the solutions
suggested are the fruit of sincere investigation and cogita-
tion. If better and more satisfactory solutions can be proposed none will rejoice more than he. The chief purpose
of this book is to stir up thought and the writer is convinced that once the American people devotes its thought
to the consideration of these fundamental problems it will
solve them all in an adequate, satisfactory and truly American way.

AMERICA

A Study of Its Problems and Their Solution

CHAPTER FIRST

THE SIGNIFICANCE OF AMERICA IN WORLD HISTORY

It is a truism that the discovery of America is epochal in the history of the world. With America there was given to mankind, particularly to the Caucasian race, the most precious gift it has ever received. Other portions of the earth's surface have since then been discovered by intrepid explorers, and gone over into the possession of various European nations, notably Australasia and the greater part of the vast African continent, but none of them have had the significance for, or exercised an influence upon, the destinies of mankind comparable to that of America. Mankind showed that it sensed this exceptional importance of America by the designation which it gave it "The New World," that is to say, a region not only previously unknown but also in which hitherto non-existent and apparently unrealizable conditions of human happiness and well being could and should prevail. America presented itself to the wondering gaze of humanity as a fairy-land of unlimited possibilities and opportunities. These opportunities were of a double nature, material or economic and social or political. Its vast expanse of territory, nearly all of it fertile and productive, favored mainly with an equable and temperate climate and inhabited only by small and scattered aboriginal tribes, marked it as the predestined home of a great civilized population, while its very newness and rawness, leaving it free and unhampered by the chains of inherited tyrannies and the overwhelming weight of traditional bigotries, hatreds and blunders made it possible for the new nation to be born on its soil to profit by the errors of the past and to so regulate its governmental system as to insure to all its citizens the priceless blessings of genuine and permanent liberty and true social and political

15

justice. Mankind in the Middle Ages, groaning under the accumulated and intolerable burdens of centuries of absolutism and feudalism, weary unto death of a social system under which no man could call his soul his own and the overwhelming bulk of the people were forced to vegetate in squalid hovels with hardly enough of the necessaries of life to maintain the vital spark in their wretched bodies while their temporal and spiritual lords and masters reveled in their gaudy palaces in unbridled feasts and banquets, looked towards the newly discovered hemisphere with eager anticipation of better things, hoping with an intense longing that there would be fulfilled therein the Divine assurance given to ancient Israel when about to enter into the Promised Land, "And thou shalt eat and be satisfied and shalt bless the Lord thy God for the good land which He gave unto thee." Since its discovery in the fifteenth century an unceasing stream of emigrants from the Old World has poured upon the shores of America, changing it in the course of little more than four centuries from an almost uninhabited wilderness to a mighty and highly civilized empire with a population of approximately one hundred and twenty-three million souls.* All of those millions who thus tore themselves up from their native roots and braved the perils of what was then the trackless wastes of the Atlantic Ocean in order to find new homes in the distant west were actuated by the one or the other of two motives, either to find relief from economic difficulties and sufferings which had grown unendurable or to obtain the precious meed of political and religious liberty. The economic motive was perhaps the impelling force in the case of the greater number but the proportion of those who were driven by no material compulsion but whose reason for desiring to settle in the New World was because they loved political and religious liberty and desired to dwell in communities of free citizens and be privileged to worship God in accordance with the dictates of their consciences, was very large indeed. Of these latter were the Puritan Pilgrim fathers, the Huguenots, the Waldenses, the Jews and the

* United States Census of 1930.

political refugees, notably those of Central Europe in the middle of the nineteenth century. America accepted them gladly and for many decades proudly proclaimed itself "The refuge of the downtrodden and oppressed of all lands." America thus became another name for an opportunity of happiness for mankind. On the whole it fulfilled this mission most excellently and brought hitherto unknown joy and contentment in life to many millions of human beings. There were, it is true, dark shadows on this otherwise bright picture. Negro slavery, introduced into this country through the unholy greed and lust for gain of some of the early settlers, was perhaps the worst and most repulsive of these shadows. It was in utter contradiction to the concepts of human liberty and personal human dignity for which America otherwise stood and it caused problems of unusual gravity and difficulty to arise in the land, for which the nation has not yet found an adequate solution. Some of the colonies, too, had illiberal and bigoted laws imposing disabilities upon dissenters from the religion of the majority. But the Revolutionary War and the adoption of the Constitution made an end of legal religious discriminations and the Civil War ended human slavery on American soil. Since the conclusion of that terrible struggle between brothers, America has been fit soil for the development of the highest type of a free and happy commonwealth. Has this greatly to be desired result been actually attained? Is the America of today really the land of human liberty and equality, of general happiness and prosperity, of just and righteous laws and institutions for which its exceptional possibilities and opportunities so eminently fit it? To consider and to find, if possible, answers to these questions will be the task of the following chapters, in which the main problems which affect contemporary America will be carefully and impartially examined from the viewpoint of their relation to the great American ideal, the establishment upon this continent of a free and happy nation.

CHAPTER SECOND

HAVE AMERICA'S OPPORTUNITIES BEEN REALIZED?

HAVING seen America as the land of opportunity, as the place where practically unlimited possibilities existed for the development of ideal conditions of liberty and happiness for a very great and important segment of the human race, we must now take up the consideration of the questions with which the previous chapter concluded: "Have these possibilities and opportunities been realized? Is America the land of ideal liberty and happiness?"

A superficial contemplation of American conditions might incline us to answer in the affirmative. Traveling through this broad continent from coast to coast we can see beautiful, well kept cities and towns, their streets thronged by well clothed, apparently care-free multitudes, we can see many palatial mansions, luxurious hotels and smoking factory chimneys, the visible evidences of wealth and prosperity. But if we are not satisfied with mere superficial observation, if we desire to base our judgment on a searching examination into conditions so as to know how they actually are, we will speedily realize the truth of the saying "Not all that glitters is gold." America is very far from being the ideal home of a free, contented and prosperous people, it is anything but a Utopia. In the America of today complete political and social equality, such as should prevail in a real democracy, do not exist; religious and intellectual liberty are not unquestioned and even material well-being, based upon economic prosperity, is, and was, already before the great depression, among broad masses of the population, sadly lacking. Great numbers are without proper cultural advantages. In various parts of the land are population groups whose culture level is far lower than that upon which, as citizens of a free and en-

18

lightened republic, they should stand. Crime prevails to a most alarming extent. From the underworld comes forth a host of hardened criminals, robbers, kidnappers and murderers, to despoil and terrorize the community. In every one of the great cities in which the North American continent is so rich there are foul and noisome slums in which multitudes dwell in misery and filth. It is true that philanthropic individuals and organizations strive manfully and with a certain measure of success to alleviate these conditions but it cannot truthfully be claimed that they have been able to make much impression upon the tremendous mass of wretchedness and unsavoriness. As for political equality that exists in theory but not in actuality. Theoretically one American citizen is as good as any other and has the same power to influence legislation and hence the institutions and destiny of the republic. Actually the greatest inequalities exist. Indeed the American governmental system seems unable to prevent such inequalities. In the State of New York, for instance, the constitution deliberately provides that the urban population shall never prevail over the rural.* The constitution of the state of New York directly ordains that the City of New York, no matter how large its population may become, shall never have more than half of the members of the State Assembly. This means that the rights, liberties and property of the people of the City of New York are practically at the mercy of the "Up Staters" although the population of the metropolis comprises more than half of the entire population of the state. At best it means that a minority of the citizens can rule over the majority and prevent it from obtaining the legislation it desires. Again the system of election of members of the Senate of the United States produces great inequality. Each state is entitled to two Senators without consideration of population. Under this system, the State of Arizona with a few paltry thousands of inhabitants has the same representation and influence

* From the viewpoint of this statement the people of the towns and cities outside of the main city are classed as rural as their ideology and sympathies are those of the rural population.

in the Senate as the State of New York with a population of approximately twelve millions.

The original method of selecting the Senate as ordained by the Constitution was even more undemocratic than that at present prevailing. The Senators were to be chosen by the Legislatures of the states but the people had no voice in their selection. This was subsequently modified by amendment, the seventeenth, which provided that they should be chosen by popular vote. This removed the most undemocratic feature by enabling the people to decide who should represent them in the Senate. But the fundamental inequality of assigning the same number of Senators to all states alike, whether great or small, still remains. A flagrant example of great injustice brought about under the forms of popular government was the Prohibition amendment to the Constitution. That the intentions of those whose efforts brought about the adoption of this extraordinary addition to the basic law of the land were good, the abolition of the drink evil and the promotion of temperance, is freely admitted, but the manner in which the attainment of these desirable ends was sought by the Prohibition amendment and the Volstead law was absolutely undemocratic and in utter contradiction to the fundamental concepts of human liberty. If liberty means anything it means that men, as long as they do not inflict direct injury upon their fellow men, shall be free to follow their own inclinations and convictions, that they shall not be troubled or molested in regard to matters of private concern and, in particular, that the state shall not dictate to them what clothes they should wear, what food or beverages they should eat or drink or what form of religion they should profess. That in a land which proclaims as its fundamental principle that "all men are created equal and equally entitled to life, liberty and the pursuit of happiness" it should be possible for a woman to be sentenced to life imprisonment for selling a pint of intoxicating liquor or for a man to be shot dead on the mere suspicion of transporting intoxicating liquor—a suspicion which turned out to be unfounded—is so glaringly wrong and illogical as to be almost unbelievable. Yet these are only two of the many hundreds of outrageous violations of elementary human rights which took place under this extraordinary piece of legislation.

It must also be pointed out that, apart from the unintended wrongs and injustices resulting from ill advised legislation, much that is intrinsically wrong, harsh and cruel, in a word, fundamentally un-American, is done in consequence of the hatreds, passions and prejudices of a great section of the population against other sections. With sorrow a true, liberty loving American, devoted to the traditional principles of his nation, must confess that there is probably no country on the face of the globe, among those that are considered enlightened, where bigotry, fanaticism, racial and religious prejudices, in short, all narrow and illiberal sentiments, prevail to the extent that they do in the supposed haven of liberty, the United States of America. How otherwise would it be possible for an organization, the Ku Klux Klan, to exist and to enroll hundreds of thousands, if not millions, in its ranks, which denies the appellation "American" to all except those who are native born, white and Protestants and which has written upon its banners irreconcilable hostility to the foreign born, the Negro and the adherents of the Catholic and Jewish faiths.* The intensity of this fanaticism was clearly shown in the Presidential election of 1928 when Alfred E. Smith, a man of exceptional intellect and governmental ability, who had to his credit three brilliant terms as Governor of the State of New York and upon whose character not even a breath of suspicion could rest, was overwhelmingly defeated largely, if not entirely, because he, Smith, was a member of the Catholic church. The fact that this action was equivalent to serving notice upon the approximately twenty millions of Catholic citizens, an element which had never failed in patriotic duty and had rendered conspicuous service to the nation, that they are but citizens of an inferior grade and that none of them can ever hope to fill the highest

---

* At the present time (1934) there exists also another organization "The Silver Shirts of America" which proclaims as its platform virulent antagonism to Jews.

position in the republic was apparently either overlooked or deliberately intended by the mass of voters.

The antipathy to the Negro on the part of great sections of the white population is most intense. To the dark skinned inhabitant of America no form of social recognition is accorded, hotels and restaurants either refuse to serve him or relegate him to some obscure corner, even conversation with him is restricted to that which is unavoidably necessary and should he begin to settle in a new neighborhood the majority of white inhabitants will leave precipitously and seek abodes elsewhere. He is treated by those who feel this antipathy as though he were hardly human, as though his very presence were contamination. How contrary this is to the very concept of human dignity needs no special statement.

Anti-Jewish prejudice, that bane of old Europe, notably of present-day Germany, is also present in America to a most uncomfortable extent. Though kept largely under cover many indications reveal its presence to the attentive observer. Into the charmed circles of the four hundred the Jew finds no entrance, fashionable hotels and clubs desire no Jewish patrons or members, Jewish would-be students of medical and other colleges are often unable to secure admission to American institutions and must go abroad in order to continue their studies. Worst of all, systematic discrimination against Jewish applicants for employment is practiced by many business establishments—although they welcome Jewish customers—and many Jewish youths and maidens find it difficult, if not impossible, because of their faith or race, to earn a living.

Nor are the Negroes, the Catholics and the Jews the only classes which suffer from the prejudice and antipathy of the intolerant elements of the American population. Almost all those of foreign origin are the victims of these hostile sentiments. Italians, Hungarians, Mexicans and Chinese are singled out for especial dislike, which shows itself in the use of contemptuous designations, "Wops" or "Dagos" for Italians, "Hunks" for Hungarians, "Greasers" for Mexicans and "Chinks" for Chinese. Three quarters of a century ago when the great Irish immigration took place they too were the victims of great antipathy and were referred to as "Micks." In recent years this antipathy seems to have died down and the Irish-Americans are regarded more or less as integral parts of the American people.

The contemplation of all these conditions forces us to the regretful conclusion that in many ways the great experiment begun so hopefully on this vast continent has not succeeded as it should, that America cannot unqualifiedly be described as a land of general prosperity, or in which the three ideals of the French Revolution, liberty, equality and fraternity, prevail. There are much suffering and poverty among broad masses of the American population, much that is wrong and undemocratic takes place with the sanction of law, many bitter hatreds and antipathies separate the people of America and make them anything but a united band of brothers. Can these evils be remedied? Can America be lifted out of the slough of despond, of sufferings, injustice, hatreds and antipathies into which it has fallen and raised to the ideal heights of happiness, righteousness, liberty and brotherhood for which it seemed predestined? To investigate these questions will be the task of the ensuing chapters.

CHAPTER THIRD

THE PROBLEM OF PREJUDICE

THE problems which need solution in order that America should be the home of a prosperous, free and united people are numerous and varied. Each of them deserves and needs special treatment and earnest and thorough consideration in order that the best possible solution be found. Overshadowing all others in importance and difficulty is the problem of how to remove the hatreds and antipathies which now divide the population of the United States into unfriendly and unsympathetic groups and to instill into their hearts the feelings of genuine national cohesion, to make them into a real band of brothers. This shall, therefore, be the first problem here considered. Before taking up the consideration of this problem it must be premised that it is one of extraordinary difficulty, that it is in fact the most puzzling and complicated problem of this nature faced by any nation in the world. It is not merely that the constituent elements of the American population are of such extraordinary racial diversity that it has been not inaptly called an ethnological curio cabinet. Other nations have among their subjects or citizens various peoples or ethnic elements. The British and French empires, for instance, extend their sway over a great number of the most diverse peoples and races. The former Austro-Hungarian empire included among its subjects upwards of twenty different peoples and in the great expanse of Russia and its Asiatic dominions there dwell more than a hundred differing ethnic groups. But in none of these is the problem at all comparable to that of America. In all of these lands or empires the various peoples belong to the original inhabitants, they dwell mainly in compact settlements in certain well defined regions in which their ancestors had their homes and in which their varying languages and cultures are maintained traditionally.* In this manner the contact and the resulting friction between the various groups is greatly lessened, in some instances to such an extent as to be almost non-existent. The historical development of America has brought about diametrically opposite conditions. The various ethnic elements which emigrated to this continent have penetrated into its most remote regions and established their homes everywhere on its broad surface. Wherever one dwells in America one cannot expect, broadly speaking, to find oneself only in the midst of one's own ethnic class but must be reconciled to an environment of many diverse types and races. Under these conditions, unless a way be found to make an end of these prejudices and antagonisms, they must naturally increase in intensity and virulence, as the numbers of the various racial and religious elements grow and the occasions of their social and economic contact increase in frequency, until they become a serious difficulty in American life and a real danger to the republic. What could be more undesirable and, indeed, disastrous to the great American experiment than that the population of this vast continent should be split into antagonistic groups, cordially detesting and abominating each other, and to whom the common appellation of American has no unifying significance and is utterly devoid of comforting and satisfying force. To the writer it seems that there is a simple and effective remedy for this most deplorable evil but which will require much courage and resolution and unswerving devotion to the basic principles of true Americanism for its successful application. Briefly stated it is genuine justice and fairness to all inhabitants of the land, avoidance of all unfair restrictions upon or discriminations against any one because

* In the old Austro-Hungarian empire, for instance, the Germans, the Poles and the Magyars had in the main clearly marked, separate territories. Where various races dwelt together, as Germans and Czechs in Bohemia, Poles and Ruthenians in Galicia, it must indeed be admitted there was invariably much tension and many conflicts.

of race, religion or color, full and unqualified according of all civic, political and economic rights to all Americans without other requirement than that they be law-abiding citizens and true patriots. The leaders of thought in America should emphatically proclaim and uphold the doctrine that there are no degrees and differences in American citizenship, that possession of that inestimable privilege means admission to a genuine brother band, the rights and immunities of every member of which are the care and the concern of all.

This does not imply unjustifiable intrusion into the domain of the private and the personal, does not mean the forcible yoking together of unsympathetic and inharmonious individuals, nor the suppression of natural and inevitable aversions and equally natural groupings and alignments. These are innate rights of free men in a free state. No man may properly be compelled to marry a person whom he does not desire nor receive as guest in his house a person who is unwelcome to him or to profess a faith in which he does not believe nor can he be prevented from making his own choice in these and similar matters. But living in one land with many persons of differing kinds he may be properly inhibited, and of his own volition should refrain, from following lines of action directed against certain classes as a whole and which tend to place them in a position of inferiority in the state and to deprive them of the right to life, liberty and happiness accorded by true American doctrine to all. In other words social and family matters should be determined by the unrestricted choice of the individual but in questions which concern the human welfare and the civic, political and economic status of the various elements of the American population these narrower viewpoints should be energetically thrust aside and no discriminations tolerated which might work injury to any class of American citizens. If an individual belonging to a certain group does not wish to come into social contact with individuals belonging to another group let him refrain from doing so; if, for instance, the members of the Four Hundred prefer the company of European nobility to that of their fellow Americans let them follow their own inclinations in the matter. These and similar things are, after all, of purely private concern and without national or general significance. But no American should be refused employment or political preferment, or should find opportunities to earn his living denied or the gates of advancement in life barred because of his faith or race, and certainly no inhabitant of the land should be treated as a Pariah, excluded from hotels and free choice of residence and subjected to countless annoyances and humiliations because of his physical type and the color of his skin. These are matters which go to the very root of our conception of the state and its relation to its citizens. They must be settled right or the nation may be shaken to its very foundations.

It is too late now to say, as many do, that it was wrong on the part of our predecessors in America to permit the development of so heterogeneous a population, that they should have forbidden the importation of the natives of Africa to serve as slaves in America, that they should have restricted free immigration to those European elements most closely akin and most easily assimilable to the Anglo-Saxon colonial stock. Wisely or foolishly, properly or improperly, the early Americans made their choice and adopted policies which brought about the development of the highly diversified population which today inhabits these United States. It is up to contemporaneous Americans to devise methods of uniting these variegated elements and causing them to dwell together in peace and harmony, in mutual respect and understanding. How to do this will be the subject of the next chapter.

CHAPTER FOURTH

THE PROBLEM OF AMERICAN NATIONALITY

In order to find a true and adequate solution for the problem of American nationality we must be clear as to what we are to understand by the term "nation." The term is far from being definite and explicit. There are various contradictory interpretations, not necessarily mutually exclusive, as there is good authority for the use of each of them. There is the racial or ethnic concept which would limit membership in a nation to those of the same blood and descent whether living in one country and speaking the same language or scattered in various territories and employing diverse vernaculars. Thus the Japanese are said to regard all persons of Japanese descent as Japanese, even if they dwell outside of the borders of the Japanese empire and have adopted, as is the case with some of their emigrant groups, the speech of other peoples. This is the case, to a great extent, also in Europe. Fully a third of the people of German descent, for instance, dwell in non-Germanic lands, but are considered by their brethren in the Fatherland and largely by themselves, as of German nationality.* It is a truism that the same is the case with the Jews, as far as these latter can be considered a national entity. Almost twenty centuries have elapsed since the Jews were driven from their national home in Palestine and scattered all over the known world. A mere fragment of the race, less than three hundred thousand out of approximately seventeen million dwell at present in their ancient land and most of them have but a slight acquaintance with their ancestral tongue,

* This concept of nationality is most strongly emphasized by the present (1933-34) Nazi government of Germany, which considers the term "German" (Deutscher) as applicable in the fullest sense only to persons of Germanic descent.

28

the Hebrew, yet a strong national consciousness exists
among them and they are customarily regarded also by
non-Jews as a nation. There is the cultural and linguistic
concept of nationality. According to this concept persons
of the same culture and speaking the same language are to
be considered members of the same nation, without regard
to their ethnic origin. This view is responsible for the
attempts of various nations to assimilate the alien groups
in their midst. In accordance with this concept of nationality the French seek to Gallicize, the Hungarians to Mag-
yarize and the Czechs to Czechize the alien elements in
their respective countries by forcing them to adopt the culture and language of the predominant groups. There is,
lastly, the purely political and geographical concept of nationality which holds that all persons born or resident in a
certain territory and subject to the government of that
territory are members of the nation which holds sway over
that region. There are varying shades of difference in these
concepts and they sometimes intermingle curiously, but
their fundamental and essential characteristics are as outlined above. The third mentioned concept of nationality,
the political and geographical, is the one legally prevalent
in the United States of America. American law distinctly
establishes the principle that any person born on American
soil or any person born in a foreign land, who has been
accepted by naturalization into American citizenship, is an
American citizen and, therefore, a member of the American
nation. This is the broadest and fairest possible conception of American nationality. It is absolutely free from
racial, religious or cultural limitations of any kind, it places
membership in the American nation on the broad basis of
citizenship, native or adopted, in the republic and does not
admit of any distinction between the various groups of
citizens. Our ancestors in America were very wise and
well advised when they adopted this broad definition of
citizenship. It is the one concept which can unite the
diverse elements of the American population into one harmonious whole and inspire them with pride in and love and
devotion to their common country. It not only permits but

inspires and encourages the development of a genuine and most enthusiastic American patriotism. If upheld and promulgated honestly, sincerely and consistently it would completely solve the problem of the attainment of a genuine, united American national sentiment or, in other words, would bring about the realization of the ideal "unity without uniformity."

Unfortunately, powerful elements exist in this country which are entirely out of sympathy with and strenuously opposed to this beautiful and legally accepted concept of Americanism. These elements are invariably found either among the Americans of English origin or those of other origin who have become so completely intermingled and amalgamated with the English-descended stock that they have lost all sympathy with or even knowledge of the peoples to whom their ancestors belonged. These Anglo-Americans hold to the view that they have the exclusive right to be called Americans and that American citizens of other racial origin, especially if the date of their arrival in this country be a few years or decades later than that of the earliest English settlers are, essentially, if not legally, aliens. The basis for this misconception is undoubtedly the historical fact that a large proportion, perhaps the majority, of the early immigrants to this land were of English stock and that the English language is its national tongue. But this historical fact gives no justification for the idea that the English-descended inhabitants of America have any greater intrinsic right to be considered Americans than the people of other ethnic origin. People of other nationality participated largely in the early colonization of the American continent. The Dutch were the first to settle in New York—New York City was originally Niew Amsterdam—and parts of New Jersey; the French settled in large numbers in the Carolinas and Louisiana and the Germans formed important colonies in many parts of the territory of the original thirteen states, especially in Pennsylvania where their language was at one time, it is said, spoken by so large a proportion of the population that the proposal was seriously considered of making it, the German, the official language of the state. Jews were present also very early among the people of New York. That, under these circumstances, the English stamp was impressed upon the young nation and the English idiom became its official speech is to be attributed partly to favorable historical conditions and partly also to the undoubtedly more forceful character of the English stock. These facts do not, however, in any way entitle the English-descended Americans to be considered as in any special manner or in any higher degree American than the Americans of any other ethnic origin. When the Thirteen Colonies sundered their connection with the British Empire they severed completely every political bond which had formerly united them to that empire; they established an entirely independent nation upon this continent, membership in which was in no way dependent upon British descent but was open to persons of the most various national origin, all of whom became, in the eyes of the law, Americans of exactly the same kind and to the same degree. It is true that the English language and culture were so firmly established in the United States that they became *eo ipso* the language and the culture of the American nation, or the basis thereof, but that, as has already been stated, was a matter of historic happening which did not, in the least, carry the implication that American nationality is, in any way, dependent upon English descent.

Immediately after obtaining the status of independence the American people showed as emphatically as they possibly could their rejection of the theory of English-descended or Anglo-Saxon Americanism by opening their vast continent to the immigration of the people of all lands without distinction of race or religion. They desired to be Americans, not Anglo-Americans or, as the unforgettable Theodore Roosevelt so aptly phrased it, hyphenated Americans.* This is the spirit in which the question of American nationality should be viewed today by all true Americans,

---

* This liberal immigration policy was afterwards, as is known, greatly restricted. Beginning with the closing part of the nineteenth century, the immigration of all Mongolian peoples was prohibited

who desire that their country should possess a genuine
national character of its own, independent of and uninfluenced, except culturally and linguistically, by the national origin of any section of its population, no matter
how strong numerically this might be. The fact must never
be left out of consideration that the people of this country,
with the exception of the comparatively insignificant group
of aboriginal descent, the so-called American Indians, are
an immigrant people, either themselves immigrants or the
descendants of immigrants, and that no one element in the
population should endeavor to domineer over the others or
to arrogate to itself hegemonic status in the nation which
all have coöperated in calling into being. As a matter of
fact such streams of non-English blood have flowed into
the land, under the influence of upwards of a century of a
generous, unquestioningly liberal "open door" immigration
policy, that the Anglo-Saxon element no longer constitutes
anything like an overwhelming majority of the population,
indeed, in all probability, does not constitute a majority at
all.* From a truly American point of view there is, of
course, nothing deplorable in this state of affairs. It merely
emphasizes the fact, already recognized by our law, that
American nationality is not racial, but purely political and
geographical, that the people of this country are neither
Anglo-Americans nor any other species of hyphenates, but
Americans in the broadest and most universal sense of that
term. The Ku Klux Klan concept of Americanism, which
would limit it to native-born white persons of Protestant

and at present all immigration is greatly restricted. But this has
been done for other reasons. Mongolian immigration was forbidden
because it threatened with its swarming millions, completely to
overflow the country and utterly change its civilization. The present
restriction is due to economic depression. In neither case has the
action been due to a desire to preserve the Anglo-Saxon character
of the American people.

* Government statistics classify the population as white and
colored, but do not make any distinctions as regards the ethnic origins
of the whites. It is, however, undeniable that everywhere throughout the country, even in New England, the non-Anglo-Saxon elements are strongly represented and in many sections are a majority
of the white population.

faith and, by inference if not by explicit statement, to those of Anglo-Saxon or Nordic descent, is abhorrent and utterly contradictory to the true significance thereof. It should be the effort of every truly patriotic American to oppose with all his force this shameful misconception of the significance of our national designation and to uphold with equal energy the true, broad and generous, and eminently fair and just interpretation of the term as embracing all native inhabitants of the land and all who have been received into the brotherhood of American citizenship. When this true concept of American nationality becomes so generally recognized and so firmly established as to preclude the possibility of successful opposition or antagonism, it will be a source of unparalleled blessing to our great nation. It will banish all antagonisms and hatreds from our midst and unite all elements of our vast population in the closest bonds of mutual respect and affection, it will add strength and potency to all our national undertakings and make America beyond cavil or peradventure the mightiest and most respected nation upon the face of the earth.

CHAPTER FIFTH

THE PROBLEM OF THE NEGRO

THE existence of a great Negro population, approximately twelve millions,* in the United States of America, furnishes an acid test of the possibility of the practical carrying out of the principles of American nationality laid down in the previous chapter.

Let us premise by at once admitting that it is a problem of extraordinary difficulty, perhaps the most difficult problem by which America is faced, certainly the most difficult of the problems arising from the diversity of the ethnic origins of its population. It is a most unusual problem. No other occidental nation has any similar problem of even approximate difficulty to solve. Even France, the majority of the population of whose colonial empire is composed of Negroes, has comparatively few of the black race resident upon the soil of its national home land, of European France. The extraordinary difficulty of the problem is primarily due to the fact that its cause, the difference of color and racial type between the Negro and the Caucasian race, which constitutes the overwhelming majority of the population of the country,** is irremovable and unalterable. While there is some scientific basis for the view that the color of the human skin is a result of climatic influence and that centuries of subjection to a temperate climate will lighten the complexion of a dark race, just as, conversely, centuries of exposure to the rays of a tropical sun will darken the skin of a white race, the process is necessarily too slow to be of any importance in the settle-

* The census of 1930 gives the number of the Negro population of the United States as 11,891,143.

** The census of 1930 gives the white population of the United States as 108,864,207 out of a total population of 122,775,045.

ment of a present-day problem. Human nature being what
it is, with its instinctive dislike of the different and its
instinctive resentment at the growth in numbers and power
of an unwanted and unwelcome element, there is nothing
at all surprising in the existence of an intense aversion to
the Negro on the part of a large section, if not all, of the
Caucasian majority of the population.* This aversion is
naturally increased and intensified if the disliked element
had originally been in a state of slavery and had been
liberated. With freedom there comes inevitably a claim
on the part of the former slaves of social and political
equality with the dominant element.

This claim is naturally—though, of course, not justly—
bitterly resented by the former owners and masters and,
combined with the rankling sense of financial loss caused
by the expropriation of what had formerly constituted a
valuable property, adds a note of personal embitterment to
the already existing antagonism caused by the difference
of race. Thus is explained the fact that, while aversion to
the Negro is general throughout the United States, it is
especially intense and bitter, amounting sometimes almost
to an obsession, in the Southern states. This antagonism
to the Negro shows itself in American life in many ways
and produces many unfortunate and dangerous results.
Race riots, bloody battles between members of the opposing
races, are not infrequent; lynchings, the slaying, occasionally in savage and barbarous forms of death, by infuriated
white mobs, of Negroes accused or suspected of crime, is
a matter of regular occurrence in the South and refusal on
the part of white workmen to labor side by side with
Negroes and efforts to expel Negroes from certain towns
or parts of towns are reported from time to time. One

---

* An exact analogy, probably the earliest known example of this
sentiment of antagonism to the unlike, is the revulsion of the
ancient Egyptians to the presence of a large Hebrew element in their
land, as narrated in the Bible. "And he (the King of Egypt) said
to his people, Behold, the people of the children of Israel are too
many and too mighty for us . . . let us deal wisely with them lest
they multiply. And they were grieved because of the children of
Israel." Exodus I, 9:11.

very unfortunate and harmful result of this anti-Negro sentiment is the fact that when Negroes begin to settle in a district of a city there is an immediate exodus of white residents with resulting depreciation of real estate values and immense financial losses. Thus, for instance, in the two greatest cities of the United States, New York and Chicago, entire large sections have suffered radical changes in consequence of this antagonism. Negroes began to seek homes in those districts, the majority of white inhabitants immediately left, the districts became thus Negro sections as other whites would not move in and the resulting losses amounted to many millions. The usual sentiment of the white inhabitants of the land over against their black-skinned neighbors is one of bewildered helplessness. They dislike and resent intensely the presence in their midst of a great multitude of an utterly different race but see no possibility of freeing themselves from that objectionable incubus. To most Americans the Negro seems—to use an apt Talmudic simile—like a bone stuck fast in the throat which can neither be swallowed nor ejected. That such a feeling does not add to the happiness of living in one's own native land is self-evident. And that such a feeling can only serve to intensify the difficulty of the problem of the mutual adjustment of the white and black races and must lead to many hostile clashes and much bitterness and animosity is equally self-evident. The peace and well-being of America require that this feeling be overcome or suppressed and that a *modus vivendi* be found through which the two races which the mysterious workings of historic causes have brought together on the soil of this continent shall be enabled to dwell together in good will and harmony and labor unitedly for the prosperity of their common country. The attainment of this goal should be made considerably easier by a consideration of the fact that the Negro is entirely free of responsibility for his presence in this land. If the existence of a black population in America is an objectionable and undesirable thing it is the white man and not the Negro who must bear the blame therefor. The swarthy natives of Africa dwelt

secluded since time immemorial in their primitive villages
in the remote recesses of the dark continent. They knew
nothing or next to nothing of the outer world and had no
thought of leaving their homes and migrating to the strange
and mysterious regions whence came the pale-faced
strangers and which, to their unsophisticated minds, appeared fraught with inconceivable dangers. It was the
cupidity and the greed for gold of the white race which tore
the simple and guileless Africans away from their ancestral
habitations and planted them in regions which otherwise
their feet would never have trodden. The African slave
trade is one of the cruelest and most inhuman misdeeds
which stain the pages of human history. The slave hunters,
armed to the teeth and in numbers sufficient to overcome
all resistance on the part of the unprepared and untrained
natives, would burst suddenly into the African villages,
would slay all who stood in their way, would seize all
whom they deemed suitable for labor, the strong men, the
younger women, youths, maidens and children, and would
drag them off to the ships which lay in wait off the coast.
There they would be thrown down into the hold, where they
would be kept confined until the vessel reached America.
The voyage, which in the days of sailing vessels lasted six
or seven weeks or longer, meant for the unhappy captives a
period of hellish suffering and agony, veritable tortures of
the damned. Crowded to the limit of capacity in the dark,
foul-smelling recesses of the ship, without decent food or
sanitary conveniences, deprived of the most elementary
human comforts, many of the involuntary passengers fell
gravely ill or perished. Often only half or a third of those
taken on board in Africa survived the voyage and reached
America. To the Portuguese attaches the disgrace of having introduced slavery into the New World. The first
recorded arrival of slaves in America took place in 1503
when Portuguese traders landed some African captives in
St. Domingo. In 1562 the English first took part in the
trade but soon surpassed all other nations in the extent of
their operations. From that time on the slave trade,

participated in by representatives of practically all
European nations, continued until the early part of the
nineteenth century, when the aroused sense of humanity
of the civilized world began to put an end to it. In 1834
all slaves in the British colonies were emancipated. In
1863, amidst the throes of the Civil War, slavery was abolished in the United States by proclamation of the war
President, Abraham Lincoln.

Slavery, as it existed in the United States, was, on the
whole, a cruel and inhuman institution. A certain proportion of the slave owners were kind hearted and humane persons who treated their slaves with gentleness and mercy,
but the number of those who looked upon their serfs as
mere chattels, who had no respect for the human quality in
them, who punished the slightest disobedience with savage
lashings and pursued the runaway slave with ferocious
bloodhounds was only too large. The dark pictures of
slavery conditions drawn by Harriet Beecher Stowe in her
famous novel, "Uncle Tom's Cabin," and by Charles
Dickens in "American Notes" are undoubtedly, in the main,
true and accurate and born of the righteous indignation
aroused in gentle and sympathetic souls by outrageous violations of elementary human rights.

It must also be admitted in fairness that the Negroes
conducted themselves well both during and after slavery,
that they have endured excellently the test both of servi-
tude and freedom. In slavery they were usually willing
and loyal servitors. Instances of deliberate idleness or rebellion are very rare. During the Civil War when their
masters and all white males were absent from the planta-
tions the Negro slaves obeyed their mistresses and cared
for the white women and children on the plantation with
touching fidelity.

And since emancipation the Negroes have striven
earnestly to fit themselves for the life of freemen. Hardly
had they been declared free than they showed their gratitude by enlisting in hundreds of thousands in the armies
of the United States, ready to lay down their lives for the
government which had delivered them from bondage and

conferred upon them the priceless gift of citizenship. From
that time to this a Negro contingent has never been lacking in the military forces of the country. Negro soldiers
have participated in the campaigns against the wild Indian
tribes of the West and in the wars of the republic which
occurred since their emancipation, the Spanish-American
War and the World War, and have invariably displayed in
preëminent measure the qualities typical of true soldiers,
courage, obedience and loyalty.

In the arts of peace the Negroes in the United States
have made extraordinary progress in the approximately
seventy years which have elapsed since their emancipation.
The erstwhile ignorant, illiterate and helpless blacks have
almost completely disappeared and a generation of self-
reliant and energetic men and women, well equipped to
take up the battle of life in a complex and highly civilized
community, has taken their place. Education, both general
and technical, has made gigantic strides among them and
a large number of individuals have acquired a high degree
of culture and pursue vocations requiring intensive training and intellectual ability. Negro clergymen, physicians,
lawyers, engineers and those of other skilled vocations are
so numerous as no longer to excite comment. Certain occupations are practically monopolized by Negroes, notably
those of hotel waiters and Pullman car porters, and are
carried out with conspicuous ability and efficiency.
Negroes have entered into all parts of the economic life
of the country and in some regions, especially in the South,
are actually indispensable.

It must also be admitted that the personal and racial
characteristics of the Negroes, as found in the United
States, are, on the whole, most pleasant and agreeable.
There are, of course, degraded and criminal elements, as
in all races, but the usual type of American Negro is peaceful, well behaved, clean, courteous, even deferential, hard
working and trustworthy. In certain fine and lofty human
tendencies the Negro shines conspicuous and has acquired
a standing and renown all his own. Many Negroes have
a strong musical sense and Negro melodies and minstrelsy

have a peculiar charm and appeal which have led great musicians, such as Dvorák, to rank them as the chief musical accomplishment of America The Negro is, too, as a rule, deeply religious, albeit his religion is frequently somewhat crude and primitive which, considering his origin and his history, is not at all surprising The spiritual and musical qualities of the Negro are interestingly combined in his religious chants or hymns, the so-called "Negro Spirituals," the quaint and touching melodies, phraseology and religious fervor of which have aroused admiration the world over.

A fair number of names indicate that the African race is not devoid of men of outstanding talent and ability. Frederick Douglass, the eminent scholar and statesman, Booker T. Washington, the distinguished educator, Paul Dunbar, the sweet singer of Afro-America, and Dr. Daniel H. Williams, distinguished surgeon of Chicago, are men who would honor any race.* Most of these men are not of pure African descent but that does not matter in this connection as a large proportion of those classed as Negroes in America have European and African blood intermingled in their veins. The so-called Negro is frequently racially more Caucasian than African. It may, no doubt, be justly claimed that the Negro is merely imitative, not original, that what he has acquired of the arts of civilization he has derived from the white men with whom he has come into contact but that he has made no contribution of his own to the sum total of human knowledge and accomplishment.

Granting that this is true, it does not alter the fact that he has made himself able to enter into the life of modern civilization quite as fully as the white races among whom it originated and attained its present high development and that he is able to bear its burdens and perform its tasks with excellent ability and success. The Negro in America bears his share of the responsibilities of organized society quite as well as his Caucasian neighbor, despite his (the

* Alexandre Dumas and Toussaint L'Ouverture are two Negroes eminent in French history, whose achievements have conferred world-wide honor upon their race.

Negro's) handicap of less than a century of escape from slavery and the latter's (the white man's) advantage of many centuries of civilized life. Indeed, no race is historically known to have made such a tremendous advance in civilization in such a comparatively short time as has the American Negro since his emancipation. He is emphatically not an African savage but just a good average American citizen with a black or dark skin. In fact the very absence of any special determinative forces in his African past has made him more amenable to the influences of his American environment and caused him to assimilate more closely to the American type than any other of the immigrant non-Anglo-Saxon peoples who have entered this land. He had little or nothing to contribute to American culture and for that very reason he was readier and more eager to absorb everything in that culture. In speech, in manners, in religion, in his views of life, in everything but color and racial appearance he has become a perfect Anglo-Saxon American.

The facts and considerations outlined above automatically answer the question, "How shall America solve the problem of the Negro? How shall the American nation deal with the vast colored population in its midst?" The answer is, With perfect justice and, even more, with friendship and kindness. Any other solution would not only be inconsistent with the traditional principles of American democracy but would ignore the heavy debt of moral obligation which the peculiar history of the Negro in his relation to America and the exceptional manner of his arrival on this continent have placed upon those responsible for that history and that arrival. The Negro should receive freely and ungrudgingly every civic and political right and should be kindly and sympathetically assisted to become fitted to take his full share in the life of America.* The law should protect him in his civic and political rights and see to it that he be not deprived of the usual comforts and

* Broad-minded and generous white Americans have recognized this obligation and given large sums for the improvement of the condition of the Negro in America. The Phelps-Stokes fund,

conveniences of civilized life because of prejudice against
his race and color.

Here arises the thorny problem of how to secure for the
Negro the enjoyment of these comforts and conveniences
since, in order to obtain them, it is usually or frequently
necessary to apply to white persons in possession or control of them and white public opinion is, as a rule, strongly
and, in the South, even intensely and bitterly, opposed to
the social recognition of the Negro involved therein. How,
for example, can the law insist that Negroes be accommo-
dated in hotels or restaurants or Pullman sleeping cars if
the bulk of the white patrons energetically rebel against
such association with them? The law is practically helpless
in matters of this kind. The case of Prohibition shows that
a really unpopular law cannot be enforced. But the law
can and should insist that public carriers make no distinctions between patrons and accommodate all applicants
equally though not necessarily in close association with
each other. It should not be possible for colored persons
traveling through the country to be unable to find a place
in which to pass the night, a restaurant in which to obtain
food to still their hunger or, if on a train, to be obliged to
remain up all night because no berth is available for them.
These are conditions unworthy of any truly civilized and
humane country and the great and generous American nation, whose warm heart pulsates with kindly emotions and
which is ready to respond to the cry of the afflicted and
the suffering everywhere on earth, should not tolerate such
conditions within the boundaries of its own land. It is not
to formal legislation that we must look for the remedying
of these evils. Laws can be evaded or nullified. But a
most determined effort should be made, if not to completely
remove, at least to soften and modify the great antipathy
which exists in the hearts of so many white Americans
against their colored fellow citizens and to implant therein
instead kind and friendly sentiments. It is a delicate and

founded by Miss Caroline Phelps-Stokes, supports liberally the
cause of Negro education in the South and Mr. Julius Rosenwald
has also been a generous benefactor of the race.

difficult task and speedy success cannot be expected. Inherited antipathies, in particular racial prejudices and
antagonisms, die hard. But the attempt must be made
for the sake of the fair name, and even more, for the sake
of the future peace and security of America. No well
wisher of America would desire to have reproduced in this
country the conditions of India where a perpetual war,
involving innumerable battles, much bloodshed and a constant disturbance of public security, goes on between Moslems and Hindus.

There need be no close social relations between whites
and blacks but neither should there be bitter antipathy and
hatred. A sentiment of friendship, of mutual respect and
esteem should exist between the two races which, though
separated by such great physical differences, the Creator
has caused to dwell side by side in the same land. Upon
white Americans devolves especially the duty of cultivat-
ing tolerance and refraining from extreme manifestations of
anti-Negro sentiments. Such exaggerated demonstrations
of repugnance as the wholesale abandonment by white people of entire sections of cities when Negroes begin to settle
therein should be sedulously avoided. The evil results
thereof, such as the tremendous financial losses caused by
the depreciation of real estate values, the great change in
character of extensive portions of the cities, converting
them into exclusively Negro districts and the emphasizing
of the antagonism between the races, are all too manifest.
These proceedings are not only injurious, they are also
stupid and futile. After all, white and Negroes do dwell
together in the same land. It is impossible for whites to
escape contact with Negroes, no matter how much they
might wish to do so. To think of settling the problem of
the Negro by removing him from the land is the wildest
figment of a diseased imagination. Apart from the fact
that the Negro is today a free American citizen and need
not leave the country except at his own desire, the mere
physical task of removing a population of more than eleven
millions from one land and settling them in another, if
such can be found, puts it beyond the bounds of possibil-

ity.* Thoughtful Caucasian Americans must, therefore, recognize that in the existence of a large Negro population in their land, they are confronted with a definite, permanent fact, a "condition, not a theory," to quote the words of the immortal Grover Cleveland, and are in duty bound to take such steps as shall make this living together as easy for both elements and as free from friction as possible. This can best be attained, in the opinion of the writer, as already stated, by according to the Negro all civic and political rights and all comforts and conveniences enjoyed by other citizens, and leaving social relations to regulate themselves. This arrangement would meet with the approval of the most representative leaders and best thinkers of the Negroes themselves, who have no desire to force themselves into social circles where they are not wanted and are perfectly satisfied with citizenship rights and living conditions which will guarantee and safeguard for them a reasonably agreeable and happy status. It would, therefore, be entirely acceptable to the great bulk of the Negroes, with the exception, perhaps, of a small minority of irreconcilables.

As a matter of fact the above suggested method is practically identical with the conditions actually prevailing, at least in the Northern States of the Union, except that it is at present carried out in a haphazard and incomplete manner and not definitely accepted as the proper solution of the problem.

It is idle to speculate whether the day will come when all social barriers between the white and black races in America will be broken down and perfect social equality prevail. It is also gravely questionable whether such social equality would be desirable or beneficial, especially if the Caucasians in America desire to preserve the purity of

* Such an attempt was made in 1820 when the republic of Liberia was established on the west coast of Africa by the American Colonization Society, which settled several thousand American Negroes there. But the movement soon came to nothing and was abandoned. At present there is scarcely any immigration of American Negroes into Liberia and there has been no appreciable effect on the numbers of the Negro population in the United States.

their race and the nation as essentially a white nation. But, whatever be one's opinion on this subject, one thing is certain, not for a very long time, if ever, will social equality prevail between the white and black races in this country. There are countries which do not draw the color line, but the United States of America is not one of them and there are no indications that Americans will change their attitude on this matter within measurable time. However, social recognition is not a very important matter and not one with which governments need officially concern themselves. Lack of social recognition will not harm any one. The Negroes in the United States are numerous enough to create their own social life and are probably happier among their own people than in the company of others.

If complete civic and political equality be accorded the Negro, if no unnecessary obstacles be placed in the way of his earning his livelihood, if he be encouraged and aided to acquire the qualifications which are needed for full participation in the complex life of modern society, and if he be protected and care taken that he enjoy the comforts and conveniences of civilized life which are open to the other members of the community, then the problem of the Negro in America will, in all essential respects, be solved.

CHAPTER SIXTH

THE PROBLEM OF THE JEW

A JEWISH problem in America! Hatred of the Jew in the classic land of liberty, which laid down in the glorious Declaration of Independence with which it proclaimed its separation from the mother-country, Great Britain, and hence from the Old World as a whole together with all its follies and brutalities, of which Jew-hatred is one of the cruelest and most stupid, as the fundamental principle of its state-theory that "all men are created equal and endowed with unalienable rights to life, liberty and the pursuit of happiness" is certainly a strange and illogical phenomenon. Here, if anywhere, the sorely afflicted descendants of Abraham, Isaac and Jacob, harried and persecuted beyond endurance in most of the countries of the Old World, had a right to expect to find a haven of refuge where they would be free to worship God in accordance with the dictates of their conscience and to seek the material comfort and well-being for which human hearts naturally long without becoming the objects of envy or antagonism, where none would molest them or make them afraid. The Jews, the world's foremost victims of religious prejudice and chief sufferers for conscience's sake, were certainly justified in expecting that in a land largely peopled by those who sought in it the religious liberty denied them in their European homes, they would be met with sympathetic appreciation of their many trials and tribulations and would receive not only the ordinary rights of citizenship but cordial and brotherly welcome. With a few exceptions, such as the churlish and grudging reception by the Dutch governor of New York, Peter Stuyvesant, of the first group of twenty-three Jewish refugees from

Brazil who arrived at that city, then Nieuw Amsterdam, in 1654, such was in general the manner of their treatment in the colonial period of American history. George Washington, who may surely be taken as an accurate representative of the sentiments prevailing in the early days of the American republic, was particularly cordial and friendly in his attitude toward the Jews. His letter, addressed officially in 1790 as President of the United States to the Hebrew Congregation of Newport, Rhode Island, gives eloquent and impressive proof not only of his personal broadminded and liberal views but also of his understanding of the fundamental principles of the American political system. "The Government of the United States," it declares in words which admit of no dubious interpretation, "which gives to bigotry no sanction, to persecution no assistance, requires only that they who live under its protection should demean themselves as good citizens, in giving it on all occasions their effectual support." "May the Children of the Stock of Abraham, who dwell in this land, continue to merit and enjoy the good will of the other Inhabitants, while every one shall sit in safety under his own vine and fig tree and there shall be none to make him afraid."

Another striking illustration of the friendly and sympathetic attitude of American Gentiles toward the Jews, prevalent in the early years of the existence of the United States, was given in 1825. In that year Mordecai Manuel Noah, an interesting figure in the early history of the United States, who had achieved much well deserved renown as a dramatist and in political life as sheriff of the city of New York and who was at the same time a warm and enthusiastic Jew, conceived the idea of establishing on American soil a quasi-Jewish state, in which all the persecuted Jews of the world should find refuge. As a beginning he purchased several thousand acres of land on Grand Island, New York, in the Niagara River, and proclaimed that there would be founded a city of refuge to be called Ararat. He assumed the title and authority of "Judge and Governor of Israel" and issued an invitation to all the Jews of the world to come and make their homes

in the new colony. On September 2nd, 1825, the proposed
city was formally dedicated with elaborate ceremonies in
the neighboring city of Buffalo. The celebration was opened
by the firing of cannon and was participated in by federal
and state officials, Christian clergymen and representatives
of the Masonic order. We are not now concerned with the
merits of the proposal which, indeed, fell flat and met with
no response on the part of world Jewry. The reaction of
Gentile Americans to it is, however, highly significant.
Not only was there no opposition to it but, on the contrary,
the scheme of establishing a Jewish colony in America was
greeted with cordiality and even enthusiasm. As far as
the sentiment of non-Jewish Americans of that period was
concerned, there would have been no difficulty in initiating
Jewish colonization on a large scale in the vast and still
thinly populated regions of America from which the development of one or more states of the Union with a Jewish
majority of inhabitants might very well have resulted. It
is very evident, therefore, that the public sentiment of
America in the early stages of its history over against its
Jewish inhabitants and the Jewish people as a whole was
a decidedly favorable one. This sentiment remained, generally speaking, unaltered until shortly before the close of
the nineteenth century when signs of a change for the worse
began to become visible. At the present time there can
be no doubt that much anti-Jewish bias exists in the United
States. The evidences thereof are only too clearly visible.
Hotels which refuse to accept Jews as their guests, clubs
which exclude Jews from membership, banks and commercial establishments and corporations which discriminate
against Jews as employees and when advertising for help
add the qualifying attribute "Christian" or "Christians
only" and schools and colleges which either close their
gates against Jewish students, or reduce their number to a
small quota, supply disheartening but irrefutable evidence
of an extraordinary change in the attitude of many Americans toward the Jew.

The coming into existence some years ago of the so-called
Ku Klux Klan, although it did not limit its hostility to the

Jew but included in its ban Catholic, Negro and foreign
born, was, for that very reason, most saddening for it
showed with startling clearness how far a large section
of the American people had departed from the fundamental
concepts of Americanism. Unfortunate and regrettable
though it is, the importance of anti-Jewish feeling in America should nevertheless not be exaggerated. It cannot by
any means be considered the general sentiment of non-
Jewish Americans toward their fellow Americans of Jewish
blood and creed. The government of the United States,
in particular, has always maintained a strictly correct,
indeed, a notably sympathetic and liberal attitude over
against the Jewish element of the citizenry. This was
conspicuously demonstrated in pre-world war days by the
unanimous abrogation by Congress of the treaty with Czaristic Russia because of the refusal of the latter to honor
American passports in the hands of Jews. It was also
amply shown at the time of the adoption of Prohibition as
a national policy by the liberal provisions made by the
Government to enable Jews to obtain the supply of wine
required by their religious observances. Many non-Jewish
Americans of the highest standing have followed the example of George Washington and shown by word and pen
their appreciation of the part which Jews have played in
history, their sentiments of friendship and sympathy for
the Jews and their utter condemnation of all anti-Jewish
prejudice, discrimination and persecution.* Special organi-
tions have been formed for the sole or main purpose of
combating prejudice against the Jews. Typical of these
organizations is "The National Conference of Jews and
Christians," whose office is in New York City and which
expresses its purpose at the head of its stationery in the
noble words "For the Advancement of Justice, Amity and

* Examples of books written by American non-Jews in defense and
favor of the Jews are "Justice to the Jew" by Madison Peters, and
"The Jew and Civilization" by Ada Sterling. The late U. S. Senator Zebulon R. Vance is the author of a masterly oration in favor
of the Jews entitled "The Scattered Nation," which has appeared
in print.

Understanding." While the evidences of anti-Jewish feeling are only too frequent, incidents indicative of sincere
friendship for individual Jews or the Jewish people as a
whole and of genuine appreciation of the achievements of
Jews of outstanding merit are even more numerous. Jews
possessing the proper qualifications are constantly elected,
even in constituencies where Jewish voters are but a
negligible factor, to positions of the highest importance
and dignity. In fact, Jews have been chosen for every position in American political life, elective or appointive, short
of the Presidency and Vice-Presidency.* Especially interesting and gratifying is the fact that Jews are looked
upon with especial favor as judges. At the present time,
1934, two Jews, Louis D. Brandeis and Benjamin N.
Cardozo, are members of the Supreme Court of the United
States. Both enjoy the highest possible reputation for
probity and rectitude and exceptional ability in their vocations. Brandeis is renowned for his liberality in judicial
matters, a renown which he shares with the oldest member
of the Court, Mr. Justice Holmes, recently retired, and
Cardozo is famous for the beauty of his English legal diction. This readiness to select Jews for the judicial office
is an unintended but none the less real testimony of faith
and confidence alike in the intellectual ability of Jews
and the purity and reliability of their moral character. A
number of Jews in various cities and towns throughout the
land have distinguished themselves so greatly by acts of
non-sectarian charity and benevolence and other important
public service as to earn the warm esteem and respect of
the entire community and to be designated, officially or
unofficially, as the "first citizen" of their places of residence.
Such a universally esteemed citizen was the late Nathan
Straus of New York City. He was easily the best loved
resident of the great American metropolis and he richly
deserved to be such for his kindness of heart was endless
and his deeds of mercy and benevolence knew no limitations

* In the fall elections of 1932 four Jews were elected Governors of
States. Herbert H. Lehman was elected Governor of New York
with the largest majority ever given to any candidate in the state.

of race or creed. Love of humanity was the guiding principle of his life and he was ever ready to put all his strength and means at the service of his needy and afflicted fellow beings. His view of human duty is well expressed by his favorite saying, which he addressed particularly to the rich, "Give until it hurts," and he followed his dictum for, although he amassed a large fortune in business, by the time of his death he had given away the greater part of his possessions. The most important and far reaching in effect of his benefactions was the establishment in New York City of stations for the supply, free or at nominal cost, of pure, pasteurized milk for the children of the poor, which has had a tremendous effect in lowering child mortality. This was an absolutely epoch-making action, testifying to Mr. Straus' profound understanding of practical charity and his breadth of vision, as, at the time of the establishment of his pure milk stations in 1890, such a method for the general improvement of public health was hardly even imagined. By this act of fundamental humanity Mr. Straus became the direct cause of saving countless human lives. His idea of pure milk stations has been copied by many other cities in America and has spread to other parts of the world. Yet Nathan Straus was a loyal and enthusiastic Jew, a lover of Judaism and an ardent Zionist. Nathan Straus, though unquestionably the most distinguished American-Jewish philanthropist, is far from standing alone. The list of great-hearted and broad-minded Jews of wealth, who have given lavishly of their substance for the betterment of human conditions, without drawing any narrow sectarian lines, is a long one, far too long, indeed, to be given here in detail. To mention only a few of the most prominent. Judah Touro (1775-1854) was one of the most distinguished philanthropists in the early days of the republic. He gave hundreds of thousands of dollars for humanitarian causes, for his time an enormous amount. Jacob H. Schiff (1847-1920) is a historic figure in American philanthropy. His charity was unceasing and inexhaustible, his benefactions amounted to many millions. Among living philanthropists Adolph Lewisohn and Felix M. Warburg are undoubtedly

the most prominent.* All of these men, though open and
outspoken adherents of Judaism and generous donors to
needy Jews and Jewish causes, are at the same time broadly
humanitarian and non-sectarian in their philanthropic
generosity.

All of this broad benevolence and patriotic citizenship
have not passed unnoticed by the representative leaders of
American thought and the American people in general and
have contributed greatly to the dispelling of ancient
prejudices and giving the Jewish people an assured position
in American life and public esteem. It is a fairly safe
assumption that the citizen rights of American Jews are
securely established and that the prejudices and antipathies
of a bigoted minority cannot avail to undermine or even
seriously shake their solid foundations in American liberty
and democracy. But the mere existence of such prejudices
is a very unpleasant phenomenon which should be extremely disturbing not only to the Jews who are its victims
but to all sincere adherents of traditional American principles of liberty and equality. Jews in particular cannot
be satisfied until they enjoy the esteem of all their fellow
citizens and the question of anti-Semitism is eliminated
from American life. A sincere and earnest effort should be
made to investigate this puzzling phenomenon of anti-
Jewish prejudice, to ascertain its causes and the facts and
conditions on which it is based, or alleged to be based, and
to see if it cannot be removed. This effort shall now be
made, if not in complete detail which would require in itself
a voluminous work, but as far and as accurately as the
limitations of space in this book will permit.

A great number of reasons, many of them contradictory
and mutually exclusive, are given by Jew-haters for the
enmity they bear the "chosen people." Broadly speaking,
they may be divided into four classes, racial, religious,
economic and social. The opinion is widespread that the
antagonism to the Jew is due to his race, which is con-

* Julius Rosenwald, recently deceased, belongs in this group.

ceived as different to that of his Gentile neighbor.* On
this account it is frequently referred to as "race-prejudice."
An impartial and scientific investigation, however, entirely
disproves this view. Antagonism to the Jew cannot be
racial for the simple reason that, despite the assertion of
bigoted race-fanatics to the contrary, there is no real racial
difference between him and the white peoples among whom
he dwells. According to the usual classification of the
racial divisions of mankind there are five major races, the
Caucasian or White, the African or Black, the Mongolian
or Yellow, the Australasian or Brown, and the American or
Red. By origin from the ancient Hebrews, the Jews are
a family of the Semites, who are a subdivision of the Caucasians. It is, however, the consensus of modern scientists
that the Jews have by no means preserved their descent
pure from admixture. Such investigators as Fishberg and
Ripley deny that there is any such thing as an unmixed
Jewish race. This is to be expected since the Jewish
religious code permits intermarriage with converts to
Judaism and in all ages there have been numbers of such
new adherents to the ancient faith of Israel. This fact is
indicated by the great diversity of Jewish facial types.
Despite a quite general opinion there is no specific, distinc-
tive Jewish type. What is usually considered such is simply
the Semitic type, which is characteristic of many other
peoples, Syrians and Armenians and largely of Southern
Europeans. Very many of the Jews do not show this type
but are closely similar in appearance to the Nordic races.
Red, yellow and light brown hair, blue eyes and fair skins,
the characteristic appearance of the Germanic and Slavonic
peoples, are characteristic also of a large proportion of the
Jews. The mere fact that Jews are often mistaken for
Gentiles and that it is often necessary to inquire in order
to know whether a particular individual is Jew or Gentile
is convincing proof that there is no real difference of race

* This is the view which has now been elevated to the status of a
governmental principle by the fanatical and reactionary Nazi government of Germany and made the pretext for depriving German Jews
of most of their rights of citizenship.

between the two. The prejudice against the Jew is, therefore, decidedly not "race-prejudice."

Next in importance as an alleged reason for antipathy
to the Jew is his religion. Hatred of the Christian to the
Jew is supposed to be due to the fact that the latter clings
obstinately to the faith of his forefathers and refuses to be
swallowed up by world-conquering Christianity. This reason has the merit of being historically true. Even in pre-
Christian antiquity much enmity to the Jews on the part
of the idolatrous, polytheistic peoples of that age had been
aroused by the stern morality and uncompromising mono-
theism of the Mosaic code. In the Middle Ages the
religion of the Jew was undoubtedly the chief, if not the
only, reason for the intense antipathy prevailing against
him. Bigotry and fanaticism were so extreme and virulent,
alike in Christian and Mohammedan lands, that the fact
that the Jew was everywhere a dissenter from the national
church and, hence, a heretic, was ample cause for placing
him outside of the pale of human society and bringing
down upon his unfortunate head the fiercest storms of
persecution. There are undoubtedly still people, even in
the modern world, who hate the Jews on religious grounds
but their number is relatively insignificant. Men, as a
rule, no longer hate each other because of differing theological views, certainly not in civilized countries, least of all
in America, to which religious liberty and the right of every
human being to believe or not to believe, as he sees fit,
is the most axiomatic of concepts. The frame of mind
which could bring about a St. Bartholomew's day or an
Inquisition is no longer fashionable. Indeed, the modern
mind is hardly enough interested in religion to care whether
a man adheres to any form of faith whatever and is certainly not disposed to hate anyone for obeying the precepts
of the Mosaic Law. Religious prejudice may, therefore,
safely be dismissed as a cause of contemporary anti-
Jewish sentiment.

A third reason frequently alleged as an explanation of
anti-Jewish feeling is the supposed economic superiority of
the Jew to the Gentile and the latter's inability to compete

with him. This supposition is so absurdly in contradiction
to the actual facts that it is hard to understand how any
one, unless already violently prejudiced, can be influenced
thereby. The Jews are far from being a wealthy people,
even in this most favored of countries. The phrase "as
rich as a Jew" is absurdly false as a generalization and
the contrary statement "as poor as a Jew" would be much
nearer the truth. There are in this country a handful of
Jewish multi-millionaires, and a moderate number of fairly
wealthy individuals but the overwhelming mass of Jews
either belong to the middle classes or live in grinding poverty. As for surpassing the Gentile economically "it is to
laugh." There are no Jews who can compare in wealth
with the Gentile possessors of huge masses of capital, the
Rockefellers, Fords, Morgans, Harknesses and so forth.
Nor is the economic level of the average Jew superior, but
probably not even equal, to that of the average Gentile.
The economic superiority of the Jew to the Gentile is a
mere delusion and certainly no reasonable basis for anti-
Jewish feeling.

A reason not infrequently given for Gentile dislike of the
Jew is the latter's supposed lack of good breeding. The
opinion prevails quite extensively that the typical Jew is
characterized by peculiar and disagreeable mannerisms
which render association with him repugnant to those not
of his kind. This opinion is largely due to the theater and
the vaudeville stage where it has become customary,
probably without direct anti-Semitic intentions, to depict
Jewish characters in a most unfavorable light. The "stage
Jew," as ordinarily shown, is indeed a most repulsive creature. His pronunciation, accent and use of the vernacular
are strangely outlandish, his gestures and gyrations most
extraordinary and his entire demeanor the acme and climax
of vulgarity and unrefinement. That this representation
has very little relation to the real Jew, as he actually exists
in life, does not diminish the contempt and antipathy
produced in the minds of the many thousands of Gentile
observers who have no opportunity to meet Jews and learn
to know them as they are. That this concept is false and

calumnious need not be demonstrated to those who know the Jews of America. By and large the manners, demeanor and language of Jews are not inferior to those of Gentiles. Of course with Jews as with Gentiles there are different classes and various degrees of culture and refinement. Not all Jews are models of courtesy and politeness. A considerable number have been reared in wretched, poverty-stricken surroundings, forced by their utter lack of means to dwell in the slums and associate with the very dregs of humanity and unable to acquire the refining attributes of culture. It could hardly be expected that their manners should not show the influence of their unfortunate environment. But it must be admitted that even these low-class Jews are ethically not inferior, but superior to non-Jews of the same social strata. Drunkenness, wife-beating and the abuse of children are not characteristic even of the lowest class of Jews. And, in their own way and according to their customary standards, they have courteous and refined manners. This is reflected, to a considerable extent, in their children although here, it must be admitted, the influence of the American city streets is distinctly injurious and often counteracts the example and precepts of parents. Nevertheless it is a well known fact in New York City, and presumably in other cities, that public school teachers eagerly desire appointment to so-called "Jewish" schools, because the pupils, instead of torturing their teachers by rudeness, boisterousness and insubordination, as is so frequently the case in the generality of schools, are almost invariably well-behaved, respectful and obedient. As for the more fortunate element of Jews who have had the opportunity of being reared under conditions of comfort and wealth and acquiring the best and finest culture of the age, no fair-minded person can deny that they are, by every test of refined living, the social equals of the best. Yet the doors of so-called "aristocratic" society are as relentlessly closed to them as to the lowliest and least cultured of their brethren.

Social repulsion does not really exist against persons or people of a type not only unobjectionable but in many

ways extremely sympathetic. The existence of antagonism
to the Jew cannot, therefore, be found in the social domain
but must be sought somewhere else. A number of other
reasons are also alleged for dislike to the Jew but they are
so illogical and indeed puerile and in many instances so
manifestly untrue that they hardly merit consideration. A
favorite accusation formerly frequently leveled at the Jews
was that they are lacking in physical courage and patriotism
and unwilling to risk their lives in behalf of the countries
whose protection they enjoy. This accusation is untrue
even as regards the countries of the Old World whose
"protection" of the Jew is often of a more than dubious
character. As regards America it is nothing but a contemptible calumny. In all periods of American history the
Jews have fulfilled every patriotic duty with the utmost
loyalty and have participated in even greater measure
than required by their proportion of the population in the
wars of the republic. In the World War the number of
Jews of all nations participating is estimated at over two
million and the number of deaths at half a million. No
military leader has ever, to my knowledge, accused the
Jewish soldiers under his command of cowardice.* In
recent years there have been given as reasons for discrimination against Jews as workingmen and employees
that they are too prone to strike and that they are not
content to remain in a subordinate position but seek to
learn the business at which they are employed and to become
independent employers themselves. These accusations are
mainly untrue. Most Jewish workingmen are quiet and
peaceful and desirous of retaining their positions without
strikes and trouble and the majority of Jewish employees
are content to remain as they are and are not ambitious
of rivaling their employers. But if a certain proportion
are resolute and determined in defense of what they consider their rights or filled with a laudable ambition to
better their condition and rise in the social scale, shall they
be condemned therefor? Shall they not rather be admired

* For interesting information on these points consult Simon Wolf,
"The American Jew as Soldier, Patriot and Citizen," Phila. 1895.

and lauded for their courage and resoluteness and intelligent ambition? Certainly these facts give no warrant for antagonism to Jews as a class or for discrimination against employment seekers for no other reason than that they happen to be Jews. An impartial consideration of these alleged reasons for a hostile attitude to Jews shows convincingly their utter groundlessness and that they are simply excuses put forward to justify a prejudice which is based upon something else. What is that something else?

The present writer believes that it is to be understood as follows. Modern anti-Jewish sentiment is a mere survival of the past, an atavistic obsession. Had there been no hatred of the Jew in the Middle Ages, it would certainly never have arisen in modern times. Medieval Jew hatred was exclusively religious in its nature or, to express it better, was based upon religious differences. It was the *odium theologicum* in an extreme and intense degree. The adherents of any one form of religion hated and detested the adherents of every other form. Christians abominated the Mohammedans, the Moslems cordially reciprocated, Catholics hated Protestants and vice versa and all united in detesting and abhorring the Jews. The Jews, as the weakest of the sects, were also, in special measure, victims of calumny and persecution. Under these circumstances an intense aversion to the Jews developed in Christian minds and became an instinctive part of their world view. To minds thus affected repugnance to the Jew is axiomatic. Nothing that he can do is right, his very existence is obnoxious. But the theological antagonisms upon which this intensity of hatred is based are essentially medieval. They are long since outworn and utterly out of touch with modern views and conditions. Antagonism to the Jew, however, still survives. It has become a sort of tradition which many Christian minds cannot easily surrender. As the inherited medieval reason will no longer suffice other reasons must be sought if anti-Jewish feeling is not to be rejected as something utterly senseless and absurd. Hence the host of illogical and mutually exclusive "reasons" for dislike of the Jew. That is all there is to anti-Jewish prejudice; only this and nothing more.

What is the duty of Americans over against this utterly irrational, un-American and disturbing anachronism of anti-Jewish prejudice? It is to crush it out of existence, not to condone or tolerate it in any form, shape or manner, as something intrinsically repugnant and loathsome to the fundamental principles of true Americanism. A man must not be judged in America by anything but his own personal worth or lack of worth, must be neither favored nor discriminated against because of race or religion. The true American will insist that this principle prevail in American life both public and private. He will look upon any one who seeks to overthrow these principles and to establish the paramountcy of one group of American citizens over another or to deprive any class or element of Americans of any rights or advantages possessed by another as a deadly enemy of the republic and all for which it stands. The true American will judge individuals as individuals, not as members of any particular racial or denominational group. In a word he will look upon all Americans as brothers and endeavor to secure for all the same opportunities, the same equable and brotherly treatment. If this view prevails in our country—as it should prevail since it is the only true and genuine American view—there will come an immediate end to the problem of the Jew in America.

CHAPTER SEVENTH

Assuming that the social and political relations of the various elements of the American population have been arranged in an agreeable and harmonious manner, that racial and religious antagonisms have ceased to exist and that all American citizens have become one united band of brothers, the wished for conditions of peace and happiness would not yet be attained and America would not yet be the ideal land which its vast extent and wealth of resources enable it to be unless its economic system be such as to assure to all or the great majority of its people a reasonable degree of prosperity and well-being. The proper solution of the economic problem is essential because the economic needs of man are fundamental to his being. It is a truism that man is a creature of dual characteristics, into whose composition both physical and spiritual elements enter, that he is, so to speak, part animal and part angel. The spiritual and intellectual side of man's being is undoubtedly the nobler and superior but the physical and animal side is basic and fundamental. The physical structure is the ground work and foundation upon which the wonderful superstructure of reason, exalted spirituality and commanding personality is erected. But the foundation must be well laid and firmly secured if the superstructure is to tower on high in all the beauty of its exaltation. The demands of man's animal nature, his bodily cravings, are imperative and insistent and only if they are duly cared for and properly gratified can his spiritual and psychic powers reach their full development and fruition and his whole being full rounded and well balanced completeness. That is what the Romans meant by their saying, "Mens sana in corpore sano,"—"A sound mind in a sound body." That is to say, the mind can only be sound if the body

is sound. The same thought lies at the bottom of the
Rabbinic adage, "If there is no bread there is no Torah,"
that is to say, a starving wretch cannot be expected to
master the intricacies of learning. Pursuing this thought
further, it tells us that no nation can rise to the highest heights of culture and civilization, of intellectual and
spiritual eminence, when a few revel in limitless luxury
and self-indulgence, while the great majority languish
in wretchedness, living lives which are mainly chains of
constant and unceasing privations and sufferings. Such
has been hitherto the usual experience of mankind. There
is no reason in the natural state of the earth for such conditions of distress and it must be confessed that up to the
present the human race has failed to attain the goal of
proper utilization and distribution of the abundant resources which a beneficent Creator has placed at its disposal. If we contemplate the earth as the place of abode
and the source of nourishment and maintenance of the
human race we can see at once that it is admirably fitted
to fulfill both of these functions. Upon the far outspread-
ing expanse of continents and islands vast multitudes of
human beings can dwell in comfort and from the vegetation
which flourishes in its fertile soil and the swarming animal
life of dry land, interior waters and seas can obtain nourish-
ing and palatable food in unfailing abundance. Of course,
not all regions of the earth are equally adapted for human
habitation. Extremes of heat and cold and other attendant
conditions render the Arctic and tropical zones difficult and
even dangerous as places of abode except for especially
hardy or adaptable specimens of the *Genus Homo;* great
stretches of land are unfitted, by reason of their desert and
arid character, to produce the food needed for the support
of human life, while other great stretches of country are
swampy and miasmatic and thus render impossible the
existence upon them of numerous and healthy populations.
It is, furthermore, axiomatic that even the fertile and salu-
brious regions of the earth cannot, unaided by human
energy and ingenuity, provide the requisites for a pleasant
and civilized human existence. Houses do not build them-

selves. They must be built and furnished by human skill and labor. Trees and plants do, it is true, produce of their own accord edible fruits, but they are not, as a rule, sufficiently dependable in quantity or regularity as to suffice for the needs of a large and settled population. Cultivation of the soil by human hands—which includes, of course, the breeding and care of food animals and birds—must be relied upon for the providing of a regular and adequate supply of nourishment for established, sedentary communities. But, admitting all this, the truth of the statement that the earth is well adapted to be a home and a source of economic maintenance for the human race remains unquestionable. The difficulties and deficiencies inherent in natural conditions can be and are overcome by human intelligence and energy. Arid regions can be irrigated, swamps can be drained and both species of territory, when their natural defects have been overcome, become unusually fertile and capable of supporting large numbers of inhabitants.* In ancient times, as Biblical and other records testify, famines not infrequently afflicted humanity and caused the death of great numbers of people. They were brought about by failure of crops, due to natural conditions such as lack of rain which human ingenuity could not combat, and deficient methods of transportation which made it impossible to convey sufficient quantities of food from one region to another. Under modern conditions such famines are practically unknown except, perhaps, in backward countries like China. Modern methods of agriculture and transportation have reached such a degree of efficiency that far more food and other products can be produced than the human race actually needs and they can be transported with ease to the most remote regions of the earth. The

* Both methods of improvement of originally unusable soil are practiced with great success in America. In the western states hundreds of thousands of acres of desert have been irrigated. In Florida much of the vast swamp region of the Everglades has been drained. In both sections gloomy wildernesses, formerly given over to wild beasts, poisonous serpents and a few wandering savages, have been converted into the smiling homes of highly civilized people and have acquired enormous financial value.

world today is suffering, strange to say, not from under-
production but from overproduction. Not from a lack but
from an excessive supply of the things needed for human
consumption.

Normally, under such conditions of abundance, poverty
should be non-existent and no human being should lack
food, shelter or the other necessaries of life. Yet, paradoxical though it may sound, such is not the case. The
markets of the world are glutted and surfeited with wheat
and oil and all substances which make for human comfort
yet millions of human beings are without the necessaries
of life, are starving or in need of charitable aid in the
midst of overflowing plenty. Without a doubt the capitalistic system which measures the value of all things in
terms of money and which makes the possession of money
an indispensable prerequisite for the obtaining of the necessaries or luxuries of life is responsible for this abnormal
state of affairs. Food products and all articles of use are,
under present conditions, raised or manufactured not primarily for the satisfaction of the needs of human beings
but for the sake of profits, of the money they will bring.
The vast populations which today inhabit the world need
and could consume with ease all or most of these products
but with the exception of the comparatively few who are
in a position through the possession of land and factories
to produce themselves what they require, cannot obtain
them unless they have money with which to pay the price.
Most human beings have no accumulated capital. They
must, therefore, depend upon that which they can earn by
the labor of their hands in order to be able to obtain the
means of subsistence. Great numbers of persons in all
lands, because of the competition of multitudes of other
employment seekers, can only find employment at very
low wages, barely sufficient to purchase enough to keep
body and soul together. Such persons vegetate—they can
hardly be said to live—in a state of the utmost misery,
subsisting on the cheapest and coarsest foods, dwelling in
wretched and unsanitary hovels, deprived not only of everything which makes human existence enjoyable but even

of what is needed to make it endurable. But pitiable and
miserable as is the lot of these unfortunates, there are, even
in the supposedly enlightened and advanced present age,
many millions whose life condition is infinitely worse.
These are the great host of the unemployed, who are not
only willing but anxious to support themselves and their
families by honest labor but who cannot, in spite of the
most earnest and unremitting efforts, find the work from
which to derive the means of support for themselves and
their dependents. These unfortunates have only the bitter
alternative of either perishing for want of the fundamental
necessaries of life or of accepting the charitable gifts of
the kind hearted or the grudging doles of governments.
These or similar conditions have existed throughout human
history. Alongside of the wealthy and moderately prosperous classes of the community there have always existed
throngs of the poverty stricken and necessitous, made so
by the inexorable demand of the capitalistic system that he
who would enjoy the comforts of life must have the wherewithal to purchase them, a demand with which these
submerged multitudes are unable to comply. Scripture
recognizes these conditions, looks upon them as inevitable
and makes them the basis for an injunction to practice
charity and benevolence. "For the poor shall not cease
from the midst of the land, therefore I command thee, saying: verily thou shalt open thy hand unto thy poor and
needy brother in thy land" (Deuteronomy, xv, 11). The
Mosaic code, it is true, made a valiant fight against poverty
and enacted for this purpose many laws which, from the
modern viewpoint, must be considered decidedly socialistic,
but it seems to take the view that legislation alone cannot
accomplish this end and that private charity will always
be needed. Modern improvements and increase of efficiency
in the production of food and other necessaries have not
changed this historical condition. Wealth has increased to
fantastic proportions, fortunes have been accumulated
which make the fabled riches of Crœsus seem beggarly,*

* In 1928 the cash in bank of Henry Ford is stated to have
amounted to more than six hundred million dollars.

but the fundamental problem of just and equitable distribution is as far from solution as at any time in the past. These vast stores of capital are concentrated in the hands of a comparatively few individuals while the masses of the people live from hand to mouth. The increase in unemployment and consequently the absolute lack of all means of subsistence has been as fantastic as the increase of wealth. At no time in the past were such enormous numbers of people so absolutely without the opportunity of self-support.* A particularly strange feature of the situation is that it is worst in the countries which are most efficient and progressive. While there are many reasons given for the great extent of unemployment, there seems to be no doubt that the one greatest contributing cause is what is called the technological factor. The invention of labor-saving devices, enabling one machine to do the work of many men, has deprived millions of persons of their livelihood.

A few instances will suffice to prove this point. The invention of labor-saving agricultural machines has made it possible to work the farms with an astonishingly small number of men. Mechanical reapers, threshers and binders and other devices have made a large proportion of farm laborers superfluous. This is undoubtedly one of the causes for the influx from the country to the city and the increasing depopulation of the rural districts.** Until

* In 1932 the number of the unemployed in the whole world was estimated at between 20,000,000 and 25,000,000. In the United States of America the number of unemployed was estimated as between 8,000,000 and 9,000,000, in Germany at over 4,000,000. The same condition was almost universal. Only two major countries, France and Russia, formed exceptions and appeared to be exempt from the plague of unemployment. Palestine, due to special conditions, also formed an exception.

** The New York *Times* of June 22, 1931, contains a striking corroboration of this thought. A correspondence from South Africa states, "The Director of Census is convinced that modern farm methods, resulting in less labor being necessary, help to account for the decrease in the rural population." Additional corroborations follow:

N. Y. *Times,* Oct. 22, 1931—World Ills Laid to Machine by

recent years the operation of subway trains required the services of a conductor for every car, and of a ticket seller and a ticket chopper at every station. At present one man opens and closes the doors of all the cars of the train and the use of the turnstile has made both ticket and ticket chopper superfluous. The former ticket seller has been for the present retained as a giver of change but automatic change giving devices have already been installed in some of the stations and will presumably soon become universal

Einstein in Berlin Speech—BERLIN, Oct. 21—Discussing the effects of natural science on man's life, Professor Albert Einstein in a lecture tonight deplored the fact that the industrial technique which was meant to serve the world's progress by liberating mankind from the slavery of labor was now about to overwhelm its creators. He characterized the great distress of the present times as the result of domination by man-made machines, but blamed technique not as much as lack of organization in economic and social life, the stabilization of which is one of the chief tasks of the present time. Regarding the direct effects of natural science upon life, Professor Einstein stressed the philosophic theory of determinism, which he said was almost generally recognized today.

The following extract from the New York *Times* of June 15th, 1932, states the present economic problem so aptly that it must be quoted in full.

CARNEGIE TECH HEAD URGES EASIER LIFE—Dr. T. S. Baker Says Science Has Given Leisure, Yet Man Blindly Worships Work—SURFEIT ITS CONSEQUENCE—More Equitable Distribution of Modern Benefits is Called the Problem. PITTSBURGH, June 14—As a technologist, replying to the current accusation that invention has rashly multiplied the productivity of man and upset the economic equilibrium, Dr. Thomas S. Baker, president of Carnegie Institute of Technology, declared in a commencement address here today that science made to mankind a gift of leisure but that men blindly kept on worshiping a tradition of work.

Addressing the institute's graduating class, he asked: "Dare we adopt a less austere guiding principle—that work is not the aim of existence but rather that man was created to enjoy as well as to labor? The present surfeit of commodities leads us to suspect there has been too much work." He continued: "The most perplexing, the most humiliating and alarming subject which the world today has to consider is unemployment. Will this condition continue? Certainly not in its present intensity; but there are reasons for believing that the United States will never require as many hours of labor as in the past.

"The sum total of work to be performed will never be as great as and drive another class of human workers from their employment and livelihood. The street cars formerly required the services of two men each, a motorman and a conductor. At present many of these cars are operated by one man who performs the functions of both. Elevators or lifts formerly could only be operated by specially trained and authorized persons. Today an increasing number of elevators alike in hotels, apartment houses and private residences are automatic. These are operated by the passengers themselves through the simple process of touching a button and are guaranteed "fool-proof," that is to say that they are absolutely safe and cannot be put out of order through

before 1929. No more railroads are needed. There are too many mines, too many farms are being tilled, the cities are overgrown.

"But most important of all the elements or conditions that mark the turning point in the history of the United States is the rapid development of technology, which has reduced to a degree that cannot be computed the gross amount of labor that must be done.

"It has been said quite frequently of late that science has upset the economic equilibrium by her discoveries and inventions.

"It must be regarded, or at least it should be regarded, as a blessing if we are forced to work less hard for our daily bread. If, as a result of the scientists' discoveries, one acre of land can produce as much food as formerly two acres furnished, the increased productivity is a gift to mankind which relieves the cultivator of the soil of one-half his labor. If the engineer has shortened the time that the laborer must give to his tasks, he has done a service of equal importance.

"Dare we adopt a less austere guiding principle—that work is not the aim of existence but rather that man was created to enjoy as well as to labor? If we accept this conception we can believe that we are entering upon a new dispensation in the intellectual and moral world as well as upon a new era in our economic life.

"The present surfeit of commodities leads us to suspect that there has been too much work. We are therefore encouraged to revise our code and to consider the desirability or the necessity of a form of existence without the strenuous qualities of former generations. The appeal for greater productivity, greater industry, greater energy, is today out of place. Our prayer now must be for greater intelligence, that we may learn to distribute more systematically and more equitably the benefits that we now enjoy.

"We can think of the ever-increasing store of scientific knowledge which is at the service of mankind as a source of wealth to be drawn on to make life easier and happier."

the carelessness or lack of skill of the passenger. Perhaps
the saddest example of what this modern inventiveness has
done is what has happened to the musical profession
through the introduction of the so-called Movietone or
Vitaphone and other systems of mechanical music. Formerly every theater or cinema required an orchestra of
trained musicians, whose profession was a highly honored
one and whose services were well remunerated. At present
most of these musicians have been superseded by mechanical musical devices which render the musical part of the
program very acceptably. It is estimated that over one
hundred thousand professional musicians in the United
States and Canada have been displaced by these devices
and are now practically breadless together with their dependents, conservatively estimated at between four and
five hundred thousand persons.

This process of what may be called the "superfluousiza-
tion" of human skill and energy is going on constantly in
practically all lines of activity and threatens, if not checked,
to attain catastrophal dimensions. The most stupid of all
proceedings is to blink these startling facts. Paradoxical
and enigmatical is the fact that these terrible evils are
brought about by splendid achievements of human genius,
which are really a magnificent tribute to the human mind
and which should be not a curse but a blessing to mankind.

The lightening of human labor should normally and logically be a most beneficial and desirable thing, freeing the
lives of modern men from the constant drudgery which was
the unavoidable lot of their ancestors and making their
earthly existence much sweeter and happier. That it has
not done so for a very large part of the human race, that,
on the contrary, it has introduced new forms of wretchedness and misery and made the very existence of millions
problematical, cannot be the fault of these wonderful inventions but must be due to some fundamental error in the
method of utilizing them. It seems to the present writer
that this fundamental error lies in the making of money
the only means of acquiring possession of the necessaries
of existence or rather in the making of the acquisition of

money—or of adequate quantities thereof—such a difficult, almost impossible process for the vast majority of the human race. The use of money is not, indeed, essentially undesirable but, on the contrary, possesses great and undeniable advantages. As a means of determining the value of commodities and of regulating the exchange of needed articles among men, in other words of facilitating industrial and commercial activity, it is probably the best and most practical system that could be devised. It is, of course, immeasurably superior to the crude method of barter employed by primitive men. Money is not only a measure of the value of material objects; it is also a most accurate means of determining the value of the imponderables, such as the services of an efficient official, the skill of an artisan or the artistic ability of a great actor or singer. If the president of a great corporation doing a business of many millions of dollars receives a salary of a hundred thousand dollars a year, or if a skilled artisan receives a hundred dollars weekly while ordinary workmen receive only twenty-five or thirty dollars for the same period or if a Caruso or a Ponselle receives three thousand dollars for a single performance at the opera, these differences are a striking illustration of the varying values of the work or services of different individuals, the accurate fixation of which is only made possible through the use of the money standard of measurement. These differences in value are, of course, due to many varying circumstances or causes with which we are not, at this time, concerned. The underlying principle of these value-differences is the very natural and logical one that the person who renders a greater service is entitled to a greater reward. With this principle no just or fair minded person can have any quarrel. It is only right and proper that those exceptional men and women who possess unusual talents and abilities and are able to render and do render exceptional services to their fellow beings shall receive as their reward an unusual share of the substance which is essential as a means of procuring the things which make for comfort and well-being. In this fact in itself there is no wrong and no social danger, pro-

vided that those humbler members of society, who are only
able to render ordinary and modest services, shall at least
be assured the modest income which shall protect them
from want and suffering. Great and terrible danger, however, does result and most disastrous consequences flow
from the unfortunate combination of the indispensability
of money and the extreme difficulty of obtaining it on the
part of large sections of the people.

Life becomes, on the whole, a desperate and unceasing
struggle for the possession of the precious substance upon
which not only the enjoyment of comfort and ease but even
the very maintenance of life itself depends. The first consequences of this all-absorbing pursuit are a perverted
concept of the purpose and meaning of life and a frightful
weakening of the moral fiber. Success in life is conceived
as a matter of accumulating money and shady practices,
of more than dubious morality, are looked upon indulgently
or tacitly condoned if they have enriched their perpetrator
who otherwise conforms to the standards of respectability
and perhaps distributes some of his ill-gotten gains in
charity. "Get money, my son," said the Yankee lawyer to
his youthful scion, about to enter the arena of business
life, "Honestly if you can, but get money." That this
fierce craving for financial power leads to savage disregard
of the well-being of one's neighbor, that all moral and
tender sentiments are ruthlessly subordinated to it, has
been deplored by all humane thinkers since the first establishment of organized society. Virgil denounced the *auri
sacra fames* "the accursed hunger for gold" which leads
men to commit deeds of wickedness and infamy.   The
Rabbis in the Talmud lament the demoralizing effect of
the struggle for sustenance. "Harsh is the task of finding
food and it causes Israel to transgress the will of their
Creator" is the Rabbinical way of expressing the thought
that the necessity of finding the means of support forces
multitudes of human beings to the violation of the accepted
canons of righteousness and morality. The Bible antici-
pates the Rabbis in recognizing this fact. "For a piece of
bread a man will sin," says the wise Solomon (Proverbs,

XXVIII, 21). Nor is his condemnation of these violations
of the moral code very severe, when they are done in order
to satisfy man's elemental cravings. "Men do not despise
a thief if he steal to satisfy his desire when he is hungry"
(Proverbs, VI, 30).

Few people realize to how tremendous an extent the
desire or the compulsion to obtain money is responsible
for crime. The obtaining of money is not the only motive
for crime. There are other motives such as perverted love
or exaggerated jealousy, offended feeling of honor, hatred
of the unlike or mere sadistic lust of destruction but there
can be no doubt that the overwhelming majority of crimes
have as their motive the gaining of some form of material
advantage for the perpetrator and that, in the last analysis,
means, under the capitalistic economic system, the obtaining of money or its equivalent. The monetary or financial
motive is such a powerful and all-prevalent factor of crime
that it is hardly an exaggeration to say that if it could
be eliminated from human conduct it would practically
mean the elimination of judges and courts of justice, of
police forces and even of armies, for lust of possession is
not only the cause of strife and violence between individuals
but between nations as well.

The accursed hunger for gold rests like a black cloud,
pregnant with misfortune, upon human society and turns
life, which might be innocent and happy, deriving sufficiency and contentment for all from the overflowing
abundance of nature, into a repellent Valley of Trouble,
filled with violence and terror, hatred and suspicion, suffering and anguish, poverty, misery and despair. The crimes
of which the desire for money is the motive are extremely
variegated. They range from acts of the most audacious
and brutal violence to contemptible petty thefts and fraud
but, however greatly they differ, the impelling cause is always the same, the desire to obtain a material advantage
which, under the existing economic system, cannot otherwise be obtained.

America, at the present time, is suffering from an unprecedented epidemic of crimes of violence. Bandits and

brigands ply their nefarious trade with an audacity unknown in the palmiest days of the highway robbers of
Italy and Spain. So-called "hold-up" men invade in broad
daylight banks, business establishments and factories and,
terrorizing the officials, employees, or customers with drawn
revolvers, seize the deposits, receipts or pay funds, as the
case may be, and make a swift "get away" with the ever
ready automobile.* "Racketeers" grow fat on illicit traffic
or tribute forced from terrorized merchants by fear of
death and wage war with rival bands of members of the
"underworld" with open contempt for established law and
absolute disregard for human life. The great majority of
these crimes remain unpunished. Only in exceptional instances are the attempted robberies baffled or the per-
petrators caught and duly punished. It goes without
saying that these unspeakable crimes, a shameful blot upon
our boasted modern civilization, are prompted by one motive, the desire to obtain money, quickly, easily and in
large amounts.

Hardly less frequent than robberies by violence are the
cases where persons in positions of trust and confidence,
to whom funds are entrusted for security and investment,
betray the trust reposed in them and misappropriate or
waste the money of others over which they happen to have
control. Directors of banks and corporations vote themselves huge salaries and huger bonuses with slight consideration of the question whether their actual services merit
and the condition of the business warrants such payments
and with even less consideration of the interests of the
stockholders whose money is thus recklessly squandered.

Innumerable are the instances where the executors of
wills or the guardians of trust funds have sought to enrich
themselves at the expense, perhaps even through the ruin,
of the beneficiaries or wards whose interests it is their
sacred duty to protect. All sorts of legal tricks and manip-
ulations are resorted to in order to make these dishonest

* In isolated instances hold-up men have even invaded private
homes of wealthy persons and robbed the occupants of money and
valuables.

actions conform to the law and to enable the scoundrels
who are guilty of them to escape the legal consequences.
Sometimes these shameful betrayals of trust spell utter
poverty and lifelong misery for the innocent victims, helpless widows and orphans, who depend for their support
upon these investments and trust funds established for them
by loving ones passed away and who find themselves utterly
penniless. These crimes are far viler and more contemptible in their cowardly trickiness than the robberies of the
"hold-up" men which, at least, have the merit of frankness
and courage, but they are inspired by the same motive, to
obtain the all-precious substance of the capitalistic system,
money.

Perhaps the most revolting illustration of the power for
evil inherent in the craving for gain is given by the part
which it plays in the political life of the nation. The lust
for "graft" which is only another term for bribe-taking or
unlawful gain is a foul canker which eats at the very
vitals of our governmental system. It is a notorious fact
that great numbers of those who seek public office in the
United States of America, whether as members of legislative bodies or the judiciary or as appointees for the carrying out of the law, look upon their positions merely as
opportunities for enriching themselves by betrayal of their
trusts and misuse of their powers. The result of all this is
unscrupulous squandering of the national resources, unendurable increase in taxation to meet the utterly extravagant and excessive cost of government and the degradation
of politics into an abominable revelry of public plunder.
Legislators become mere members of predatory organizations sworn to implicit obedience to their "bosses" as bandits are to their robber chieftains and the noble art of
government becomes a mere method for the more efficient
despoiling of the people. Even the courts, which should
be the sacred refuge of Justice and the citadels of aid and
deliverance for the oppressed and the injured, cannot escape the universal corruption. While many members of
the judiciary are unquestionably high-minded men, filled
with a firm determination to administer their responsible

office in strict accordance with the dictates of righteousness and the law, it is also true that many of the wearers of the ermine are of a far lower type, and regard their positions primarily as an opportunity for private profit and know no scruples of any kind, if only they can be sure to remain undetected. In New York City during the years 1930 and 1931 several magistrates were removed from office for gross abuse of their judicial functions and prerogatives. It is not surprising that men of low moral caliber come to sit upon the bench since nominations to judicial office must be bought and paid for, can admittedly only be obtained through the payment of thousands of dollars to the political leaders in control thereof. Many of the police are more than suspected of being in complicity with the "underworld," of selling immunity in the commission of crime for cold cash. When a police officer, receiving a salary of three or four thousand dollars annually, is shown to have deposited in bank fifty or a hundred thousand dollars in a few years and explains the fact by saying that he and his family lived very economically or that he was very fortunate in Wall Street speculation, or some other equally absurd explanation, the matter would be comical if it were not so utterly sad. Of course, the taking of bribes and the abuse of public office is nothing new nor is it characteristic of America alone. It existed in Bible days. The great lawgiver of ancient Israel, Moses, found it necessary to enjoin upon his people in words that sound strangely modern, "Thou shalt not take a bribe, for a bribe blindeth the eyes of the wise and perverteth the words of the righteous" (Deuteronomy XVI, 19). Isaiah, the fiery champion of righteousness, rebukes the public officials of ancient Jerusalem and we seem to hear the voice of earnest reformers in modern New York or Philadelphia, "Thy officers are corrupt and associates of thieves, every one loveth bribes and seeketh rewards" (Isaiah I, 23). Official corruption is practically coeval with the civilized world. A Russian proverb of the Czaristic time shows how prevalent it was in that vast empire. "Three persons do not exist, a Jew who was never beaten, a *moujik* (peasant) who was never drunk and a *Tchinovnik* (public official) who never took a bribe." But it may well be doubted if "graft" and official corruption ever existed anywhere or at any time to the extent and involving such a deep effect upon the national life as today in these United States of America. The lust for gold exercises its influence for evil in numberless forms and extends its ramifications into every part, not only of public, but also of private life. Disputes over money matters change the love and harmony which naturally exist between members of the same family into strife and hatred. How often have groups of brothers and sisters, who had always lived together in perfect accord and amity, been changed into bitter enemies when the will of a deceased parent seemed to discriminate unjustly against some and in favor of others.

How frequently it occurs that executors of wills, appointed because they were relatives, uncles, brothers or cousins, of the other heirs and therefore presumably desirous of protecting the interests of these latter, utterly disregard the call alike of moral duty and of kinship and seek to turn the estate over to themselves even though they thereby reduce their own flesh and blood to penury and destitution. Sons and daughters have murdered their parents for the sake of obtaining their inheritance more quickly and because they did not have the patience to wait until they, the parents, would, in the natural course of events, pass away and leave them their possessions. Others, not base enough to go to that extreme, have nevertheless had in their hearts the sentiments of murderers, have begrudged the parents their right to life and wished them dead so that they, the children, might inherit their property. Cruel and heartless parents have insured the lives of their minor children and then brought about their death for the sake of the few hundred dollars they, the parents, might thereby receive. Unscrupulous merchants misrepresent the value of their wares, conscienceless contractors substitute inferior material for the superior quality for which they are paid, cowardly sneak thieves abstract valuables from unguarded homes and unwary individuals and all are actuated by the same motive, the lust for gain which they could not otherwise obtain.

But why multiply instances? They are as numerous and as variegated as the aspects of life. As long as the possession of money is indispensable to human comfort and wellbeing, as long as the attainment of this possession is fraught with great difficulties for most human beings and is impossible to many millions of others, so long will the conditions resultant from these facts continue to draw a trail of blood and tears, of crime, wretchedness and misery over the world.

Money or money's worth, which is the concrete form in which capital presents itself, is naturally the basis upon which capitalistic society is erected. Nowhere is this truer than in America. All things are measured by and have their propelling force in money. No great movement for the promotion of a moral or supposedly moral cause is launched but an appeal is made for the money without which it cannot be carried on. Institutions for the promotion of art, health or charity, universities and schools for the dissemination of science and culture, propaganda organizations desiring to influence the public mind in favor of the views of some particular group or clique, all depend for their success upon this one indispensable factor, money.

The question now arises, "Is there any efficient and adequate substitute for capitalism?" "Can society be organized upon a noncapitalistic basis which shall do away with the injustices, inequalities and other evils inherent in the capitalistic system while retaining the practicality and efficiency which characterize it?" An alternative question is, "Can the capitalistic system be so modified as to eliminate its wrongs and hardships without decreasing its efficiency?"

These are, of course, very old and familiar questions. Earnest thinkers, desirous of promoting the welfare of their fellow beings, have since the earliest times sedulously endeavored to find solutions for the social and economic problems which afflict mankind and to devise methods for the organization of society which shall do away with the manifold ills inseparable from unmitigated capitalism.

The Republic of Plato and the Utopia of Sir Thomas More were attempts to picture such ideal states, in which none should suffer undeservedly and the prosperity and happiness of all should be assured. In modern times the systems proposed for the cure or alleviation of the social and economic ills to which human society is heir, have been mainly two, Socialism and Communism. It is not the intention of the author of this book to enter into a detailed description and analysis of these two social-economic systems, their likenesses and their differences. Such an attempt would lead us entirely too far and is, besides, not entirely germane to the theme of this chapter, which is the consideration of a practical and feasible method of dealing with our own economic difficulties, of finding a solution for the economic problem of America. For, if anything is sure it is that the viewpoint of America is neither Socialistic nor Communistic, that the broad masses of the American people are far removed from seeing in either of these doctrines either anything which is abstractly right or which might be a remedy for the economic ills from which it, the American people, is suffering. All that we need is to consider the fundamental concepts of these two systems and to see how far they offer a solution for the economic problem as it exists in our country.

Broadly defined the basic view of Socialism is that the state must care for the welfare of all its people and for that purpose it must control all the wealth of the land and, in particular, must own all the so-called public utilities, the things, such as railroads, telegraph and telephone lines, which are needed by the people as a whole. Communism goes further and declares that the entire wealth of the land must belong to the entire people and be shared by all in common, that there must be no such thing as private property or private enterprise.* Some forms of Socialism ap-

---

* The line of demarcation between Socialism and Communism is by no means perfectly clear. The Encyclopedia Britannica (11th Edition) defines the two systems thus. "Socialism is that policy or theory which aims at securing by the action of the central democratic authority a better distribution and, in due subordina-

proach the Communistic doctrine so closely as to be practically identical with it, while Communism, in its practical working out, as in present-day Russia, has accepted modifications strongly akin to or identical with the practices of Capitalism. We need not consider here Socialistic or Communistic tenets concerning which there is room for difference of opinion in all schools or which may be theoretically acceptable to all minds, such as the duty of the state to care for all its people or the desirability of the collectivization of industry. For us the crux of the whole matter is in the question: "Will the abolition of private property and the compulsory collectivization of all economic activity solve the economic problem, in particular the economic problem of America?"

tion thereunto, a better production of wealth than now prevails."

"Communism is the name loosely given to schemes of social organization depending on the abolition of private property and its absorption into the property of the community as such."

According to these definitions there appears to be a perfectly clear distinction between the two systems. Socialism merely seeks "a better distribution of wealth" while Communism depends upon "the abolition of private property and its absorption into the property of the community as such." Socialism would, according to this, be perfectly compatible with individualism, albeit a fairer and juster individualism than at present prevails, while Communism would, *eo ipso*, exclude all individualistic property rights and enterprise. But the notion of state ownership of the means of production and industrial participation, as held by some socialists, is so extreme as to be very slightly, if at all, different from Communism while some Communists consider their system socialistic. Thus Leon Trotzky, exiled Bolshevist leader, in an article in the New York *Times*, July 19th, 1931, constantly refers to the avowedly Communistic regime of Russia as Socialistic. It will be the policy of the present writer to ignore these party names and to consider concrete proposals, without distinction as to the particular school of economic thought to which they may belong, in so far as they offer, or fail to offer, aid in the solution of the economic problem of America. Much attention has been recently aroused by a proposed new system called Technocracy, supposed to have been originated by Howard Scott. The writer sees nothing worthy of especial consideration in this system. In laying stress upon the dangers of technological unemployment and the inefficiency of the price system it states nothing new. It does not distinctly advocate communistic methods of distribution but, should that be its underlying idea, it would, naturally, be open to the objections which apply to Communism.

A definite and categorical answer to this question cannot at the present time be given for the reason that the whole matter is largely theoretical and no man is able to say how the Socialistic or Communistic system would work out in actual practice if applied to the economic management of an entire nation. We have not in history any example of a nation conducting its economic life on purely socialistic or communistic principles. Present-day Russia, under the Bolshevist régime, has definitely committed itself to Communism and is strenuously endeavoring to create upon its vast territory with its enormous population a genuinely communistic union of nations. But the Russian effort, up to the present, is only an experiment, an experiment, moreover, concerning the ultimate success of which the opinions of competent observers are very widely divided. The optimists claim that it will be a glorious success and is destined to revolutionize the whole world; the pessimists assert that it is already a complete and inglorious failure. All that seems to be positively known is that economic conditions at present in Russia are very bad, that the bulk of the people are suffering extreme privations and that many of the ordinary conveniences of civilization are either unobtainable or only obtainable at extremely high prices. For, be it noted, communistic Russia has not abolished money. Desired commodities must be bought with money and the prices vary according to the law of supply and demand just as in bourgeois capitalistic countries. We cannot, therefore, expect any help from Russia in the solution of this problem and may omit it from consideration. We must rely upon our reasoning powers, aided by our knowledge of human nature and history, for an answer. Relying upon these sources our answer must be: "Socialism or Communism, understanding by these terms any economic system which would abolish private property or forcibly collectivize industry or labor, would be an unsatisfactory substitute for the capitalistic system now prevailing. Its success is doubtful but even its success would not be desirable in the interest of the true welfare of the human race."

Such a system would not, in all probability, work satisfactorily because it is contrary to human nature. In every human heart there dwells a deep instinctive longing for something of one's own, for personal, individual ownership of the things which are necessary for comfort and the enjoyment of life, for personal power to decide one's own career, to choose one's road in the world. No normally constituted human being can be really satisfied, can be truly contented, if he has no domain of his own, be it ever so small or insignificant, over which he can hold sway and exercise control without let or hindrance. To be merely one of a vast multitude all of whom receive food and raiment and the other elementary requirements of life in equal measure in accordance with a mechanical routine and procedure decreed from above, to be merely a number, without personality or individuality, without power to shape one's destiny or hope of greater reward for better performance, such a condition is utterly loathsome and revolting to every true human soul. And yet such must be the condition wherever and whenever a serious attempt is made to put the principles of communism into practice. The moment there is any departure from the doctrine that the earth and all its products are the common property of all human beings, the moment one individual is permitted to accumulate more possessions or to receive a larger reward for his labor or services than another or to select a career according to his individual fancy which does not, in the general judgment, contribute to the common welfare, in that moment the communistic system perishes and is no more.

The communistic system, if really carried out, tends, on the one hand, through its very universality and the indiscriminating equality with which it guarantees equal sustenance to all men, to develop the worst and least worthy traits in human character and, on the other hand, to bring about a tyranny in government as stern and unrelenting as any exercised by an absolute monarch. What incentive has any man to industry or faithful performance of duty if he cannot expect special recognition for his services, however meritorious, and if, under all circumstances, his support and maintenance are guaranteed? The natural tendency would be to shirk and evade, on pretense of sickness or other pretext, all work that could possibly be avoided. The government, however, could not possibly permit any such remissness since to do so would mean to demoralize the entire system. It would, therefore, be obliged to resort to the severest measures in order to force all workers to perform the tasks assigned to them. The result must be the adoption of a rigorous system of tyrannical compulsion and terrorism which would reduce the entire population to a condition of abject, trembling slavery and drive every vestige of liberty from the land. Such, indeed, appears to be the actual state of affairs in Russia. While direct compulsion to work has not been shown, except in isolated instances, the penalties involved in standing outside of the regular industrial system, such as deprivation of the right to purchase at the governmental stores, deprivation of the right to education and so forth, are so severe as to coerce even the most recalcitrant into humble submission to the governmental desires. We have heard, too, from time to time of the summary execution of the best of the land, learned scholars, distinguished scientists, skilled engineers and artisans for alleged counter-revolutionary activity, which, in simple English, means that they were opposed to the communistic system. What becomes of human dignity under such circumstances? It simply does not exist. It is dead, drowned in a flood of blood and terror.

Such a system cannot, in the nature of things, be permanent. It is not in man to submit forever to a system which violates and outrages the profoundest sentiments of his heart. History, as far as it gives a lesson, tells us that communism cannot succeed. When English colonists first settled in Virginia they organized their colony on a communistic basis. The result was privation and almost starvation. Few were those who would work since the community had undertaken to support all. Many later communistic settlements in America, while not as unsuccessful as this, nevertheless failed to maintain a permanent existence. Communism may safely be dismissed as a solution of the economic problem of America. The dignity and self-respect of the American people, their love of independence and self-determination, their desire to reap the legitimate rewards of talent and industry, are such, that they would never submit to a system which would reduce them to virtual slavery as the price of a guaranteed modicum of material support.*

In thus completely rejecting the claims of Communism, and in a lesser degree, of Socialism, to offer a solution of the economic problem of America, there is no desire on the part of the writer to indite a panegyric on the Capitalistic system at present prevailing in this land or to cover up or conceal its many grave defects. Capitalism as an economic system has its good and its bad sides, brings both advantages and disadvantages to mankind. These must be examined closely and impartially in their influence upon human welfare in order to determine which effects, the good or the bad, predominate, whether another economic system should be substituted for it or whether it can and should be modified and if so in what manner and to what extent. What is Capitalism? For the purposes of this discussion it may be described as the economic system according to which all objects and commodities needed or desirable for human existence, comfort or benefit and all human abilities, talents or services have a more or less definite financial or monetary value, that these commodities or benefits can normally only be obtained by giving for them money or its equivalent and when obtained become the property, that

* No consideration is given in this statement to special features of Communistic or Socialistic thought some of which are outside of the economic field. Thus there is in them a distinct anti-religious trend which is particularly emphasized, for instance, in the Bolshevistic system of Russia. This has, of course, absolutely no connection with the economic question. To the present writer this tendency seems quite absurd. The economic issue, which is the main element of these systems, should not be obscured by mixing it with religion which has to do with an entirely different set of human thoughts and emotions. Here only the salient economic principles of these systems are considered as they affect the economic problem of America.

is to say, the personal and inalienable possession of the individual or group obtaining them.* It will at once be seen that this is a hard and relentless doctrine but one likely to be efficient. And, as a matter of fact, the capitalistic system possesses undoubted advantages to which the strong hold which it has maintained over human society since time immemorial must unquestionably be ascribed.

Its first great advantage is that it corresponds to the natural cravings of the human mind. As already stated men instinctively desire possessions of their own. Under the capitalistic system this craving is gratified. Whatever a man lawfully has is his and none can dispute his right thereto.

Its second great advantage is that it is clear and definite. Under the capitalistic system a man knows exactly how he stands financially, what is his and what some one else's. The distinction between *meum* and *tuum* is not blurred and obscured as it must inevitably be where Communism prevails.

A third most fundamental advantage is that it rouses all human powers to energetic fulfillment. Shirking or evading work on the part of the worker is practically eliminated for its main motive is removed. The worker knows that he is giving and receiving a definite *quid pro quo,* that he is rendering so much work for so much pay and it is the normal impulse of a man to keep his pledge and agreement. There is, of course, a certain amount of shirking and disloyalty but, under any reasonably efficient control, it is exceptional and negligible.

Capitalism impels men to better accomplishment and stirs up their inventive ability. The worker knows that if he performs his task with especial efficiency his position will be securer and his wage probably larger. Inventive

* No consideration will be given in this discussion to the question as to what constitutes capital. This topic treated so elaborately by Karl Marx in his work "Das Kapital" and which occupies such an important place in the theoretical structure of Socialism and Communism, is of no particular importance to the economic problem of America.

minds realize that if they can devise some new machine
which will increase human power or well-being their reward may be very great. In every branch of human activity, in agriculture, commerce and industry, in science
and exploration and even in the more ideal pursuits of art
and music, poetry and the drama, abstract learning and
literature, the hope of rich reward for work well done spurs
men on to the best and highest achievement. Best of all,
the capitalistic system confers upon men a great measure,
perhaps the greatest measure possible in organized society,
of personal liberty and self-determination. It dictates to
no one his vocation or what kind of work or labor he shall
perform. It leaves him at perfect liberty to follow his own
taste and inclination in these matters and even to abstain
altogether from every form of gainful occupation, if he so
chose, provided only that he have the wherewithal from
some other source to defray his expenses. It asks nothing
of any man except to pay what he owes and if he can find
a way to get through life without incurring debt he need
pay nothing. It thus makes it possible for men to take up
an infinite variety of pursuits and occupations, to do the
things which really interest them, and thus gives to civilized life that wonderful diversified and variegated quality
which is its chief charm and the most convincing demonstration of the wealth and great extent of human ability
and achievements. These undeniable great advantages of
the capitalistic system are forceful arguments in its favor
and undoubtedly the reason for the apparently impregnable
position which it has always occupied and still occupies in
human society.

But these arguments, true and strong though they be,
tell only half the tale, show only one side of the picture.
The undoubted advantages of the capitalistic system are
offset by disadvantages so grave and terrible that, in con-
templating them, one is forced to wonder whether the
benefits of capitalism are not too dearly purchased at the
price of the evils which it entails. If the purpose of any
economic system is to enable the human race to draw its
sustenance from the rich storehouse of nature in security

and unfailing abundance and with the least possible degree of toil and anxiety, then must the capitalistic system be declared a failure. The evil conditions, both material and moral, which result from the capitalistic system, have already been described and need not be considered again. The question now arises, "Is there a remedy for these terrible evils, is there any conceivable method of avoiding the suffering and the wretchedness, the sin and the crime which now seem inseparable from every form of human society, even the highest and most advanced, and changing it into a gathering of contented, happy and virtuous people?" This is, of course, a question of the highest interest to all mankind but most especially to the American people whose vast continent seemed destined, as has been pointed out in the early chapters of this work, to be the place where the grievous problems which have tortured mankind since the dawn of history, among them the sorest and most grievous of all, the economic problem, would find adequate and satisfactory solutions and which had thought that it had, in a measure, solved them. Before attempting an answer the writer would premise by saying that there can be no hope of remedying the ills of mankind unless the existence of these ills be recognized and an honest desire be felt to find their cause and, when found, to remove it.

For centuries the world has either been blind to the existence of these evils or has considered them as inevitable as the passing of night and day and the change of the seasons. When Scripture said "For the poor will not cease from the midst of the land" it expressed the general opinion of mankind not only in antiquity but throughout the succeeding centuries up to comparatively recent times. With the exception of the handful of visionaries who dreamed beautiful dreams of happy Utopias where all should dwell in contentment and bliss, and the Socialistic and Communistic theorists who were always a more or less insignificant minority, mankind, especially its so-called solid and conservative elements, has always considered life in its economic aspects as essentially a battle, a warfare of all against all, to which apply the words "Every man for

himself and the devil take the hindmost." That the charitable and sympathetic impulses of kind-hearted and benevolent men and women have been stirred by the sight of so
much misery and wretchedness and have alleviated some
of their worst effects has not altered the intrinsic brutality
of the unmitigated capitalistic viewpoint.

But a change has come over the spirits of modern men.
Many of the greatest modern thinkers, men of moderate
and conservative views, far removed from radical and revolutionary tendencies, have come to see that "all is not well
in the state of Denmark." It is no longer heresy to criticize the prevailing economic system and to point out its
many incongruities and inconsistencies and the inhuman
and shameful social conditions for which it is responsible,
and these distinguished men have not hesitated to give
frank expression to their opinions. A few of these utterances will be quoted here in order to show how momentous
this change of attitude has become.

Senator Arthur A. Quinn of New Jersey, President of the
State Federation of Labor, at a conference at Rutgers
University of labor leaders and economists, reported in the
New York *Times* of June 9th, 1931, attacked the present
economic system as causing an unfair distribution of wealth.
The old methods, he said, are no longer working out. The
bulk of wealth produced goes to the few and, strange to
say, the greater the wealth produced the greater are the
problems of the poor. Neither capital nor labor as such,
he declared, are to blame "but the system itself." Men
who had devoted their lives to the study of economics and
men active in the labor field should get together "to study
the way out."

The words of the New Jersey Senator, while eminently
conservative in spirit, show distinctly that he realizes that
there is something wrong in the operations of the present
economic system and that it is necessary to devise a new
method to remedy it or, as he expresses it, to seek "a way
out."

William G. McAdoo, former Secretary of the Treasury
and United States Senator from California, in a lecture

delivered in San Francisco, reported in the *New Yorker
Staats Zeitung* of June 4th, 1931, recommended the formation of a National Economic Council, whose chief purpose
would be to prevent overproduction and unemployment.
Planless development of industry, he said, leads to the
wasting of values. Industry must serve primarily the needs
of the people and only secondarily the acquisition of profits.
In the whole world, he concluded in a striking peroration,
the sun is setting upon the theory that profit is the chief
purpose of industry. Mighty changes in the social order
are taking place everywhere in the world and the United
States cannot stand in the background. These words of a
distinguished American, former holder of the public office
which has most to do with financial and economic matters,
the Treasury, are deeply significant of the change which
has come upon American thought.

Dr. Nicholas Murray Butler, the distinguished president
of Columbia University, in his commencement address on
June 1st, 1931, reported in the New York *Times* of the
next day, gave utterance to some forceful and noteworthy
thoughts to the same purport. Dr. Butler revived the question raised half a century ago by Henry George, single
taxer, in his book "Progress and Poverty" as to why there
is still so much poverty and want in such a highly civilized
world and why there is such a profound gulf between those
who are prosperous and those who are not. After con-
trasting the tremendous surpluses of the necessaries of life
with the millions of those in dire need, Dr. Butler said that
a sluggish, self-centered and somnolent public opinion
should be stirred to look deeply into these questions before
it is too late. Too late for what? Too late to stem the
tide of discontent, of disorder and of political and economic
revolution. Great masses of men will not indefinitely sit
quietly by and see themselves and those dependent upon
them reduced to penury and want while that which we call
civilization has so much to offer, commands such stupendous resources and seems capable of accomplishing almost anything.

Somewhere and somehow there is a gap, a want of balance in our social, our economic and our political system which we have not found ways and means to fill or to supply. Dr. Butler does not directly suggest a remedy for these evils which he so greatly deplores but he does state emphatically that supine inactivity will not do, that earnest thought and energetic activity must be devoted to solving the social and economic problems of the age and that the solution must be sought along broad-minded, liberal and progressive lines.

These quotations are quite sufficient to show how seriously the great minds of America are considering the problems created by the new economic conditions now prevailing. Two other statements by public men of importance shall, however, also find a place here because of the clear and definite proposals for an improvement of existing economic conditions which they contain, proposals which a generation ago would have been considered radical in the extreme.

Senator James Couzens of Michigan, although reputed the wealthiest member of Congress, attributed, in a statement published in the press generally on April 22nd, 1931, the prevailing unemployment and attendant ills, to unrestrained greed. The capitalistic system, he said, must be put in order by those in charge of it or suffer regulation by the people. Although he prefers the scheme of private initiative upon which American business and industry have based their phenomenal development, Senator Couzens stated that he doubted whether the American people can continue to rely upon it.

It is very interesting to note that a man of great wealth, undoubtedly, therefore, a beneficiary of the capitalistic system, has such a poor opinion of the system through which his millions were amassed. It reminds of the Talmudic saying, "Alas for the dough concerning which the baker himself testifies that it is bad."

Thomas L. Chadbourne, author of the Chadbourne plan for the control of sugar production, in an address on July 7th, 1931, before the Virginia Institute of Public Affairs spoke as follows: "Constructive measures will have to be piled one upon another if the capitalistic structure of society, under which you and I and our forefathers have lived, is to justify itself. There are but three possibilities before us, chaos, collective leadership or collective control. The last means governmental control of industry, such as exists in Russia. The advocates of unrestrained competition, as it exists today, are the best friends of the Russian Bolshevik theory while the advocates of collective leadership in each industry are the worst enemies of the Bolshevists. The law of supply and demand, the law of the survival of the fittest, the fine old business maxim, 'Competition is the life of trade,' all of blessed memory—these three old comrades have had a stormy road to travel since the World War."

The noteworthy point of these utterances is the frankness with which the speaker, himself an adherent of capitalism, albeit in an improved form, rejects the most favorite principles of the capitalistic system, particularly that concerning the benefits of competition and openly advocates the collectivization of industry. A stronger proof of the revolutionary change in the views even of conservative economists could not possibly be found.

It now devolves upon the author to say what he has to offer in the way of suggestions or proposals for the healing of the economic evils primarily of America but also, in a general way, of the whole world or, at least, of all organized civilized nations. This he will now endeavor to do but before stating what he believes to be the true solution or solutions of the economic problem he must put forward two premises which the reader will please bear in mind. The first is that he does not offer his suggestions or proposals as the sure and guaranteed remedy for all the economic ills to which the body social and political is heir. "Humanum est errare" "To err is human" is a true rule from which the author does not claim to be exempt. Personally, however, he is convinced that the measures which he advocates will really, if put into practice sincerely and energetically, bring healing to the sore economic sickness of modern society. Whether he is right or wrong in this view only experience can show. The second premise is that we must distinguish between two kinds of proposals for the remedying of economic ills, the first kind practical proposals for improving the condition and increasing the profitability of particular industries, the second general suggestions for the improvement of the economic system with a view to bringing about a more equitable distribution of wealth and removing the hardships and privations under which so large a portion of the community suffers. To the first sort of proposals the author will give no attention except incidentally but will concentrate his effort upon the second species.

In attempting to find a solution for the economic problem of America we must first try to picture to ourselves the characteristics of an ideal economic system, to make clear what objects it must strive to attain and then endeavor to ascertain whether these objects and ideals are capable of realization. In the opinion of the writer the ideal economic system must pursue the following aims which are essential and indispensable for the attainment of the best results from both the practical and the ideal viewpoint.

First. It must be a system which will conserve the energy, ambition and liberty of action of men, it must not exercise a paralyzing and deadening influence upon their decisions and strivings but shall leave them free to develop their individual powers and capacities to the fullest extent for their own good and the good of the community in general.

Second. It must be a human system, that is to say, it must be actuated not merely by a fierce craving for the accumulation of wealth by individuals but by a sincere desire for promoting human welfare and making the world a better and happier place in which to live. It must, above all, have as its object to prevent all avoidable suffering. It must assure to every worthy person, as far as human efforts can do so, a sufficiency of the things needed for comfort and well-being and especially to preserve in this country what has become known as the American standard of living.

Third. It must be a system which upholds human dignity, it must recognize that all human beings are essentially alike, that the accidents of wealth and poverty do not make any real difference between men but that all are intrinsically entitled not only to a reasonable degree of material well-being but also to respect and honor. In conferring benefits, therefore, upon the weaker elements of society, the ideal economic system will do so in such a manner as not to infringe upon their honor and self-respect by treating them as inferiors and unfortunates to be pitied, but shall regard them as fully equal members of the community whose interests and well-being are as thoroughly entitled to consideration and protection as those of the wealthy and powerful.

These postulates *eo ipso* exclude both communism and unmitigated or unmodified capitalism from consideration as the ideal economic system for America. Communism is excluded because, as we have seen, it stands in irremediable antagonism to postulate one. Under the communistic system individual aspirations and ambitions are necessarily eliminated since the individual is a mere cipher in a nebulous multitude. America, with its strong insistence upon individualism, with its intense desire that individual talents and energies shall have the opportunity for the achievement of individual success can never accept an economic system which directly negatives these aspirations. Unmitigated capitalism is just as emphatically rejected for it stands in complete contradiction to postulates two and three. Pure or absolute capitalism is a brutal and unfeeling system, it has no trace of human sentiment or sympathy about it. Its one object is to amass profits, to heap up money for the capitalist. It takes no consideration for the happiness or health of the worker but desires to exact from him the maximum of labor for the minimum of pay, it is equally callous to the interests of the consumer and seeks to force him to pay the highest possible amount of money for the smallest amount of service rendered or commodities supplied. Its ideals are "cheap labor" and "big returns"; it follows the policies expressed by one of its most typical representatives "charge what the traffic will bear" and "the public be damned." Its attitude towards questions of humanity is sufficiently evidenced by the abject wretchedness of the masses in those regions of the world, notably in the Orient and Africa, where it exercises unrestricted and unlimited sway. It follows, therefore, that the ideal economic system must be some form of capitalism but very greatly modified, a form which will retain the undoubted benefits and advantages of capitalism but shall be free from its defects, a system which, while preserving the self-determination, liberty of choice and incentives to ambition of the individual, shall defend and safeguard the interests of the masses and assure a fair share of the national wealth, reasonable comfort and well-being to all the people. This is the conclusion to which the best minds of the nation have come or are coming, as evidenced by many utterances, some of which have been quoted above. It is the opinion, among others, of that most eminent economist, Professor Edwin R. A. Seligman of Columbia University, whose views, based upon vast knowledge and mature judgment, are entitled to the most earnest attention and careful consideration. Professor Seligman, in a recent statement, said that capitalism should prevail in the future as in the past but that it should be strictly regulated in accordance with an increased sense of social responsibility. "Unadulterated individualism must give way to 'socialized individualism.' Capitalism will continue to exist but it will be held in control by legislation and a much larger share than hitherto of the gains of the very wealthy will be taken by the state for the purpose of promoting the welfare of the community at large."

With this view of the eminent Columbia professor the present writer finds himself in general accord. The question, however, remains as to how this larger share of the national wealth which is to be taken for the benefit of the people, is to be employed. On this point, on which Professor Seligman did not express himself, the writer has some very decided opinions. He would first like to stress that the use made of these national resources must be thoroughgoing and decisive, that the action taken must be radical and go to the heart of the economic problem as a whole. No half measures, no mere temporary relief or superficial palliatives dealing only with partial and limited aspects of the problem will do. In the very nature of things these incomplete expedients are doomed to failure. Many such superficial proposals have been made during the present period of depression, all equally inadequate. The suggestion, for instance, has been repeatedly made that unemployment, now prevailing to such an alarming degree, should be guarded against by unemployment insurance. It is really surprising that such a proposal should have been seriously made. A moment's reflection will show its utter absurdity. One cannot insure against a permanent condition. A man, whose house burns down regularly, cannot obtain fire insurance. A chronic invalid cannot forever receive sick benefits. Unemployment has become a permanent condition, caused mainly by technical improvements rendering human labor superfluous. It cannot be insured against.

Another method suggested for relieving the distress caused by unemployment and used to some extent during the present crisis, is the carrying out of public works, building roads, draining swamps and so forth. This method, while good in itself when the public work done is necessary and desirable, is nevertheless totally inadequate as a solution of the problem of poverty and unemployment. The government cannot provide work for the whole host of the unemployed and cannot continue this form of relief indefinitely without reference to the real needs of the nation. Such work, furthermore, is totally unsuited to many of the needy unemployed. Musicians and, indeed, all artists, for instance, are constitutionally unfitted to build roads or drain swamps.

The giving of doles by the government to the unemployed, as in England, or charitable aid from public or private funds, as in America, is an especially objectionable method of attempting to solve the economic problem. Charity, private or public, while undoubtedly necessary under the present economic system, is intrinsically degrading to the human spirit. To be obliged to accept alms, doles or any other form of charitable aid which implies that the recipient is a poor unfortunate, a superfluous and supernumerary member of society, who must be cared for by others while himself contributing nothing to the community, is a humiliation to which no human being should normally be subjected. It cannot be considered a permanently satisfactory solution of the economic problem.*

Other suggested methods of coping with the economic problem, specifically the problem of unemployment, are, the reduction of the days and hours of labor,** the lowering of the tariff and the abolition of prohibition. They are all open to the same criticism, inadequacy and also other shortcomings. To reduce the days of the working week to five or less and the hours of the working day to eight or less, is in itself a splendid and most desirable innovation, if done purely for the sake of human welfare, of freeing men and women from the heavy burden of drudgery which has hitherto embittered their lives and of giving them more leisure for recuperation or for cultural, artistic or spiritual occupations. But if intended as a solution of the problem of unemployment it is subject to two serious, indeed fatal objections. The reduction of the time devoted to work

* This statement does not, of course, apply to assistance or relief granted to persons who are in special need of aid because of handicapped or unfortunate conditions of life or who have suffered injuries in the service of the state. Widowed mothers, the aged, and disabled veterans of war are, as a matter of course, entitled to the special aid of the state in the form of regular payments or pensions. But the problem with which we are now concerned is that of the healthy and able-bodied workers, ready and willing to support themselves but unable to do so because of unemployment or insufficient wages.

** In the press of August 5th, 1931, an address of William Green, President of the American Federation of Labor, before the Massachusetts Bureau of Labor, is reported in which he advocates the reduction of the weekly days of labor to three, if necessary, to give employment to all the unemployed. The present wage scale is to be maintained and no reduction in pay is to be permitted because of reduced hours of labor.

might give employment to all if the potency of labor saving machines could be limited or if the march of inventions could be halted. But neither contingency is at all probable. Labor saving devices have already much more than doubled the power of the individual worker and the progress of invention may very well reach the point where one working man will be able to accomplish as much or more as at present a thousand men. Besides, how, in justice, can an employer be expected, under prevailing conditions of capitalism and competition, to pay a worker the same wage for three days' labor as for six.

The lowering of the present extremely heavy and, in some respects, almost prohibitive tariff will, in the opinion of many, create a more friendly sentiment towards America on the part of foreign nations and thus bring about a great increase in our export trade. Admitting that this view is correct, the most that could be expected would be a somewhat heightened prosperity and employment for a number of workers. These results, desirable in themselves, would not suffice to solve the economic problem as a whole.

The abolition of prohibition was undoubtedly a great step forward in the direction of improved economic conditions in the United States. The removal of the hastily adopted and sadly ill-advised eighteenth amendment from the constitution and of the absurd Volstead law from the statute book brought fresh life and vigor to a number of industries and assisted greatly in relieving the unemployment problem. It benefited the distressed farmer by creating a demand for vast quantities of his grain, it enabled coopers and bottle manufacturers to dispose of increased amounts of their products, it furnished employment for hundreds of thousands of men in brewing, transportation and sale of alcoholic beverages. But in spite of the tremendous benefits which followed the abolition of prohibition, that alone could not suffice as a solution for the economic problem. That problem is greater and vaster than any other single issue before the American people and requires a greater and mightier remedy than can be given by any one individual element of the economic totality. What shall that remedy be?

In the opinion of the writer the first requisite for a successful attack upon the economic problem would be the creation of a National Economic Council, whose task it would be to study from all angles the economic question, particularly as it affects America. It should be composed of, let us say, seven men of the highest ability and character obtainable, representing the various elements most especially interested in the solution of the economic problem, two industrialists, two labor leaders, two theoretic economists and one humanitarian, that is to say, a high-minded thinker, devoted to the promotion of the general welfare of mankind. Its powers would be purely advisory, that is to say, it could recommend to Congress such measures for the solution of the economic problem as, after earnest study and due consideration, it should deem advisable but the power to accept or reject and, if accepted, to enact the same into law, would reside in Congress or, better yet, in a national referendum. These recommendations would be unrestricted in their scope, embracing proposals of any nature which might, in the judgment of the Council, be of aid in improving economic conditions. More specifically stated, these proposals might be either partial or general, having as their object either the improvement of some particular aspect of the economic problem, as it shows itself today under the capitalistic system or the definite and permanent solution of the problem as a whole.

To the existence of such a Council the writer attaches the highest importance. It is, in a measure, comparable to a council of war, when the best and ablest generals of an army assemble to consider what tactics shall be adopted in order to defeat a powerful and tricky enemy or to a medical consultation, when skilled physicians, specialists and experts of various kinds, deliberate on the best method of healing and restoring to normal health the victim of an obstinate and malignant malady. Debates in the halls of legislation on the economic problem and its solution are inevitable and almost certain to be wearisome and con-

fusing as well as productive of intense partisan bitterness
and hostility but these conflicts would, in all probability,
be much softened and agreement on needed legislation much
more easily reached, if well considered reports and recommendations emanating from a competent body of eminent
men and economic experts were prepared and ready for the
guidance of the legislators.

The writer will now take the liberty to offer some suggestions which he believes the Council should adopt—or at
least earnestly consider—as adapted to bring solutions to
some of the particular economic evils of the present system
and to the problem as a whole.

First. The problem of overproduction. This is one of
the most grievous problems at present afflicting producers
of all kinds. It is particularly trying to the farmer. A
flood of agricultural produce overwhelms the markets forcing prices down to absolutely unremunerative levels. This
is notably the case with wheat and cotton. The government
has tried to assist the wheat and cotton growers by authoriz-
ing the Farm Board to spend several hundred million dollars of the people's money in buying up these products.
The result, instead of being beneficial, has been disastrous.
The Farm Board has in its possession millions of tons of
wheat and bales of cotton which it cannot and dare not sell
and the prices of these commodities are lower than ever
before in history. But such proceedings are utterly futile
as a means of strengthening the market for the simple reason that they encourage overproduction, which then forces
down the price. There is just one remedy. Whenever the
production of an article exceeds the absorbent capacity of
the market to such an extent as to force the price down to
non-remunerative levels, the government, by exercise of its
power of eminent domain and in the interest of the producers themselves, must limit the production. This is undoubtedly an unusual use of governmental power but new
conditions force new actions and *salus rei publicae summa
lex est*, public welfare is the highest law. It is better for
a farmer to raise five hundred bushels of wheat at a profit
than five thousand at a loss. It goes without saying that

this power of limitation of production must be exercised conservatively, that the object should be merely to insure a reasonable profit to the producer and that the interest of the consumer should also be considered. But the fact remains that the only cure for overproduction is limitation of production and governments must have the courage and energy to carry this out when conditions make it necessary.*

Second. The problem of over-mechanization. This is undoubtedly the most dangerous problem now threatening the economic life of the nation. The increased potency of labor saving machinery, rendering the labor of millions of people superfluous, raises the bitter question, "What shall become of these displaced masses?" It is the problem of unemployment in its harshest and bitterest form. Many suggestions for remedying this evil have been made, all equally inefficient. There is just one real remedy for this machine made plague. It is to restrict the use of labor saving machinery. This proposal undoubtedly sounds both reactionary and radical. It will be said that it means turning the hands of the clock backward, reversing the course of mechanical inventiveness which has made the civilization of the present age so vastly superior to that of

---

* It may be—and undoubtedly will be—argued that this is a reactionary, purely capitalistic proposal, that over-production is merely another name for under-consumption and that to restrict production means merely to deprive the hungry populations of the world of food and other necessaries which they urgently need and could very well consume, if only they could obtain them. This objection has much plausibility but is not correct. It must first be remembered that under the capitalistic system—and we have seen that for various reasons the capitalistic system must be upheld—commodities must bring a profit or they cannot be produced. Secondly, it is perfectly possible, under modern methods of production, that commodities can be produced in quantities greater than the entire population of the globe even if possessed of the money with which to purchase them, can consume, in which case there is undeniable over-production. Thirdly, it is the task of humanized or socialized capitalism to see to it that all persons possess the means of purchasing the necessaries of life. As a matter of fact the Farm Board has appealed to farmers and planters to restrict production but they will not do so voluntarily.

past centuries and increased the comforts and enjoyments of life to a degree undreamed of by our ancestors, in a word, that it is contrary to the whole spirit of progress. It will be argued that the present conditions of technological unemployment are not new in the history of the world but that whenever in the past a machine has been invented which has improved or increased production it has always meant the displacing of a certain number of workers but that the final result has always been the employment of greater numbers of workers and the betterment of the condition of the working classes and that the same results will follow now when industry has been adjusted to the new conditions.

These assertions and arguments are all fallacious. The proposal to restrict the use of unemployment-creating machinery is not antagonistic to true progress, neither can the conditions in the past resulting in the displacement of workers through the introduction of labor-saving machinery be compared to the conditions existing in this age of intensified mechanization and automatization. When, for instance, in the early decades of the nineteenth century, power looms and sewing machines superseded hand weaving and hand sewing, a certain number of weavers and seamstresses were thrown out of employment but the great increase of population which rapidly followed and the vastly increased demand for cloth and ladies' dresses which accompanied it, furnished full opportunity for the use of the new machines and in the end greatly increased the numbers of workers employed. The present technological unemployment is, in the opinion of practically all who have studied the question, radically different. The machines invented in recent years are startlingly efficient. With uncanny, almost demoniacal super-ability they accomplish, with the aid of a mere handful of men, tasks formerly requiring the labor of thousands and for these displaced multitudes no new opportunities of employment present themselves for the mechanizing process has penetrated into every branch of industry. It is a gloomy, almost hopeless prospect, if a *laissez faire* policy be adopted.

As regards the relation of machinery to progress we must distinguish between two species of mechanical devices. One kind improves human conditions and adds to the powers of man and the comforts and happiness of life. The other makes no fundamental change in conditions but merely renders human labor unnecessary and creates unemployment. Examples of the first are the automobile and the airplane which have vastly increased man's power of locomotion and in so doing created tremendous industries and multiplied many times the opportunities of employment and the demand for various commodities or the telephone which has so greatly increased man's power of communication and also called into being a great new industry with many new opportunities of employment. Such inventions are of the highest service to mankind and must be sedulously upheld and encouraged. To antagonize or restrict them would be a real blow at progress.

Examples of the second kind are, for instance, mechanical musical devices. They certainly do not surpass or even equal the performance of human musicians. All they do is to displace the human musician thus depriving many thousands of persons of their livelihood and discouraging the study of one of the finest arts known to man. Or the door-closing device, through which one trainman can open and close all the doors of a train whereas formerly as many men were needed as there were cars to the train. These devices do not improve the opening and closing of the car doors. On the contrary it is less efficiently done than hitherto. All they accomplish is to reduce the number of men needed.

The writer maintains that such devices, and many more of a similar nature, could and should be prohibited. To do so would not in the slightest degree antagonize progress but would be a distinct benefit to the economic life of the community.

The National Economic Council should also concern itself with the various suggestions which have been made for the betterment of economic conditions. The chief of these are, the introduction of a shorter working week, of five or four days out of the seven, of a shorter working day, of seven or six hours or less; of unemployment insurance and of a minimum wage for workers. The objects sought to be attained by these suggestions are the employment of a greater number of workers, the protection of workers from want during periods of unemployment and the maintenance of a high standard of comfort and well-being, the so-called American standard of living, for the workers. These are all praiseworthy and desirable objects and the writer is in thorough sympathy with all of them. Especially is he in sympathy with the idea of the shorter working week, not only on economic but also on social, cultural and spiritual grounds. But, for reasons already stated, neither this nor unemployment insurance, is, in his opinion, capable of bringing a real solution of the economic problem. A minimum wage, assuring to the worker sufficient income to enable him and his family to live in comfort, is certainly an excellent thing for the worker fortunate enough to be employed. For the unemployed it is without meaning. However, these suggestions are all worthy of earnest consideration by the National Economic Council, which should determine the manner and extent in which they are capable of application.

The writer comes now to the final proposal which he desires to make. This concerns the finding of a solution of the economic problem as a whole and he recommends it most earnestly to the consideration of the National Economic Council, if such a body shall be formed, and of all friends and well wishers of humanity. He freely admits that it is unusual, even radical. But he sincerely believes that it is a real solution of the economic problem which is the plague and bane of the modern world, that it will remedy at least the worst evils of poverty and unemployment and that it will do this without either infringing upon human dignity, encouraging indolence and shiftlessness or lessening energy and ambition. In order to contemplate accepting it we must divest ourselves of preconceived notions of the absolute sacredness of individual property rights and must recognize that fundamentally a land belongs to the collectivity of people constituting the nation which possesses it. It is absurd to speak of belonging to a great and wealthy nation and rejoicing in that fact if one does not own a square inch of the soil of that nation or enjoy an iota of the streams of wealth flowing from it and does not know, perhaps, whence to-morrow's meal will come. It is often said by those who wish to be considered practical, hard-headed men, that "the state owes no one a living" but that is only true in a very limited degree. Certainly no state making any claim to civilization and humanity could calmly permit its citizens to perish of starvation for no fault of theirs and every such state should consider it its duty to promote the welfare of its nationals by all means in its power. It has always been recognized in law that the ultimate right to the soil and property of a land is vested in the nation which exercises the political sovereignty over that land, that individual property and other rights are conferred by national authority and held in accordance therewith and subordinate to the interest of the nation. These are the ideas which lie at the bottom of the power of eminent domain and of taxation. The state has the admitted power to tax the possessions of individual citizens to such extent as the national interests require, sometimes almost to the extent of confiscation. The state exercises this power now for the benefit of needy and helpless persons, such as widowed mothers, the aged who have passed seventy and are without means and for disabled veterans. It is only a step further to the proposition that not only the suffering and helpless classes of the community are entitled to share in the national income but that every citizen, by virtue of his or her membership in the nation, is entitled to a portion thereof. This doctrine, although it may appear novel and to some minds even startling, has already to a considerable extent been accepted and acted upon in this and other countries. The writer, while on a trip in Europe, learned of a town in Bavaria named Gocksheim which owns some wells of asphalt the product of which is sold for the general benefit of the community and is sufficient not only to free all the citizens from taxes but also to pay each one an annual dividend of several hundred marks.* The government of the United States also, indirectly but nevertheless actually, recognizes this principle in at least two ways. In its dealings with the Indian tribes it looks upon them as wards of the nation entitled to support and protection against want and privation. It also recognizes the collective ownership by the tribes of the soil of their reservations and the right of each member of the tribe to a share of whatever wealth may be derived therefrom. Some of the Indians have grown very wealthy from the products of their land, notably the Osages, who have acquired immense riches from oil found in their tribal territory. The United States also recognizes this principle in its dealings with its own citizens as regards the disposition of the public domain. Every citizen of the United States has the right under the Homestead Law to preëmpt 160 and, in the case of certain kinds of land, 320 acres of any unoccupied part of the public domain. It is true that the greater part of the once vast public domain has long since gone into private possession but its doing so took place in tacit recognition of the principle that individual citizens are entitled to a share of the land of the nation. If this principle is valid in regard to land, which is the source of all wealth, it is only logical to infer that it is also valid in regard to the wealth derived from the land.

The principle, therefore, which the writer believes should prevail as the basis for the definite and complete solution of the economic problem is that, in the last analysis, the

* Arthur Brisbane in the New York *American,* of August 14th, 1932, tells of similar achievements by American towns. Three towns in Kansas, Belleville, Chanute and Colby, are able, through the income derived from public utilities administered by the municipal government, to dispense their citizens from the payment of taxes. It would not seem difficult to increase the income from such utilities to such an extent as to make it possible to pay dividends to its citizens. New York City possesses such tremendously valuable utilities in its unrivaled water front, its rights of way, concessions for places of refreshment in parks and numberless other privileges, that, by wise administration in the interest of the community, it should be possible to lessen greatly if not entirely to remove, the burden of taxation from the citizens.

land, together with all that is therein and all wealth derived
from its utilization, belongs to the entire people and must
be administered for the benefit of all. The right of private
property shall continue to exist and those who have acquired
exceptionally large amounts of wealth through special
services or abilities or the pursuit of legitimate commercial
or industrial activity shall continue to be entitled to enjoy
the fruits thereof, subject, however, to the limitation that
the possessors of large wealth must contribute their due
share to the maintenance of the state and to the assuring
to the less fortunate citizens of the minimum of a decent
and comfortable existence, according to American concepts.
The right of private properly must, by no means, be so
interpreted as to signify that a comparatively small group
shall be able to revel in inordinate luxury while millions
of their fellow citizens languish in wretchedness and misery.
The nation must regard itself as one great family, of which
all Americans are children, and just as in all normally loving and devoted families the spirit of mutual helpfulness prevails and the prosperous and well-to-do members do not
permit the less fortunately situated to suffer want and
privation, thus also in the great nation-family the wealthier
elements must give of their superabundance in order that
the gaunt spectre of hunger and destitution shall be banished from the land. This must, however, be done through
the regular channels of legislation and as a part of the
normal institutions of the nation; it must not be left to
private initiative and must not have the form of charity,
whether individual or public. Charity, while beneficial and,
indeed, indispensable under existing conditions and in exceptional cases, is highly undesirable as a permanent public
policy affecting numerous and normally self-supporting
elements.* Charity humiliates and degrades the recipient.

* In the press of August 14th, 1931, Governor Pinchot of Pennsylvania is quoted as advocating a huge bond issue, of five or six
billion dollars, by the national government, the proceeds of which
are to be used for subventions or doles to the unemployed. This is
a very unwise recommendation which, if adopted, would be futile.
It would create pauperism and when the proceeds were exhausted,
new bond issues would be required *ad infinitum*. It would be

The mendicant who, without shame or hesitation, stretches out the palm that he may live in idleness from the unearned gifts of the charitable, is, perhaps, the lowest type of humanity. If worthy and industrious persons are forced by utter necessity to cast aside their self-respect and accept such humiliating assistance they deserve sincerest commiseration. The bread line is a shameful and repellent sight which should not be seen in democratic and wealthy America. That it is in utter contradiction to the concept of American citizenship is self-evident. That the vote, the symbol of the power of the people to shape their own destiny, should be cast by starving beggars, is revolting to every mind that holds a higher concept of the value of American citizenship. Poverty, at least in its harshest and bitterest form, must be abolished in America. In a country of the extent and limitless resources of America poverty must not be permitted to exist and it must be done away with in a manner which shall not injure the self-respect or lessen the energy and ambition of Americans or lower the concept of American citizenship.

In order to realize this apparently fantastic ideal the writer proposes a new economic system for America, a system which shall be neither unmitigated Capitalism nor Socialism nor Communism and for which he suggests as the most fitting and appropriate designation Fraternalism.

As its name indicates Fraternalism is based upon the concept that all Americans are brothers, members of the same great nation-family and placed by the Divine Father in the same land and as brothers not only in duty bound to help each other but also entitled to share in the common patrimony, the wealth of the great land which the Father gave to them.*

merely repeating the blunder of the British dole system which has put the British government into a position of embarrassment from which there is no apparent escape.

* This concept is, of course, applicable to all nations in all lands and may even, under certain circumstances, be realizable for all mankind and the world as a whole. Here, however, we are only concerned with America and its problems.

Is this a practicable proposal and can it become a reality? The writer believes that it is entirely practicable, that, indeed, all modern trends lead in this direction and that it might be fulfilled somewhat in the following manner: Without abolishing the right of private property or interfering, beyond reasonable control, with the commercial or industrial activity of individuals, the principle should be recognized that the wealth of America is fundamentally the wealth of the nation and that all Americans are entitled to share therein. This share should not be large enough to paralyze industry or stifle ambition but should be sufficient to do away with undeserved poverty and suffering. The plan might be carried out about as follows: Estimating the population of the United States at 125,000,000 souls and the average income at $800 per person annually, would yield a total annual income of one hundred billion dollars.* A great fund, to be known as the Fraternal Fund, should be created for the benefit of all Americans, without distinction of age, sex or social station. This should be entirely distinct from the ordinary and normal taxes which should continue as usual. Only those persons who, after the payment of all regular taxes, had a clear income of more than $5,000 would be obliged to contribute to the Fraternal Fund one half of their excess. Allowing one half of the total income of the nation for the regular taxes and for incomes of $5,000 or less would leave the sum of fifty billion dollars available for the Fraternal Fund. Of this one half would remain in the private possession of the owners and one half, or $25,000,000,000 would go into the Fraternal Fund. It would thus be possible to pay every American annually approximately $200. This sum, given as the right of every American, would not injure self-respect. It would not decrease commercial activity and would not be large enough to lessen energy and the desire to earn more but it would

* It is, of course, understood that these figures are purely tentative. The present income (1933) of the American people is much less than one hundred billion dollars. The gist of Fraternalism is that a certain proportion of the national income shall be distributed among the entire citizenry.

suffice to take away the bitterness of poverty. It would aid prosperity and business by increasing the purchasing power. To the unemployed it would be a veritable godsend but it would not embarrass the government. Well-to-do persons who would not care to take their share would, of course, be at liberty to leave it in the fund to increase the share of the less fortunate.

This plan is not as revolutionary as it may appear nor does it involve any injustice to any one while its advantages are great and numerous. It is not revolutionary because the principle that the property of the individual may be taken for the benefit of the state is already well established in the law and practice of the nation. It involves no injustice to any one because the opportunity to amass wealth is given to individuals through the grace and good will of the nation. It is, therefore, only right and fair that the individual shall return to the nation a part of the wealth which it enabled him to acquire. It is true that the amount which the wealthy individual is obliged, according to this plan, to turn over to the Fraternal Fund, one half of his income above $5,000 annually, is rather heavy and there would, no doubt, be much squirming and wailing among the possessors of a plethora of mammon at the thought of surrendering so many of their beloved dollars, but no one would suffer any real hardship on that account. Five thousand dollars annually are sufficient for the support of any average family in reasonable comfort and to surrender one half of the excess income above that amount for the benefit of one's brother Americans would not entail any privation. Besides, every member of the family would be entitled, as an American, to the annual payment from the Fraternal Fund, which would increase the family income by that amount. It would decrease the profits of business or investments by one half but inasmuch as it would not be levied except when there were profits and when the annual income exceeded $5,000 annually that would involve no hardship. Certain rich persons could not enjoy all the luxury to which they have been accustomed but there is no harm in that either to the nation or the individuals themselves. Indeed, the thought that they are thereby staving off a social revolution and thus assuring to themselves the enjoyment of a very substantial portion of their wealth, ought to reconcile the very rich to the idea of the Fraternal Fund. It is certainly better to give up half of one's income than to lose it all. That is exactly what happened in Russia and is by no means impossible in America. No less a thinker and observer than Dr. Nicholas Murray Butler has lifted his voice in warning that a social revolution threatens in America unless a speedy solution is found for the economic problem. There is already a strong Communistic element in this country and it can easily become many times stronger if unemployment and hunger continue to increase. The American workingman has hitherto been conservative and pro-capitalistic because he earned large wages and was comfortable. But now that unemployment and destitution are the lot of millions these conservative sentiments are rapidly vanishing. These considerations ought to make every wealthy man an active advocate of Fraternalism.

The adoption of Fraternalism would bring several important advantages to the public life of America. It would take away the sting of unemployment and would go a long way towards abolishing poverty. If every man, woman and child in the country enjoyed an annual assured income of $200 they would contemplate the possibility of unemployment with equanimity. If there were, say, five persons in the family there would be an annual income of $1,000 which would suffice for a modest livelihood. The vast sum of twenty-five billion dollars poured into the nation annually would greatly stimulate every line of business and thus create many opportunities for employment. It would obviate the necessity of much charity and save the vast sums annually spent for that purpose. It would greatly stimulate patriotism for every American would have a substantial reason for gratitude to and love for his country. As a natural consequence of this it would put a complete and permanent end to all communistic, indeed to all subversive tendencies which live on discontent and hunger.

Fraternalism will definitely solve the economic problem and make of America the land of happiness and plenty which its first settlers hoped it would be.*

* Since this chapter was written Franklin D. Roosevelt, as President of the United States of America, has introduced the so-called N.R.A. system for the solution of the economic problem of America. That is an action of such importance that it will be considered in a separate chapter.

CHAPTER EIGHTH

THE PROBLEM OF RELIGION

THE American people, in its overwhelming majority, is a religious people. The statement is probably true that nowhere on earth, not even in those lands which maintain a state church as one of their national institutions, is religion more firmly intrenched in the hearts and affections of the people than in the United States of America. This is a particularly interesting phenomenon in view of the fact that, according to the Constitution of the United States, church and state are completely divorced and religion receives no manner of direct governmental aid or assistance. The Constitution of the United States of America provides in the third clause of Article VI that "no religious test shall ever be required as a qualification to any office or public trust under the United States"; and in its first amendment that "Congress shall make no law respecting an establishment of religion or prohibiting the free exercise thereof." The attitude of the American nation over against religion is, therefore, that of complete official non-participation. The government of the United States has no official concern with the religious views of the citizens. Religion is absolutely and entirely the private concern of the individual citizen in which the state has no official interest. As far as the government is concerned there is no necessity for the existence of any form of religious faith or observance. If an individual has religious views the government does not object and does not interfere with his manner of carrying them out as long as they are unobjectionable morally and if his views on religion are decidedly antagonistic, the government is equally well satisfied.

We are not now concerned with the question whether this attitude is right and proper or whether it is for the

THE PROBLEM OF RELIGION 111

best interest either of the nation or the individual citizen
but merely with the fact that this is the official attitude
of America as laid down in the Constitution, the fundamental law of the land. Absolute neutrality in matters
of religion, complete separation of the affairs of the state
from those of the church is, therefore, an essential characteristic of true Americanism, politically considered. This
does not mean that the state-view of America is anti-
religious, that the status of the church is that of a system
and an organization unwillingly and reluctantly endured
and barely tolerated. Such is by no means the case. The
governmental attitude of America, based upon a correct
understanding of the American folk-psychology, has always
been, and still is, non-religious but not anti-religious. Indeed there are those who claim with much justification
that the adoption of the policy of neutrality in matters
religious embodied in the Constitution was not due to indifference or antagonism to religion on the part of the
Americans of that period, but, on the contrary, to their
excessive religious zeal. According to this view there were
so many sects in America at the time of the adoption of
the Constitution and the adherents of each were so insistent
on the merits of their particular denomination that it would
have been impossible to establish any one of them as the
national church of America without arousing the bitter
enmity and hostility of all the others. For the sake, therefore, of peace and harmony in the new republic it was
necessary to avoid partiality to any denomination and
to adopt the policy of strict neutrality in matters of religion.

That this was the ideal policy may, perhaps, be ques-
tioned but that it has been of any injury to the cause
of religion in America can not be seriously asserted. As
already stated, religion flourishes in America as probably
in no other civilized land. Every form of Christianity and
Judaism claims its thousands or millions of adherents and
their zeal and generosity is testified to by the host of fine
or even magnificent churches, synagogues and other religious edifices and institutions which are to be found in

every city and town in the land, all erected without one
cent of governmental aid.* But the finest result of this
policy of religious neutrality is the spirit of tolerance between the various denominations which it has fostered.
Since religion is purely a private and voluntary matter no
denomination, no matter how numerous its adherents, can
assume an attitude of superiority to others, it must and
does recognize its sister denominations as entitled to the
same respect as it claims for itself. This effectually pre-
vents sectarian rivalry assuming any dangerous form and
is in accordance with the best spirit of religion. Nowhere
else in the world is there such mutual esteem and cordial
coöperation between various religions as in America. This
is the true American attitude over against religion and it is
the devout prayer of every true American that it may
ever continue to exist.

Unfortunately this liberal and brotherly attitude is only
characteristic of a part, though probably the great majority,
of contemporary Americans. A considerable number of
people, drawn mainly though not exclusively from the
Protestant churches, have apparently no concept of the
fundamental American position in regard to religion, appear to believe that Christianity is the established faith of
the land and are constantly endeavoring to influence the
public life of the nation in accordance with this concept.
Their efforts are incessantly directed towards the attainment of mainly three ends, forcing the observance of the
Sunday and Christian holy days upon all the inhabitants
irrespective of their religious adherence, permeating the

* Owing to the neutral attitude of the American government it
would, of course, be possible for any form of religion to exist in this
country, but, as a matter of fact, only Christianity and Judaism are
represented to any appreciable extent. The other great world religions, Mohammedanism, Buddhism, Brahmanism, Confucianism
and Shintoism are hardly represented at all outside of the comparatively few immigrants descended from peoples professing those faiths.
A certain form of Mohammedanism known as Bahaism has found
a limited number of adherents among native Americans. Christian
Science, although repudiated as Christian by some, may nevertheless, in the opinion of the writer, be classed as a Christian sect.

public schools with the spirit of official Christianity and
lessening the power and influence of those folk-elements
not of their creed or otherwise not conforming to their
narrow and bigoted concept of Americanism. These efforts may, and to a great extent actually do, have the effect
not only of infringing upon the religious liberty of those
elements of the population who do not happen to profess
the prevailing creed but even of restricting their civic rights
and reducing them to a position of inferiority, making of
them, in fact, citizens of the second or third class. Take,
for instance, the case of the Sunday laws. These laws are
distinctly religious in their concept and motive. They are
designed to enforce the observance of the Sunday as a
religious rest-day on all citizens, irrespective of their religious views, and although this purpose is somewhat obscured by the alleging of the intention of affording
opportunity for recreation and the promotion of health,
yet the real motive is clearly evident to all who care to
observe.* These laws work a great hardship upon all
those who observe the seventh day (Saturday) as Sabbath, the Jews and the Seventh Day Baptists and Ad-
ventists. Even in those states which grant exemption from
the Sunday law to the observers of another day as holy
time, the disadvantage wrought by the law is only partially compensated by the exemption. The stigma cast
upon these dissenters by the official recognition of the Sunday, the rest-day of another faith, remains as a permanent
badge of inferiority, and the exemption granted is usually
so hedged in by restrictive conditions, as, for instance, that
merchandise must not be publicly displayed or that work
or labor done must not disturb any one in his observance of
Sunday, as to lose much of its value. Such legislation in

* In twenty-four of the forty-eight states of the Union exemption
from the Sunday law, complete or partial, is granted to those who
conscientiously observe another day of the week as holy time. In
the other twenty-four states no exemption is granted. Only three
states, California, Oregon and Washington, are without Sunday
laws. In the District of Columbia there is no Sunday law but the
advocates of Sunday observance are constantly strenuously endeavoring to secure such legislation.

favor of the rest-day of a particular faith, and hence of that faith, is manifestly improper in a land where church and state are separated and where all citizens are supposed to have equal rights. The only proper procedure in this matter would be either to have no Sunday laws whatsoever or, if it be deemed desirable, on hygienic or social or economic grounds, that all persons abstain from work or business on one or more days of the week, to enact laws to that effect but to leave the choice of the day or days to the free and uninfluenced decision of the individual.*

The attempts of these religionists to influence the public schools in the direction of their particular views of religion and life are far more objectionable, even, than the efforts in behalf of Sunday observance. They are, indeed, a direct and terrible menace to the whole spirit of true Americanism. The public schools are presumably the place where the children of all the various elements of the population shall meet in perfect harmony and amity and without a shade of disturbing antagonisms or controversies. The object of the public school is not merely to give the pupils a certain modicum of knowledge but to rear a generation of true Americans, who, although drawn from the most diversified racial and religious stocks, shall feel themselves a true band of brothers, united through love for and patriotic attachment to the one common country.** But,

* This, in the opinion of the writer, would also have the advantage of being the only method by which the observance of a day of rest could be enforced upon the unbeliever without contravening the clear intent of the Constitution. The unbeliever, who does not care to observe the precepts of any religion, is a fully equal citizen. He cannot, according to the Constitution, be forced to observe the Sunday, since no religious test is required for citizenship. But a law ordaining a rest day on purely secular grounds and leaving the choice of the day to the individual, would be an entirely different matter and would be unquestionably binding on all citizens.

** After writing the above the writer read an address delivered by the late President Coolidge in 1923 before the Annual Council of the Congregational Churches, in which he expresses himself as follows: "Our local schools which are sanctioned by the States and cherished by the National Government are institutions of enormous value not

if this lofty ideal is to be attained, all pupils must meet
on a basis of perfect equality and impartiality and stress
must be laid only upon those things which unite, to the
complete exclusion of everything which tends to create
disunion and to arouse discontent and resentment. There
is no subject on which people are as sensitive as that of
religion and nothing that will more quickly arouse bitter
resentment than the attempt to place an institution, supposedly general and for the benefit of all, under the domination of any one group or any particular faith or creed.
The public school must, therefore, scrupulously adhere to
the spirit of the Constitution, accord to all elements of
pupils an impartial and equally cordial welcome, be non-
religious though not anti-religious, and, above all, refrain
from giving to any one religious group or its representatives or customs or holy days greater recognition than or
preference to any other. It must be admitted that the
public schools do not always adhere to this principle of
impartiality and non-sectarianism. Jewish parents have
grievances in this regard which they have often voiced without receiving much consideration for their just demands.
Selections from the Bible are often read and though, if
these are taken from the Old Testament, there is no implication against Judaism, Jewish parents feel that religious
exercises should be left to the families or churches of the
pupils. The chief grievance, perhaps, is that Christmas
entertainments take place at the closing exercises before
the midwinter vacation. Another great grievance is that,
while the Christian holy days are scrupulously observed
through suspension of instruction, Jewish pupils or teachers
often encounter difficulties in being excused for the Jewish

only in providing learning for our youth but also in removing the
prejudices which naturally exist among various racial groups and
bringing the rising generation of our people to a common understanding." The similarity of thought between the views of the
distinguished former President and those here given will be at once
noticed. Ex-President Coolidge is universally recognized as a sound
and authoritative interpreter of true Americanism and it is naturally
gratifying to the writer to have his concept upheld by a personage
of such distinction.

holy days without loss of standing or emolument. Sometimes examinations are set for the Jewish holy days and
Jewish pupils are given the choice either of transgressing
the commandments of their faith or of being unable to
advance regularly in their educational progress. All these
things are in flagrant violation of the spirit of true Americanism and the public school will not be able to perform its
task of rearing a genuine, united and harmonious generation of Americans from the diverse elements of the population until every trace of sectarian bias and discrimination
is banished from its midst.

The worst and most reprehensible form of this illiberal
activity is, however, the sowing of dissension among the
various elements of the American citizenry by harsh accusations against the adherents of minority creeds, in particular, by impugning their loyalty on the ground of their
religious affiliations. Twofold evils result for the citizens
affected, economic injury and lowering of their status as
citizens. It would be hard to imagine anything more completely contradictory to the fundamental concepts of
Americanism. The Jews and the Catholics are the special
victims of this libelous hostility and it is interesting to note
that the enmity to the latter appears to be more intense and
virulent than that directed against the former. The reason
for this apparently anomalous condition is probably that
family quarrels are usually bitterer than those with out-
siders. Catholics and Protestants are both members of the
great family of Christendom and therefore, according to this
view, the *odium theologicum* between them is far intenser
than that against the Jews, who, though by no means lacking in foes and detractors, are nevertheless, as rank out-
siders, looked upon with a certain measure of indulgent
tolerance or indifference. Be this as it may, Catholics in
America are undeniably objects of extreme enmity and of
a most extraordinary campaign of denunciation and vilifi-
cation. This was strikingly illustrated in the Presidential
campaign of 1928 when Alfred E. Smith, a man of great
ability and sterling integrity, with an enviable record as

Governor of the State of New York, was defeated, partially, no doubt, because of his anti-Prohibition views, but, in all probability, mainly because of his Catholic faith. A flood of scurrilous pamphlets was let loose against him attacking him in unmeasured terms and declaring him utterly unfit for the august post of Chief Magistrate of the Republic, and a host of clergymen, among them Bishop Cannon of the Methodist Episcopal Church South, poured forth all the venom of tongue and pen in a determined effort to prevent his election. The chief argument which was relied upon to turn the electorate against him and which was only too successful, was the accusation that as a Catholic he would be obliged to set his loyalty to the Pope above that to America and to prefer the interests of the Roman church to those of his native land. Smith issued a dignified and temperate statement in which he declared himself a sincere American patriot who would, if elected, administer his high office in that spirit and that he had been taught to regard the Catholic faith as a purely spiritual obligation and the priesthood as clothed with authority only in things spiritual. His statement did not suffice to quiet the tempest of anti-Catholic sentiment. These anti-Catholic accusations were made with the utmost vehemence and, if we are to believe them, the Pope is the head of a dark conspiracy to make all America Catholic, to subordinate the American nation to the domination of Rome and to re-introduce the Inquisition and all the other horrors of the Middle Ages. Without desiring to participate directly in this controversy and speaking simply as an unprejudiced American and impartial observer, the writer must say that these accusations appear to him to lack all substantial foundation and to be little more than figments of an overwrought imagination. There is certainly no tangible evidence to substantiate the accusation that the Pope is plotting to become the ruler of America and to overthrow the American political system in general and its guarantee of religious liberty in particular. It seems unreasonable to suspect him of harboring such

vain and visionary schemes inasmuch as the position of
the Roman Catholic Church is far better in the United
States of America than almost anywhere else in the world.
Under the American system of the separation of church
and state Catholicism has prospered mightily. Its adherents number many millions, its magnificent cathedrals
occupy the choicest locations in all the great cities of the
land, its wealth has grown to impressive proportions and is
constantly increasing, its ecclesiastical rulers are permitted to administer all this entirely unhampered and to
develop their wonderful church organization in accordance with their own intentions and desires not only without any opposition on the part of the government but even
with its benevolent acquiescence. Contrast this for a
moment with the treatment accorded the Roman church in
such ostensibly Catholic countries as Spain and Mexico,
where it is engaged in a bitter conflict with the government not only to maintain its ancient prerogatives but even
to retain possession of its property and to preserve its very
existence, and we are forced to the wondering question:
"Why should the Roman Pontiff desire anything better than
the undisturbed peace and unparalleled prosperity of his
church in the United States and why should he risk the destruction of all this well-being by arousing the wrath of the
American people through shamelessly ungrateful and at the
same time utterly stupid and futile plots to overthrow their
national institutions?" The writer holds no brief for the
Catholic church and as a descendant of that people, the
Jews, which has suffered most grievously from the savage
persecutions of the Middle Ages and whose sons and
daughters have perished by thousands in the *Autos da Fe*
and dungeons of the bloodthirsty Inquisition, he certainly
is not prejudiced in its favor, but a simple regard for truth
compels him to say that it is not proper to identify the
methods of medieval Catholicism with those followed at
the present day and that the Catholic church is certainly
not pursuing at present a policy of persecution and suppression of the heretic and non-Catholic. Its strongest

weapon at the present time is excommunication and that is
a very feeble one.

But let us think what we will of the Roman church, its
doctrines and its policies, it is certainly shamefully unjust
to accuse the individual Catholic citizen of America of lack
of patriotism or sincere devotion to the welfare of his
country. American Catholics have always been among the
most loyal and devoted citizens and have proven their
patriotism so emphatically upon a hundred battlefields and
in every domain of civic endeavor that it is quite a work
of supererogation even to defend them. That Alfred E.
Smith, for instance, would be a traitor to America and its
Constitution and that he would obey the commands of the
Pope of Rome in matters political and to the hurt and
injury of his country, is an accusation so extravagant that
it is difficult to see how it could even be seriously propounded to intelligent persons. Certainly nothing in his
personal character or political record gives any warrant
for such a supposition. The argument that it is Catholic
doctrine that the Pope is superior to all earthly potentates
and that all governments must acknowledge his supremacy
and that a consistent Catholic in public office must permit
his official actions to be controlled by the wishes of the
Holy See, is utterly without force or validity. If there is
anything sure it is that Catholic statesmen do not seek
such consistency and look upon such doctrines as pure
matters of theological theory without any relation to
practical politics. The statesmen who are guiding the
destinies of Catholic countries today are practically all
members of the Catholic church, but that fact does not
make them subservient to the church or one whit less energetic in defending the state against ecclesiastical intrusion
into its domain. It is certainly absurd to imagine that
American statesmen, who in religion are Catholics, would
permit that fact to militate in the slightest against their
loyal performance of their duty to the nation of which
they are citizens. Accusations of disloyalty against Catholic citizens on the ground of their religion must, therefore,

be relegated to the domain of fable, as the product of fanatical hatred and suspicion.*

An especially undesirable and unfortunate result of this attitude on the part of so large and influential an element in the country is the constant and unremitting effort to override the plain provisions of the Constitution and to identify the governmental system of America with Christianity. This agitation is carried on with great force and energy by special organizations, such as the Lord's Day Alliance, the National Reform Association and the New York Sabbath Committee. These organizations are well financed through the generosity of wealthy adherents to these ideas, indeed, their funds are so ample that they are able to maintain fine offices with a large staff of high-salaried officials, to issue great quantities of propagandistic literature and to keep special representatives at the various State Capitols to watch all proposed legislation with a view of preventing the introduction of liberal laws or the liberalizing of existing statutes. Another extremely unfortunate result is the intensive participation of the clergy in politics. Impassioned clerical orators launch violent tirades against particular parties or candidates and fill the columns of the press with their denunciations of them, presumably, of course, on purely ethical grounds and in the interest of the public welfare. Nevertheless they expose themselves to the suspicion, on the part of unfriendly critics, that a leading mo-

* It is a frequent phenomenon in history that dominant majorities accuse unpopular minorities of all kinds of wicked conspiracies against the weal of their neighbors, not of their creed. The Jews have been especial victims of this. In the Middle Ages the Jews were accused of poisoning the wells and of killing Christian children for the purpose of mingling their blood with the unleavened bread of the Passover. At the present time anti-Semites sometimes assert that Jews cannot be patriots because they hope for the re-establishment of the ancient Hebrew state in Palestine. A scurrilous pamphlet of dubious authorship "Protocols of the Elders of Zion" accuses the Jews of secretly seeking the overthrow of all Gentile nations and the establishment of Jewish world dominion. These accusations have more than once been the basis of pogroms and massacres of Jews. They are too stupid to need refutation.

tive is a desire for publicity, an insatiable craving to stand in the limelight.*

Admitting the entire sincerity of their motives there can still be little doubt that the attempts of these organizations and clergymen to force the legislation of the country to conform completely to their religious views is opposed to the spirit of the Constitution and, therefore, un-American. It is a grave question, also, whether the attempt to influence the opinions and actions of the legislators outside of the mandates given by their electors does not constitute an improper interference with governmental functions and, furthermore, whether the formation of organizations for the direct purpose of forcing upon the nation laws and statutes which are very clearly at variance with the spirit and intent of the fundamental law of the land is not really a species of sedition. There can be no doubt that in time of war attempts by organizations or individuals to interfere with the settled policy of the nation would be speedily and radically suppressed and there does not appear to be any logical reason to make a distinction in this regard between war and peace. The participation of the clergy in politics is altogether a matter which is open to great question. Those who favor it argue, of course, that clergymen are as truly American citizens as are the laity, that American citizens have *eo ipso* the full right to participate in politics and to endeavor to influence their fellow citizens to their heart's desire and that there is no reason why an American citizen should be asked to relinquish this intrinsic right of citizenship because he happens to be, by vocation, a clergyman. But this argument, plausible though it may sound, is specious and deceptive. The objection to the participation of clergymen in politics is not to their participation as citizens but as clergymen. Were it possible to divorce the clergyman from the citizen, there could not and would not be any opposition. But such a divorce is not possible.

* The majority of these "political" clergymen are Protestant but a few Jewish ministers and Catholic priests have also been infected by the same germ and attempt to sway the political destinies of the nation in accordance with their higher wisdom.

When a minister fulminates against a certain party or candidate or policy, the impassioned orator is not thought of as Mr. Smith, Murphy or Cohen, but as Rev. Dr. Smith, Father Murphy or Rabbi Cohen. The clerical politician throws, intentionally or unintentionally, the entire weight of his influence as a clergyman, as a church dignitary, in other words, as a man of God who is revered as such, upon the scales in behalf of the cause which he advocates. This constitutes, in the opinion of the writer, a direct interference of the religious forces, of the church, in the political controversies of the nation, and is clearly contrary to the concept of the separation of church and state imbedded in the Constitution. It is so even when the point at issue is a purely secular one, in no wise related to questions of religion. But when the clergymen of a certain denomination or denominational group fiercely oppose a certain party or candidate because it or he favors a certain policy which they as clergy disfavor or because the candidate is a member of a church which they oppose on theological grounds, then the issue becomes a sharply religious one and in utter disharmony with the whole concept of Americanism. It is unquestionably the clergyman's prerogative and duty to preach righteousness and virtue in his church and thus inspire his congregants to become citizens of the highest type, who will strive to fulfill their civic obligations in accordance with the finest ethical principles, but he has neither the right nor the privilege, if he desires to abide faithfully by the genuine concept of Americanism, to betake himself personally to the arena of political strife and to debase his cloth by vulgar battling for the political victory of a particular party or candidate over another.

Some of those aligned with the religio-political elements who are striving to bring about the subjection of the land to ecclesiastical domination appear to realize the inconsistency of this attitude on their part as Americans with the constitutional concept of the United States as a land in which church and state are separated and the government is neutral in matters of religion. They seek, therefore, to defend their action by vigorously rejecting this concept and vociferously asserting that the American nation is a Christian nation and that the tenets of Christianity are an integral part of the laws and moral standards of the land. They make much of a judicial opinion of Mr. Justice Brewer in which he is said to have stated definitely that the United States is a Christian nation. The implication is, of course, clear that adherence to the Christian faith is, if not exactly a legal obligation, yet, in a manner, an essential part of the make-up of a true American and that those citizens who dissent from the prevailing faith do not measure up to the full requirements of American citizenship and might even be considered, to a certain extent, disloyal. It cannot be denied that this view is widely disseminated even among Americans of high standing and intellectual power. It crops up in the most unexpected places, particularly in the public addresses of high officials who appear tacitly to assume that Christianity is the basis of American civilization. Some years ago the writer received a letter from one of the most prominent university presidents of the land, who, since the letter was personal, shall be nameless, in which he asserted that the American nation is definitely a Christian nation, that its institutions reflect the spirit of Christianity and are based upon that foundation and that, while religious liberty is granted and no citizen is required to be a member of a Christian church, yet the non-Christian citizen must submit in all things to the views of the Christian majority and must in particular not seek exemption from any state law because it conflicts with his duty as a member of a non-Christian religion and that, therefore, the desire of Jewish citizens to be exempted from the Sunday law because they observe the Sabbath on Saturday is unjust and improper.* Without going into the

---

* The idea that the United States is a Christian nation because its ethical standards and social views and some of its customs are derived from Christian teachings, is scientifically incorrect and unworthy of a scholar. Nations are constantly borrowing from each other in cultural matters without, on that account, being identified with the nation from which they have borrowed. America has bor-

merits of the legal points involved on which he does not claim to be an authority, the writer must assert his emphatic conviction that such argumentation, in the face of the explicit statements of the Constitution, is an inexcusable perversion and misuse of the reasoning faculties. How can the United States be said to be a Christian nation when its Constitution expressly prohibits Congress from making any law establishing religion and provides that no religious test shall ever be required for public office? No nation can be considered as adhering, nationally and legally, to any particular faith if it has not established a state church or conferred a higher status upon one religion than upon others. The United States has never officially accepted Christianity as its national faith nor even officially recognized Christianity as superior to other religions. The fact that the majority of the American people are Christians— if it be a fact, which is by no means certain since, according to the Census, less than one-half of the population are church members—does not make the United States a Christian nation in any legal and political sense. Only the deliberate acceptance by the nation of Christianity as its national faith could make the United States a Christian nation. This acceptance has not only never been given but has, on the contrary, been expressly avoided and guarded against. The truth, therefore, remains that the United States is a secular nation pure and simple, that it has not, as a nation, accepted any faith but leaves religion to the domain of the individual conscience, that, to quote the majestic words of its glorious Constitution, it "makes no law respecting an establishment of religion or prohibiting the free exercise thereof." To those who would, with specious reasoning, seek to obscure the clear meaning of these plain statements and to demonstrate that they signify their contrary, apply the words of Scripture, "Who is this

rowed much in matters of apparel and manners from France but has not become French. Christianity is based upon the Bible and its ethical standards are those of the Bible. But the Bible is a Jewish book. There would be even more justification, therefore, in calling the United States a Jewish nation.

that darkeneth counsel by words without knowledge?"
(Job XXXVIII, 2).*

It would be an injustice to the great body of Americans
to accuse or even to suspect them of harboring these reactionary and illiberal views. It would be equally unjust
to suspect the entire body of clergymen of narrow and
bigoted views. A goodly number of them, possibly the
majority, though this is not clear, are imbued with true
American sentiments and cheerfully accord to those not of
their faith the recognition they ask for themselves. The
writer is in possession of a letter written to him by the
late Bishop Potter in which that distinguished prelate writes
that he will gladly coöperate in securing for his Hebrew
fellow citizens all their constitutional rights. There are
also societies such as the National Conference of Jews and
Christians and The Fellowship of Faiths, formed for the
express purpose of doing away with religious prejudices
and antagonisms, the membership of which is composed
largely of clergymen of all denominations. We may, therefore, safely say that there is still much liberality of sentiment among the American clergy. The overwhelming
majority of the American people, clergy and laity, are unquestionably loyal to the historic concept of Americanism
as a system of liberty in all true significations of the term
and particularly in matters religious. This is evidenced
by the fact that the reactionary and fanatical forces, despite
partial and local successes, have never been able to win any
general victory or make any serious breach in the citadel
of American liberty. The usual history of the reactionary
movements has been that, after an initial period of enthusiasm and threatening growth, they have languished
and failed. Such was the fate of the so-called Know
Nothing movement in the middle decades of the nineteenth

* These words are not to be understood as meaning that those who
seek to undermine the fundamental American concept of the separation of church and state do not know the declarations of the Constitution. They know them perfectly well but they do not put
their knowledge into their words. They speak contrary to their
knowledge, *wider besseres Wissen,* as the German phrase strikingly
and accurately expresses it.

century and such apparently will be the fate of the Ku Klux Klan which had a phenomenal growth and national importance in the early years of the twentieth century but has now fallen into decay and into what Grover Cleveland used to call "innocuous desuetude."

The edifice of liberty erected by the fathers, though sorely battered in parts, still stands, in all essential respects, firm and unimpaired and the statue of "Liberty enlightening the world" is not a mere sad jest.

Nevertheless the inroads which have been already made upon the traditional spirit of American liberty are extremely serious and threaten, if not courageously and resolutely resisted, to establish ecclesiastical domination so firmly in this land that it can never more be overthrown. That, therefore, is the duty which devolves upon all true Americans, loyal to the traditions of America's glorious past, to resist with the utmost energy this threatening ecclesiastical encroachment and not to permit the respect for religion, which is its right and proper due, to concede to fanatical clerics undue and unwarranted influence over the secular affairs of the nation. Especially must be resisted with unyielding determination all attempts to discriminate against or lessen the civic rights or privileges of any class of citizens because of their religion. The true solution of the religious problem in America will come when clergymen will look upon their task as essentially religious and ethical but not political and when all American citizens will enjoy genuine civic equality without regard to their religious affiliation and when the only tests of fitness for office will be, as the Constitution would have it, character and ability.

CHAPTER NINTH

THE PROBLEM OF PROHIBITION *

PROHIBITION, that is to say, the legal interdiction of the sale, manufacture and transportation of alcoholic beverages, is not in itself a problem of America or of any other country. It is merely one method of many designed to promote temperance. The real problem is that of temperance, how to discourage or completely to prevent the use or rather the abuse of alcoholic drinks with its well known injurious consequences and to train the citizenry to habits of moderation and sobriety. There is practically no disagreement on the proposition that over-indulgence in intoxicating drinks is to be condemned, that intoxication is not only an unworthy and degrading condition, from the viewpoint of personal ethics, but also one fraught with manifold social and domestic ills and that it is a meritorious service to promote self-control and temperance in this as in other habits. Apart from ethical and social considerations exces-

* It might be thought and many, no doubt, think that Prohibition is no longer an American problem. The fact that in 1933 the American people in a remarkable series of state elections rejected with practical unanimity the Eighteenth Amendment, thus emphatically repudiating National Prohibition, would seem to warrant the conclusion that Prohibition has gone the way of slavery and the disfranchisement of women and is now without significance in American life. Such, however, is not at all the case. Slavery and female inequality of citizenship have been definitely abolished and there is no thought of any attempt to restore them. But the advocates of Prohibition do not concede defeat and have not accepted the new status of the liquor traffic. They are as bitterly opposed to it as ever, as evinced by many recent pronouncements of Prohibitionist leaders and organizations. They hope for a reversal of the popular verdict and are sparing no effort to bring that about. There are also many details of administration under the new conditions which are as yet not worked out. The whole question is, therefore, still actively controversial and needs to be considered in all its aspects.

127

sive indulgence in alcoholic beverages is recognized by the
medical profession as extremely injurious to both physical
and mental health. By the name Alcoholism—a term first
used by Dr. Magnus Huss of Stockholm in 1848—medical
science designates the inordinate and persistent use of
alcoholic beverages and condemns it as a most unhygienic
practice causing extremely dangerous morbid conditions in
the human organism, such as delirium tremens, gastric
catarrh and fatty degeneration of the bodily organs.

Not only is there at the present time practical unanimity
of sentiment as regards the evil effects of excessive indulgence in alcoholic drinks but these evil effects have been
recognized since the very dawn of history. The Bible
describes them most graphically, indeed, so graphically that
it is worth while to quote the passage in its entirety. "Who
hath woe? who hath sorrow? who hath contentions? who
hath babbling? who hath wounds without cause? who hath
redness of eyes? They that tarry long at the wine, they
that seek mixed wine. Look not at the wine when it is red,
when it showeth its color in the cup, when it floweth
smoothly. At the last it biteth like a serpent and stingeth
like an adder. Thy eyes shall behold strange things and
thy tongue shall utter confused words. Yea, thou shalt be
as one who lieth down in the midst of the sea or as one
that lieth on the top of a mast. They struck me, I felt it
not, they beat me, I knew it not. When I awake I shall
seek it again" (Proverbs XXIII, 29-35). In these verses
of the Book of Proverbs the deleterious effects of alcoholism
are described with extraordinary vividness and poetic force,
the psychic depression which follows upon a debauch, the
senseless quarrelings and physical injuries resulting from
drunken brawls, the mental wanderings and the lack of
normal sense perception, the irresistible attraction of strong
drink for the confirmed inebriate and the uncontrollable
craving which forces him to indulge again and again despite
his knowledge of its evil effects.

It was only natural that these deplorable results produced
a strong antagonism to the liquor habit on the part of
moral and well-behaved persons, especially on the part of

its chief victims, women, and that throughout history there
has been a constant effort to do away with drunkenness and
its attendant evils. The first organized efforts to counter-
act the evil effects of intoxication appear to have been made
in America. Altogether antagonism to the use of alcoholic
drinks and the liquor traffic, while existing more or less in
all countries, has been and is most active and pronounced
in Anglo-Saxon or English-speaking lands.*

The first recorded association for the purpose of influenc-
ing public opinion against the evils of intemperance was
formed in Massachusetts in 1813. A year later similar
associations were organized in Connecticut and Vermont.
A strong impulse was given to the movement through the
organization, on an extensive plan, in Boston, in 1826, of
The American Society for the Promotion of Temperance.
The first annual report of this organization announced the
formation of thirty, and the second of two hundred and
twenty auxiliary associations. By 1831 more than 2,200
branch societies with a membership of approximately
170,000 persons had been formed. The great success of the
American movement soon brought about similar activity in
Europe. In 1829 the first temperance society was formed
in Ireland and within a year sixty organizations with 3,500
members had sprung into existence. A well-known and
greatly-beloved Catholic priest, the Rev. Theobald Mathew,
known as Father Mathew, rendered especially noteworthy
service to the cause. In 1838 he began a campaign for
temperance and in less than two years he succeeded by his
fiery enthusiasm and persuasive eloquence in inducing more
than 1,800,000 of his countrymen to renounce the use of
ardent liquors. In 1829 the first temperance society was
formed in Scotland, at Maryhill near Glasgow, and the
movement quickly spread through the rest of the United
Kingdom. The first temperance society in England was
organized at Bradford in 1830. By the close of that year
there were in England some thirty associations with some
ten thousand members. At first the term temperance was

* It is interesting to note that the Mohammedan faith strictly
forbids the use of intoxicating liquors.

interpreted to mean abstinence from spirituous liquors such as whisky and brandy while light wines and malt beverages were considered permissible but a more radical party which opposed the use of any kind of alcoholic drink soon arose. As early as 1817 a total abstinence society was formed in Skibbereen, Ireland, and in 1830 at Dunfermline, Scotland, and shortly afterward in Glasgow and other Scottish towns. In 1832 a campaign against intoxicating liquors of all kinds was started in England by Joseph Livesey and by 1838 the Total Abstainers or Teetotalers had won a complete victory within the movement. Since then the term "temperance," in this connection, has become identical in significance with "total abstinence."

At first the temperance or anti-liquor movement was strictly private and voluntary with no thought of governmental or legislation compulsion. But mere propaganda and moral suasion did not satisfy its more ardent advocates. They realized that they would never be able in that way to attain their ideal of universal abstinence and they began to agitate for legislative prohibition of the liquor traffic. The State of Maine was the first to yield to their importunities and adopted in 1846 a law prohibiting the manufacture or sale, within its borders, of all intoxicating liquors except cider. Since then the progress of prohibitory legislation has been steady and comparatively rapid. One by one a majority of the states of the Union, particularly in the South and West, and several countries of Europe, notably Finland,* adopted the system of governmental prohibition of intoxicating liquors. Undoubtedly the greatest victory won by the legislative prohibition movement was the adoption in 1920 by the Congress of the United States and thirty-six of the forty-eight states of the Union of the Eighteenth Amendment to the Constitution and the subsequent enactment by Congress of the Volstead law enforcing the amendment. By this amendment and this law the manufacture, transportation and sale of beverages containing more than one-half of one per cent, by volume, of

* Since writing the above, Finland, by an overwhelming vote of its citizens, has given up Prohibition.

alcohol were forbidden everywhere in the territory of the United States. It was a tremendously radical piece of legislation, completely subverting—or at least seeking to— the life habits of a great proportion of the approximately one hundred and twenty million inhabitants of the land and seriously restricting the liberty of all. Was Congress and were the approving State Legislatures well advised in adopting legislation of this revolutionary kind, fraught with immeasurable and ungaugable consequences? Is prohibition intrinsically justifiable? Does it benefit the nation? Does it improve the health of the people? Does it increase respect for law and make the task of government easier? Does it lessen crime? Does it promote temperance? Does it improve the economic condition of the people? Is it financially beneficial to the government? These are some of the harassing and disturbing questions for which answers must be found in order to reach a proper judgment on the matter. The writer will consider them frankly and impartially and endeavor, to the best of his ability, to find honest and logical answers.

He will premise by saying that he has no intention of impugning the sincerity of those who by their constant and long continued agitation finally succeeded in bringing about the enactment of this legislation. He is willing to admit that they were actuated by the purest of motives, that they were sincerely convinced that the use of alcoholic beverages is one of the gravest offenses of which men can be guilty, that it is equally damaging and destructive to the health, morals and material well-being of those who indulge in it, that the only way to do away with it is by legal prohibition, that such prohibition is capable of being enforced and that by bringing about its inclusion in the Constitution and laws of the land they were rendering a great service to the nation.* But the sincerity of purpose of those who advo-

---

* This concession does not extend to the politicians and legislators through whose instrumentality the Eighteenth Amendment and Volstead law were actually passed. Many of those were, no doubt, actuated by mere motives of political expediency or, as the current phrase picturesquely puts it "They did not drink as they voted."

cate a certain measure has nothing to do with the actual
advisability or desirability of that measure. Honest
fanatics, the sincerity of whose motives was above all
doubt, have frequently in history sought to accomplish
the most tyrannical, cruel and pernicious aims and, as the
poet says, "the way to hell is paved with good intentions."
The merits or demerits of prohibition must, therefore, be
considered with absolute objectivity and without consideration of the motives of those who advocate it. Considering the question thus the writer could come only to the
conclusion that the national prohibition of alcoholic
beverages is a mistaken policy and that it not only did not
accomplish its purpose but was followed by evils far worse
than those it sought to remedy. The reasons why, in the
opinion of the writer, prohibition is a wrongful and pernicious piece of legislation which had inevitably to be erased
from the statute books are many. He will endeavor to
state the chief and most important ones.

PROHIBITION IS A GRAVE INFRACTION OF PERSONAL LIBERTY

The first and foremost reason is because it is an unpardonable invasion of the natural, not to say constitutional, rights of every free man and American citizen. It
is in utter contradiction to the spirit of liberty which is the
proud heritage of every American through its tyrannical
intrusion into the domain of men's private and personal
habits of life. The Constitution of the United States was
adopted "in order to secure the blessings of liberty to us and
our posterity." What a tragical perversion of the intent
of the Constitution it is when an amendment is added to it
which robs Americans of man's most fundamental liberty,
the liberty of choice as to what he shall eat or drink, and
stamps as a crime the use of a substance which, when consumed in excessive quantities, is undoubtedly injurious but
which, used in moderation, is harmless and even beneficial
and has been so used, since time immemorial, by uncounted
millions of the human race without evil consequences. If
this is not a matter in regard to which men should be free

and have the unquestioned right to self-determination, it is hard to say what is. It is true that the Eighteenth Amendment and the Volstead law did not, in so many words, forbid American citizens to drink intoxicating liquors but in effect they did. When you prohibit the manufacture, transportation or sale of alcoholic beverages your intention is to prevent the ordinary citizen from drinking them through making it impossible for him to obtain them and when you enact laws having that effect you actually deprive the citizenry of their inherent rights in these regards. And that this constitutes outrageous tyranny, similar to that which caused our forefathers to rebel, no open-minded American will deny. The favorite argument of prohibitionists that the drinking of alcoholic liquors is a practice so harmful and so attended with evil consequences as to justify, and even to compel, governments to forbid it, is, if not utterly groundless, certainly extremely exaggerated. The use of intoxicating beverages does not necessarily involve harmful results.* They resemble many other things in this regard that when carefully and prudently used they are beneficial but when imperfectly or improperly used they may cause disaster. Yet what reasonable man would wish to prohibit all things the misuse of which might result in a calamity? Such a principle would make it necessary to prohibit most of the finest inventions of human genius,

* Prohibitionists frequently compare intoxicating liquors to the noxious narcotic drugs, opium, morphine, heroin and cocain, concerning the dangerous character of whose use, except for strictly medical purposes, there is practically universal agreement, and argue that just as all nations have agreed to limit the production and prohibit traffic in these narcotics for non-medical purposes, so there should be an international agreement prohibiting the manufacture and sale of alcoholic liquors except for medical use. The comparison is misleading and the argument is incorrect. The terribly dangerous and degenerative effects of the use of narcotics is matter of common knowledge and denied by none. Persons who indulge in them are known in vulgar phrase as "dope fiends." But alcoholic beverages are only injurious when used in excess. Used in moderation and in connection with food, they, especially the milder sorts, wine and beer, are not only not harmful but are, according to the experience of the race and the testimony of competent medical authorities, beneficial to health in various ways.

railroads, steamboats, automobiles and airplanes, to name only a few. Besides in a truly free country a man cannot be deprived even of the liberty of doing things which are harmful to him, if he so desire. Any other practice would mean subjecting the individual to the most galling control and dictation, where his every action would need permission by higher authority. What, under such conditions, would remain of liberty? This one reason should have sufficed to render the adoption of prohibition impossible in America, the classic land of human liberty, and now that, through the determined and long continued efforts of liberty-loving Americans it has been repealed, it is sincerely to be hoped that it has been finally and definitely erased from Constitution and statute book.

PROHIBITION IS WRONG PSYCHOLOGICALLY

Prohibition is furthermore an utterly stupid and hopeless piece of legislation because it is wrong psychologically. It is designed to promote temperance and sobriety but one cannot make people temperate and sober by compulsion through brute force. The only way to make people adopt these desirable qualities is by education and moral suasion, by appealing to their reason through showing them the evil consequences of over-indulgence and to their moral natures by urging them not to make themselves responsible for the misery and wretchedness which are sure to result from their vicious self-gratification. Most persons are so constituted that they are amenable to appeals to their reason and ethical sentiments. But when the attempt is made to compel them to abide by certain standards with which they do not agree and to abstain from certain practices which they do not consider fundamentally wrong, the usual result is to rouse their pugnacious instincts and the determination to defy or evade what they consider an unjust interference with their private lives. People even find a certain pleasure in secretly violating such interdictions. As Scripture puts it, "Secret bread is pleasant and stolen water is sweet" (Proverbs IX, 17).

Prohibitionists err when they liken a prohibition law to other laws and say that just as patriotic, law-abiding citizens obey all other laws of the state so they must obey a prohibition law as well. The simple fact is that a prohibition law is not the same as other laws, that it stands in a class by itself. Theft, murder or fraud are generally recognized as crimes which must be prevented by all the force of the state. Those who perpetrate these crimes are looked upon by the normal majority of people as dangerous individuals who must be punished and suppressed. Therefore public sentiment stands behind these laws and though desperate individuals violate them, there is no general rebellion against them and especially no denial of their needfulness or justification. Not so with a prohibition law. Vast multitudes of people are utterly opposed to it, loathe and abominate it and consider it a tyrannical and insufferable interference with their natural rights. Hence came the anomaly that hosts of persons, otherwise eminently respectable and law-abiding, in fact, in all other regards model citizens, openly flouted this law and had no moral compunctions in violating it. A law which does not rest upon public approval is unenforceable. The government spent many millions of dollars and employed a whole army and navy of officials in an attempt to enforce this law, an attempt which was notoriously and ridiculously—or tragically —futile. A law which is thus silently but resolutely resisted by a great proportion of the people cannot endure. The time speedily came when the best minds of America recognized that an attempt to force something upon the American people which the American people is resolutely determined not to accept is utterly hopeless and foredoomed to failure.*

* In the New York Times of October 4th, 1931, a radio address by Senator Bingham of Connecticut is quoted, in which the learned Senator expresses himself as follows: "When we attempt to make people good by law, when we attempt to call something illegal which their conscience tells them is not wrong, we destroy that very respect for law which ought to permeate the Republic. Too much government makes people less self-reliant, less able to look after themselves, less strong in character." Senator Bingham did not directly mention prohibition, but the reference is unmistakable.

PROHIBITION CAUSES CONTEMPT FOR ALL LAW

It would be bad enough if prohibition merely aroused contempt for itself. A nation which desires to be respected cannot afford to enact even one law which meets with almost general disrespect and disregard. Unfortunately, however, these undesirable sentiments are not limited to the one law which aroused them. They are certain to spread and to create an ideology of contempt and disesteem for law in general. The opinion is aroused that law is merely the clothing with state power of the prejudiced and narrow-minded views of legislators or of bigoted and fanatical groups which control and shape the policies of legislators. When that point of view is created, the sincere respect, almost reverence, for law, which, as Senator Bingham puts it, ought to permeate the Republic, vanishes completely and the citizens, instead of according, as they normally should and would, willing and cheerful obedience to the law duly and properly adopted by their representatives, resent it bitterly and look upon themselves as the victims of tyranny, compelled by brute force to submit to a law which they consider utterly stupid and hate and despise. The more intelligent and cultured elements of the citizenry are, of course, able to differentiate and to recognize that, while one particular law may be ill-advised and injurious, the bulk of legislation may be just and even liberal, but the mass of the people cannot make such fine distinctions. In their resentment against the wrongs and hardships inflicted by this one law, they infer that such is the character of all law. Thus is created the type of the Anarchist, or what we might call the Misonome, the man who hates law and government in any and every form and as a matter of principle. Once these views pervade the mentality of any large section of the population the stability of the Republic is seriously endangered and the menace to its future becomes very real. And that this became the mental attitude of a considerable portion of the people, causing them to despise law and look upon it as the product of the combined illiberality and grafting instincts of legislators, is painfully evident to all who know the facts.

PROHIBITION CAUSES AN ENORMOUS INCREASE
OF CRIME

The most immediate and direct manifestation of this misonomic mentality is a tremendous and appalling increase in crime. Recent years have seen an unprecedented and, indeed, terrifying growth not only in the number of crimes committed in this country but, what is far worse, in the hardihood and death-defying audacity which characterize them. It would, of course, be wrong to attribute all this terrible increase in crime to the influence of the prohibition law alone. Many causes combined to bring it about. The great war, with the spirit of reckless daring and the disregard alike of property rights and human life which it engendered, was one of the most potent causes; the capitalistic system, with the injustices and inequalities which it creates, has been another potent cause, the invention of easily carried and easily concealed deadly weapons and the automobile with its uncanny power of quickly removing a criminal from the scene of his crime, all of these causes have been most influential in bringing about this extraordinary increase in criminality. But, making allowance for all these other causes, the fact remains undeniable that the Prohibition law was the agency mainly responsible for the frightful increase in crime which is the curse and the disgrace of contemporary America. The reference here is not to the technical crime involved in the violation or evasion of the prohibition law itself because those who transgressed it considered it only *malum prohibitum* but not *malum in se*, a mere man-made crime without moral turpitude, but to actual deeds of malfeasance, such as robbery and murder.* The Prohibition law brought

---

* An idea of the tremendous extent to which the national prohibition law was violated can be gained from the reports of the Federal Prohibition Bureau. For the year ending June 30th, 1931, for instance, the Bureau reported that 66,189 cases came up for prosecu-

into existence a class of criminals hitherto unknown to criminology and whose designations, bootleggers, racketeers, rum-runners and hi-jackers, were as strange and unfamiliar as they are ugly and repulsive. A huge illicit traffic in alcoholic beverages sprang into existence, conducted by reckless and desperate men, the operations of which were often attended by bloody conflicts with officers of the law or with rival gangs of racketeers. The battles between the opposing gangs were particularly savage and human life was of absolutely no value in these struggles of unscrupulous competitors for the lucrative secret liquor traffic of the nation. It may be and sometimes is argued that the murder of criminals by other criminals is not a matter which concerns the rest of the community and that no one need worry over the death of law breakers but rather consider it a case of "good riddance to bad rubbish." Such a viewpoint is extremely narrow and mistaken. A community in which such violent and desperate crime exists to such an extent is not in a healthy ethical or social condition. When nine or ten men can be lined up against a wall and deliberately done to death by members of a rival gang, as happened in Chicago, it reveals a condition which, although the victims were lawbreakers, nevertheless must fill the minds of all thoughtful Americans with anxious apprehension. Nor are these battles between rival gangs entirely free from danger to others. In an attempt by a gang of racketeers to slay some of their rivals by a fusillade of shots in a crowded New York street a little boy was shot to death and a number of bystanders, absolutely unconcerned with the feud, were more or less severely wounded.

tion in Federal and State Courts of which 59,086 resulted in conviction. A total of $5,607,331 in fines was inflicted. Prohibition agents made 62,902 arrests, seized 8,261 automobiles, 67 boats, 21,373 stills, 27,834 fermenters, 5,002,229 gallons of beer, 1,833,276 gallons of spirits, 291,582 gallons of wine, 4,076,014 pounds and 142,785 gallons of distilling and brewing materials, and 30,818,559 gallons of mash. As discoveries and seizures notoriously took place only in a small percentage of cases the enormous extent of the violation of the prohibition law is clearly evident.

Now that Prohibition has been repealed much, if not all, of this crime may be expected to pass away, although its effects will undoubtedly be felt in abnormal criminality for a long time.

PROHIBITION UNDERMINES THE HEALTH OF THE PEOPLE

A most deplorable result which followed the adoption of Prohibition was its terrible effect upon the health of the people. That was a result which was evidently not in the least anticipated or expected but which might easily have been foreseen. Deprive a man, who has not great power of self-control, suddenly of some article of food or drink which he has been accustomed to use, especially if that article be a stimulant, and he will inevitably seek a substitute and will never consider whether that substitute is wholesome or productive of the most evil consequences to his health. This result is entirely natural and to be expected, because life-long habits which have become a second nature cannot be instantaneously eradicated. If the attempt is made to do so it will simply mean that the persons affected will endeavor by all means in their power to evade the interference with their habits and to obtain a substitute for the article of which they have been deprived. This is exactly what happened in the case of Prohibition. Millions of persons had been accustomed to the use of alcoholic beverages and were suddenly deprived thereof by the Prohibition law. They resented violently this interference with their established and traditional habits of life, an interference which they considered unjustified and tyrannical, and resolved that they would not submit to it, but would continue, as far as possible, to use alcoholic beverages in their accustomed manner. This sentiment created an enormous demand for alcoholic liquors which it was no longer possible to satisfy legally. Actual public demands, whether legal or illegal, will always find those who will endeavor to gratify them, because of the immense profits to be thereby obtained. This result followed also in the case of Prohibition. Every effort was made by bold and venturesome men, so-called bootleggers, to provide the host of customers with the liquor which they demanded. Vast quantities of liquor were brought into the country on rum-running boats and in trucks or airplanes over the land frontiers and probably even greater quantities were produced in so-called "moonshine" stills, that is, secret stills in remote and hidden places. The imported liquors were mostly of good quality, having been made in the usual and normal way, but much of the domestic product, made hastily and carelessly and used too soon, was pernicious and even deadly in its effects. Much alcohol was produced by redistillation from industrial alcohol and was utterly unfit for beverage purposes and even wood alcohol, a deadly poison, was mingled with the drinks sold to ignorant or unsuspecting patrons. The government was naturally most successful in its efforts to prevent the illicit importation of liquor. Most of the liquor consumed in the country was, therefore, a domestic product and much of it of the most unwholesome and poisonous kind. The results of the use of this pernicious stuff were most deplorable. Blindness was an ordinary consequence of drinking liquor containing wood alcohol and many deaths resulted from its use. The results in weakened health of those who escaped the more extreme consequences cannot be definitely ascertained but there is no doubt that whole classes of the population are still suffering from impaired vitality produced thereby. A law which is responsible, even indirectly, for such conditions is nothing more nor less than a scourge of the people.

PROHIBITION CORRUPTS THE MORALS OF YOUTH

Another most deplorable result of Prohibition was the corrupting and demoralizing effect which it had upon the manners and morals of the youth of both sexes. Previous to the adoption of Prohibition the young people of this country, both male and female, were, on the whole, not at all addicted to drink and their manners while not straitlaced nor as restrained as in some European countries, were not open to serious objection in respect to propriety. After the adoption of Prohibition a marked deterioration in both regards became plainly evident and was the subject of general complaint and sorrow. In ante-Prohibition days the drinking of alcoholic beverages was not characteristic of young people as such and the behavior of adolescent youths and maidens or of those in the early stages of manhood and womanhood departed but rarely from accepted standards of good breeding. During the Prohibition period there were constant complaints of the loose and dissolute conduct of young people attending social functions and at other times. The carrying of hip flasks containing intoxicating liquors to social gatherings and unrestricted indulgence in their contents, things utterly unknown before the advent of Prohibition in so-called "better society," became matters of everyday occurrence. Drunkenness, wild hilarity and undue familiarity between the sexes, necking and petting parties and similar forms of looseness were the natural result and so ordinary as hardly to arouse comment. Female modesty appears to have well nigh disappeared, except in the case of a comparatively few young women with old-fashioned ideas. Many of the youthful members of the one-time gentler sex participated in these orgies without any perceptible indication of disapproval or discontent. With this looseness of conduct there went naturally vulgarity of language and freedom of speech in matters sexual which one did not need to be old-fashioned to find indecent and shocking.

For this awful degeneracy of behavior, so startlingly in contrast to the courtesy and refinement formerly characteristic of American manners, Prohibition was directly responsible. It was so radically contrary to the result which Prohibition was expected to bring about, the development of a sober and consequently well-behaved and well-mannered American generation, that it could not but give the most extreme Prohibitionist pause and cause him to ask himself whether the adoption of this policy was not a sad mistake. Certainly no true American could desire to uphold a policy which brings about the existence of a drunken,

dissolute and unmannerly youth in America. Such undoubtedly appeared to be the goal towards which the youth
of America was tending, under the influence of the conditions which were caused by this ill-advised and hastily
adopted law. This observation undoubtedly had much to
do with bringing about the change of public sentiment
which resulted in the crushing overthrow of the Eighteenth
Amendment.

THE VOLSTEAD LAW WAS NOT SCIENTIFICALLY ACCURATE

The Volstead law, the legal instrument, by which it was
sought to enforce the Eighteenth Amendment, was not well
adapted for its purpose, because it was not based upon scientific fact. The Eighteenth Amendment prohibited the sale,
manufacture or transportation of intoxicating beverages and
the Volstead law defined as intoxicating any beverage containing one-half of one per cent of alcohol. This was not
scientifically correct. It is a matter of common knowledge
that a beverage must contain much more than one-half of
one per cent before it can possibly be intoxicating. It could
easily contain three or four per cent of alcohol without
being able to intoxicate any normal person. Congress
would, therefore, have acted in entire conformity with the
Eighteenth Amendment if it had fixed the quantity of alcohol permissible in beverages at three or four per cent. At
all events, in fixing this proportion it should have been
guided not by sentiment or prejudice but by a strict regard
for facts. Since the Eighteenth Amendment only forbids
beverages which are intoxicating Congress should have
defined the concept "intoxicating" in such manner as to
agree with the actual truth of the matter. In order to
ascertain the facts it should have consulted scientific experts and should have fixed the permitted proportion of
alcohol in accordance with the scientific truth as stated
to it by these authorities. Then, at least, it would have
to be admitted that Congress had done its duty without
prejudice or partiality as made incumbent upon it by the
Eighteenth Amendment to the Constitution. Since Congress

did not do this, popular opinion saw in the Volstead law
not the proper and legitimate instrument for the carrying
out of the intent of the Constitution but a vehicle of
tyranny, enacted for the purpose of forcing upon the people
the views of a narrow-minded clique which happened to be
in control of Congress. This added greatly to the bitter
resentment and dislike of the entire system of Prohibition
which prevailed so extensively among the people. It was
quite generally thought that the purpose of Congress in
fixing the quantity of alcohol permitted in beverages at the
ridiculously low amount of one-half of one per cent was to
render the beverages insipid and unpalatable and thus force
those accustomed to use alcoholic drinks to desist therefrom
through disgust at their insipidity. This was resented as
an underhanded and disingenuous method of increasing the
severity of Prohibition and indirectly aiding professional
Prohibition organizations, such as the Anti-Saloon League,
in their efforts to suppress completely the use of alcoholic
beverages.

The writer is not in a position to say that there was any
truth in this suspicion but the practical working out of the
law did seem to lend support to this view. The liquid
known as beer under the Prohibition system in this country
was certainly a wishy-washy, tasteless and nondescript
substance unworthy of the name which it bore. Unhappy
Americans, deprived of all opportunity to obtain the genuine article, were obliged *nolens volens* to swallow it but
foreigners, accustomed to the noble brews of their native
lands, would have none of it. Their only sentiment, when
brought face to face with the fact that that was the only
kind of beverage permitted by law to American citizens,
was that of uncomprehending wonder that in a country
supposed to be a free republic such intolerable interference
with the personal liberty of its citizens should be possible.

It may be that there is no intrinsic connection between
law and truth or justice. Law is necessarily whatever law-
making bodies declare to be such. But there is an inner
conviction in the minds of the people that law should only
be an expression of justice, a method for putting justice

into practice and that, therefore, its basis and antecedent presumption should be admittedly and incontrovertibly true. A law, such as the Volstead law, which was in flagrant contradiction to this popular sentiment, is sure to be detested. It is not a wise or safe policy for governments to adopt laws which are thus looked upon.

PROHIBITION WORKED GREAT FINANCIAL INJURY TO THE COUNTRY

Prohibition was the cause of great financial injury alike to the government and the people of the United States. Had it been productive of high and undeniable moral benefit to the people, that would, perhaps, be no argument in its disfavor but, conditions being what they were, even the most enthusiastic advocate of Prohibition could hardly claim that the results accomplished by it justified its retention at the expense of disrupting, in great measure, the economic structure of the land and placing new and heavy financial burdens on the government while, at the same time, diminishing its resources. The financial injury thus caused showed itself in a multitude of ways but may be classified, broadly speaking, under three general headings. First there was the direct damage done to the economic life of the nation through the suppression of two of the greatest industries of the land, the liquor traffic and the brewing industry, which affected not only them but also many subsidiary industries, annihilating at one fell stroke the vast revenues which they formerly produced and depriving of employment an uncertain but very large number of people, in all probability a million or more; secondly the loss to the government of the great sums formerly paid by these industries for taxes and licenses, and thirdly, the huge amounts paid by the government in its vain attempt to enforce the law. As to the amount of money lost and other economic disadvantages caused by Prohibition there is considerable diversity of opinion but there is practical unanimity that the financial damage done was very great and that the repeal of the Eighteenth

Amendment and the Volstead law was immensely beneficial to the country and helped greatly to alleviate the economic misery and depression under which the nation, in the years following 1929, suffered gravely and unprecedentedly. A few expressions of opinion, by earnest thinkers and economic authorities, will serve to show the general sentiment.

Edward F. Hutton, a prominent financier and industrialist, in an article printed in the New York *American* of September 27th, 1931, stated his view thus: "Our President has spoken of the 'Valley Forge of Depression.' Business conditions, as we find them today, would not set up any argument with that statement. When the opportunity is at the door of our Government to release at least a million men from the ranks of the unemployed by permitting beer, it would occur to the average man what an outrage it is and what an unnecessary burden is being placed upon the shoulders of the taxpayers and citizens of this country to face this problem when the modification of the Volstead Act would do so much to cure our entire picture. As for the Government's need of greater tax revenue it is probable that over a billion dollars could be raised by permitting the sale of beer. In the year 1914, in round figures, there were 66,000,000 barrels of beer manufactured, which was the output of 1,347 brewing and malting establishments. There was a Federal tax of $1.00 a barrel, which gave a revenue to our Federal Government of $66,000,000. A few years later there was additional taxation, making a total tax of $6.00 per barrel, which gave the Government revenue at the rate of $396,000,000 per year, based on 1914 production. With the modification of the Volstead Act the Government could very easily put a tax of $8.00 on a barrel. It is estimated that 130,000,000 barrels of beer would be sold yearly if the Volstead Act were modified. . . . Therefore, with a tax of $8.00 per barrel, the Government could get over a billion dollars per year revenue if 130,000,000 barrels were used. . . . According to the United States Fuel Administration, the breweries used 2,000,000 tons of coal in 1917, which represented in car loadings 40,000 cars. The other items, according to these figures, such as brewing materials, machinery appliances, beer in kegs or bottles, brewers' grains, totaled 123,666 cars. These figures were based on the 1917 consumption of beer, which was less than the year 1914, due to the fact that in 1917 many brewers went out of business, so, if we calculate on the increased consumption mentioned above, it would run in the neighborhood of 210,000 carloads. . . . To be conservative, at least 1,000,000 men would be taken from the ranks of the unemployed. We would increase car loadings by hundreds of thousands of cars. I think the railroads need the business. . . . The people who would be given employment are not alone those who worked in the breweries, but those who mined the coal, who mined and smelted the copper, who planted and harvested the grain, who built the cooperage; the wagons, trucks and railroads that hauled the freight; the waiters who served the beverage; those who manufactured the linens for aprons, caps and tablecloths; the bottles, the glasses, and the million dollars' worth of pretzels that gave joy to life."

Mr. Hutton's simple and graphic words show with incomparable clearness and lucidity the tremendous assault launched by Prohibition upon the economic well-being of America, the enormous damage it inflicted and the inescapable necessity of abolishing it in order to restore normal prosperity to the sorely afflicted land. But in order to show that he did not stand alone in his views a few more utterances by leading Americans shall be quoted here.

Hon. Charles H. Tuttle, former United States Attorney and Republican candidate for Governor of New York State in 1930, addressing a meeting of the Kiwanis Club at the Hotel McAlpin, New York City, on September 16th, 1931, spoke, in part, as follows: "The Eighteenth Amendment has failed because it is wrong in governmental and ethical principle. At present there is neither prohibition nor abstinence but, in effect, only local option in enforcement and personal option in observance. Repeal is undeniably a long road, unfortunately, beset with obstacles unrelated to its merits. Some remedies, however, are immediately practicable and in applying them we can also attain other useful, and indeed necessary, objectives. Legalizing again the making of beer is one such move. . . . It would give work to hundreds of thousands, it would form a new outlet for grains and thus tend to lessen the farm debacle. It would aid in meeting the treasury deficit and lighten the burden of the taxpayers by supplying a new and large source of revenue and by reducing the direct and indirect cost of the crime which flows from the organized business in illegal beer; it would be a blow at the speakeasy."

Mrs. Archibald B. Roosevelt, a prominent directress of the Women's Organization for National Prohibition Reform, in a radio address from Station WGBS demanded the repeal of the Eighteenth Amendment. Among the many reasons which she adduced, was also that of the financial injury caused by Prohibition, on which she expressed herself as follows: "I do firmly believe that the repeal of the Eighteenth Amendment would be an important factor in restoring prosperity to this country. Faced with a probable national deficit of $1,500,000,000, one need not be an economist or a statistician to appreciate that the loss of over $1,000,000,000 annually with a law which has failed disastrously, is not good economics. Over $40,000,000 a year is wasted by the Federal Government in a futile attempt at the enforcement of this law. About $982,000,000 is lost annually in Federal and State revenues and finds its way into the pockets of bootleggers, racketeers and corrupt officials."

Hon. James W. Gerard, former Ambassador to Germany, in an address before the Young Men's Board of Trade of New York City, on October 28th, 1931, termed Prohibition "this noble but rather ghastly experiment" and called attention to a different but very significant aspect of the financial loss caused thereby. Mr. Gerard said that during an average year American visitors spend in Canada $285,-000,000 for alcoholic beverages and in Europe $730,000,000, totaling over $1,000,000,000, to say nothing of the great amounts spent for the same purpose in Bermuda, Cuba and Mexico.

It is, of course, true that, even if there is no Prohibition in the United States, American travelers spend much money abroad for alcoholic drinks. But it is a notorious fact that hundreds of thousands went abroad, who otherwise would not have done so, for the sole purpose of evading the Prohibition law and indulging in alcoholic drinks to their heart's content. It is therefore a conservative estimate to place the amount of money spent for alcoholic drinks in foreign countries by American citizens, directly brought about by Prohibition, at $500,000,000 which amount must be added to the terrifying total of financial loss caused to the United States of America by the "noble but somewhat ghastly" experiment which its legislators, in their wisdom, saw fit to inflict upon the country.

Bradstreet's, the publication of the well known business agency, investigated the business men of the country in order to ascertain their opinion concerning the economic effect of Prohibition. Six questions were submitted to a few leading business men in each town or city throughout the country, of which repeal or amendment of the Prohibition enforcement law was one. The publication itself was neutral and expressed no editorial opinion. The result of this investigation was published in the press on November 8th, 1931. Of the total number replying 69% were opposed to the Volstead Act, 55% favoring total repeal and 14% modification; 24% believed that no benefit to business would result from a change and 7% had no definite opinion.

These clear and well grounded statements certainly indicate that Prohibition was, financially and economically, a disaster of unprecedented magnitude to the country and that leading thinkers and a great majority of those conducting the business affairs of the nation recognized that fact. Over against these overwhelming and incontrovertible facts the attempts of the fanatical Prohibitionists to deny its destructiveness and to claim that it brought about prosperity, were merely puerile. The terrible effects of Prohibition on the well being of the American people were patent on every hand, in tremendous real estate losses, in complete destruction of great business profits, in loss of employment and consequent poverty and suffering for vast multitudes of people, in senseless expenditure of American money in foreign lands, in huge loss of revenue coupled with increased expenditure to the Government. It was a frightful incubus, an "old man of the sea" resting on the back of the American people. America's people had no choice but to rise in their might and throw off this unendurable burden with such vigor and completeness as—let us hope—to rid themselves of it forever.

THE SALOON IS NOT NECESSARILY BAD

In this connection it is proper to call attention to an erroneous and misleading view which is often expressed by vehement upholders of Prohibition and other unrelenting enemies of what is uncomplimentarily referred to as "the demon Rum." That is the view that the saloon, the place where alcoholic drinks are sold and served, is incurably and irretrievably evil, that the saloon of pre-Prohibition days was a vile sink of iniquity, and that the saloon is at all times, by reason of its intrinsic nature, hopelessly vicious and pernicious, a stench in the nostrils of all decent persons, an institution for whose existence there is no possible justification and which must be mercilessly uprooted and exterminated for the sake of morality and decency and all the finer qualities of human life. So strong is this antipathy to the saloon that many even of the opponents of Prohibition are afraid to defend or justify it in any way and hasten to assure their listeners or readers that they do not favor the return of the saloon and that having been once eliminated from American life, it must remain permanently excluded. Forsooth, the experience of the American saloon is a demonstration of the truth of the homely adage, "give a dog a bad name and hang him." The American saloon as an institution is a victim of the deservedly bad reputation of some individual saloons. It is undoubtedly true, and no attempt is made here to deny the fact, that some of the old-time saloons were resorts of the vicious and the criminal, that robbery, savage fighting and even murder took place within their recesses. Nevertheless to condemn

saloons as a whole because of the offenses of some is unfair
and unjustified. Even in the old "wide open" days many
of the saloons—probably the majority—were decent, respectable and unobjectionable. It was a matter which
depended almost entirely upon the character of the proprietor. If the proprietor was an honorable and law-
abiding person and a friend of peace and quiet, he saw to it
that his saloon reflected those qualities. If he was a scamp
and an actual or potential criminal, his saloon became a
"dive," a low and abominable resort, in which the vilest
crimes were concocted and perpetrated. But it is safe to
say that only the minority of saloon keepers belonged to
this latter category. The great majority undoubtedly saw
in their vocation merely a legitimate opportunity to earn
their livelihood. They considered that they were pursuing
a lawful occupation, for which there was a need and considerable demand and they had no desire for avoidable and
unnecessary conflicts with the law and the police. Therefore, at the risk of incurring the opprobrium which is visited
upon the defenders of unpopular causes, the writer must
express his conviction that this undiscriminating condemnation of the saloon is neither right nor fair, that it is based
upon unreasoning prejudice. The saloon is not intrinsically
nor necessarily evil; on the contrary, it may, when properly
conducted, render a valuable social service. Reflection
upon the causes which brought the saloon into existence
and the purposes for which its customers patronize it will
show that this is the case. The saloon has been well called
"the poor man's club." The poor man visits the saloon or,
at least, did so while the saloon existed, in the main, for
exactly the same reason as the rich man his elegant and
luxurious club, for social intercourse and recreation. After
his exhausting toil of the day he desires to go to a place
where he can meet pleasant companions of his own social
type and pass a few hours agreeably in conversation and
the enjoyment of such beverages and other refreshments as
accord with his taste. It must be admitted that the American pre-Prohibition saloon was not particularly well
adapted for the fulfillment of this purpose. Too little at-

tention was given to arrangements for meeting the social needs of its patrons and it was largely not a resort in any true sense of the term but merely a place where one could imbibe a hasty draught and depart. The bar at which one drank in a standing posture accentuated this tendency and almost forced the patrons of the saloon to make their stay very short. In the last analysis, however, it is clear that it was the social craving and the longing for rest and recuperation which drove men to the saloon, especially the multitudes whose home conditions were sordid, dreary and uncomfortable. To these latter the saloon offered at least a temporary respite from the naggings and revilings of slatternly and sharp-tongued wives, the crying and clamor of peevish and fretful children and the bleak and repellent atmosphere of foul and gloomy tenements. The saloon undoubtedly had much about it that was evil and sinister and but little that was cheerful and beneficial. But the right method of dealing with it was not the crude and stupid procedure of destruction but the wise and purposeful policy of improvement. Not suppression but reform was what the saloon needed. All the evils which followed in the wake of Prohibition, in particular the coming into existence of thousands of so-called "speakeasies," secret resorts where those who felt the need of alcoholic beverages and the sort of social entertainment which the saloon formerly supplied gratified their desires in an atmosphere of surreptitiousness and law breaking, were the direct consequences of the fact that legislators took no consideration of the social instinct of human beings and their natural right to satisfy it with no other restriction than that dictated by decency and good behavior. It would have been true statesmanship to encourage the establishment of clean, respectable and well-conducted places of public resort—call them saloons or cafés or taverns or by any other name or designation which may be agreed upon, since the name is a matter of indifference—where men could go, alone or accompanied by their wives and children, and pass a few pleasant hours and where they could obtain pure and wholesome drinks, alcoholic and non-alcoholic, and good food at moderate prices and at the same time enjoy conversation with friends or read newspapers or periodicals or listen to good music and innocent entertainment. We can learn much in this regard from Europe, where cafés, gardens and inns, all licensed to sell alcoholic beverages, exist in great numbers and are patronized by practically the entire population, whose enjoyment of life they greatly increase without in any way violating public decency or sobriety. It may safely be stated that on the continent of Europe where the liquor trade, though subject to police regulation, is perfectly free and lawful, there is much less drunkenness than in Prohibition America where no saloon could legally exist and where all traffic in intoxicants was rigidly prohibited. There is no valid reason why we in the United States cannot solve our drink problem in the same logical and sensible manner. The late Bishop Potter of the Episcopal Church of New York recognized this truth and established at one time what was known as "the church saloon," a place of public resort under church auspices, conducted, of course, in the most unquestionably respectable manner, to which whole families could go and pass an evening sociably and pleasantly and obtain a great variety of refreshments, including alcoholic beverages. The present writer does not recall precisely what was the ultimate fate of this "saloon" but it is his impression that it flourished for a time, successfully performed its social purpose of providing an unobjectionable *rendezvous* for the poorer element of the community and enjoyed great popularity but was finally given up because of the opposition of narrow-minded church people who could not appreciate the broad social outlook of the liberal Bishop. Be that as it may, it is evident that there is no unAmerican heresy in advocating that upon which a great American and an eminent ecclesiastic such as Henry Codman Potter set the stamp of his approval. Along these lines lies, in the opinion of the writer, the solution of the problem of the American saloon. When American social workers will have the wisdom to perceive the desirability, and American legislators the intelligence and courage to enact laws that will make possible the establishment of clean, attractive and respectable places of public resort, where alcoholic liquor will neither be banned nor be the only beverage supplied, the old time "dive" will disappear and the saloon will cease to be a problem.

Summing up, the conclusion of the matter when all has been heard (Ecclesiastes XII, 13) is; prohibition is no solution of the drink problem, no remedy for the evils of drunkenness and no proper or advisable method for the promotion of temperance. Shall we, therefore, come to the conclusion that the problem is insoluble and that there is nothing for us to do except to submit to the undeniable evils of intemperance since all attempts to overcome them are doomed to failure. That conclusion is by no means inevitable. There is a way, indeed there are several ways to lessen or overcome excessive alcoholic indulgence and to promote moderation or temperance but along lines quite different from those followed in the system of Prohibition.

FORCE IS NO PROPER METHOD OF PROMOTING TEMPERANCE

The first thought which must be held fast is that force must be avoided in all efforts to promote temperance. Force is right and proper when it is a question of suppressing ordinary, vulgar crime. The robber and the murderer, the sneak thief and the hold-up man can be dealt with in no other way. They deliberately and audaciously violate fundamental principles upon which the safety and well being, indeed the very existence, of human society depend. Their unscrupulous and contumacious attempts to override the law must be resisted by the same instrument which they employ—force. It is interesting to note that criminals of the types mentioned do not usually resent the employment of force to suppress their malefactions. They know in their hearts that they have brought their sufferings upon themselves and that the state has no other recourse in its dealings with them than the employment of force, stern, relentless and unpitying force. It happens not infrequently that feeling the hard hand of the law puts criminals of this sort into a penitent frame of mind and that they resolve henceforth to amend their ways or, as they word it in their own parlance, "to go straight."

But when the illegal action for which a law violator is punished is a mere *malum prohibitum*, a matter of personal habit or custom such as the imbibing of an alcoholic drink, which the lawmakers of the land have seen fit to prohibit or make unattainable, then the attempt to enforce such a law is bitterly resented as intolerable tyranny and unpardonable invasion of the natural rights of human beings, which it is a meritorious deed to disregard and disobey. It is utterly futile to rely upon force as a means of insuring the carrying out of such a law. Disapproving citizens will always find ways and means to evade the hated law and to obtain the prohibited article which they desire. Temperance policies must, therefore, if they are to be successful, be so shaped as to influence people voluntarily to renounce excessive indulgence and practice moderation. Voluntary, unforced resolve to control one's appetites and cravings, is an essential requisite for all hopeful and fruitful work for the promotion of temperance among the people. When people realize that excessive indulgence in alcohol is gravely injurious and that moderation and sobriety are productive of physical and mental health and economic success then temperance will be the rule and drunkenness and alcoholic excess the exception.

EDUCATION THE CHIEF PROMOTER OF TEMPERANCE

Education is the great force which can be relied upon to bring about voluntary temperance and renunciation of excessive indulgence whether in alcoholic drinks or other substances of possibly noxious or toxic effect. The Socratic dictum "men sin only when folly enters their minds" still holds good.* People, at least normally constituted people, endeavor, as a rule, to do the things which are beneficial to them, they do not usually deliberately set out to injure

* It is interesting to note that the Rabbis of the Talmud set up almost the identical principle, "No man transgresses unless the spirit of folly enters into him" (Sotah, 3a).

themselves. Men are, of course, largely under the influence of passion but its sway is only absolute over ignorant and uninformed minds. It is only necessary to convince a normally constituted person that overindulgence in alcoholic beverages results in ruined health, shattered nerves and inability to perform properly the duties of one's vocation, leading finally to complete downfall and hopeless poverty, while, on the other hand, moderation or abstinence and regular life habits mean perennial health and vigor and consequent success and prosperity, to induce him, as a matter of course, to adopt the latter policy. But in order that this method of education shall be successful it must be free from exaggeration, unfounded statements and false pathos. Such expressions as "the demon rum" and unbridled denunciations of the drinking of intoxicants as a foul and damnable crime in itself, produce a reaction of disgust in most minds and defeat their purpose. Alcohol is not absolutely and necessarily bad, a mere, unmitigated poison. It has its good sides and useful purposes. Its stimulative power is not only valuable but indispensable in various forms of disease and the majority of physicians strongly condemned the restrictions placed by the Prohibition law upon their liberty of prescribing alcoholic beverages for their patients. Even for persons in normal health but who are temporarily suffering from exhaustion or exposure a moderate amount of an alcoholic drink may be most refreshing and invigorating. Most people know these facts and are repelled by the fanatical denunciation of alcoholic liquors as the vilest of vile substances, without one redeeming feature. Such statements are unqualifiedly false. The moderate use of alcohol, remaining on the safe side of intoxication, is not harmful.

The educational method of promoting temperance must therefore confine itself to pointing out the undeniable evils of overindulgence but refrain from fanatical advocacy of total abstinence. By pursuing a sane and moderate policy in its efforts to promote temperance, it can undoubtedly induce the majority of persons to recognize the wisdom of sobriety and the restraint of appetite and thus remove most of the evil conditions which were the ultimate cause of the adoption of Prohibition.

IMPROVED PUBLIC RESORTS TEND TO PROMOTE TEMPERANCE

A most effective method to promote temperance would be the establishment of pleasant and attractive places of public resort. In the discussion of the saloon it was shown that the gloomy and unsociable character of the old time saloon was one of the chief causes of excessive drinking. Unless the patron of the saloon imbibed frequently he had no business in the place and his presence was not desired. Such a resort had no social value and might easily become a public danger as indeed many of them did. But an improved "saloon" rejecting the evil characteristics of the old time resort of that name and introducing many new and attractive features, is an entirely different matter. It must inevitably be of great social benefit. Its very atmosphere would militate against drunkenness and vice and, without banning alcoholic drinks, would nevertheless promote temperance and decency. It would even promote friendly and harmonious relations in family life by bringing husband, wife and children together in pleasant and agreeable association for several hours and thus introducing a kinder and more affectionate spirit into the home. It would tend directly to diminish excessive indulgence in intoxicating liquors. Men do not yield to drunkenness when with their families and in the midst of well behaved and well mannered people. To provide clean and respectable resorts of this kind would, therefore, be a distinct contribution to the cause of temperance.

IMPROVED ECONOMIC CONDITIONS WOULD REMOVE THE GREATEST CAUSE OF DRINKING

Probably the greatest service to the cause of temperance would be rendered by improving the economic condition of the masses, that is, by introducing more happiness and well being into their drab and comfortless lives. All who have studied social conditions among the poorer classes know that the lack of comfort and convenience in the home and the constant struggle and worry which accompany the poor in their efforts to gain a livelihood are the chief causes of excessive indulgence in alcohol. As to the question of how to improve the economic condition of the masses this is not the place in which to discuss that. That question has already been treated—whether adequately or not is for the readers to decide—in the chapter on the economic problem in general. Here the writer merely wishes to call attention to the fact that the very best method of combating intemperance and drunkenness, far better even than the two which have just been recommended, education and the provision of pleasant and decent resorts, and incomparably superior to any method based upon the use of force, would be to so improve the economic conditions of the working classes as to render it possible for them to dwell in roomy and well furnished homes, enjoy all reasonable comfort in life and occupy a respected position in the community. That would make them solid and substantial citizens and citizens of that social type have no desire—because they have no need—to seek consolation for misery in the cup which brings forgetfulness. Incidentally improved economic conditions would tend to imbue the workingman with conservative sentiments, would make him a staunch defender of the existing institutions of the republic and unreceptive to the incitements of radical and revolutionary agitators. The hungry and dissatisfied are the material from which subversive movements draw their recruits, the well fed and contented will always prefer the actual comforts of the present to the most alluring Paradise of a seductively pictured but uncertain future.

Summing up the conclusions reached in this chapter Prohibition is a failure because it is an invasion of the natural human—and probably also the constitutional—rights of American citizens. It is unenforceable because it meets with the stubborn and unyielding resistance of vast multitudes of citizens, based upon their conviction that it is an arbitrary interference with personal habits without moral justification. It breeds contempt for all law and is largely responsible for the crime wave which afflicts the nation. It added heavily to the expense of government while decreasing even more heavily the income from which that expense must be defrayed, thus increasing grievously the already almost unendurable burden of taxation under which the citizenry groans. And last and worst it did not advance the cause of temperance which cannot be promoted by force but only by the three sane and reasonable methods described, education, the provision of respectable and unimpeachable places of resort and the improvement of economic conditions. It did not even succeed in abolishing the saloon which, whatever its demerits may have been, was at least open and subject to police control, but merely in substituting therefor the far worse and utterly uncontrollable speakeasy. The best thing to do with the absurd blunder of Prohibition was to efface it, as the American people have done, from Constitution and statute book. The next step is to substitute for it a rational method, based upon a sympathetic understanding of human nature, of dealing with the drink problem.

CHAPTER TENTH

THE PROBLEM OF GOVERNMENT

IT is a truism that the fate of a people depends very greatly upon the kind of a government it has. The only proper purpose for which governments exist is the promotion of the welfare of the people but since this welfare depends mainly upon the laws and conditions, political, social and economic, which prevail in the land and these are created and determined by the governments, it follows as a natural corollary that it is of fundamental importance to the people to secure a government which shall have the sincere desire to promote the national welfare, the wisdom to recognize the methods and actions by which that aim can be attained and the power and energy to carry them out effectively. It is not possible to state dogmatically which of the known forms of government is best adapted to promote the happiness of the governed. Aristotle, the master mind of ancient Greece and probably of all history, has well stated the various possible forms of human government and pointed out the merits and defects inherent in each of them. According to his well known arrangement there are three possible forms of government, monarchy or that form in which the sovereignty of the state is vested in one individual; aristocracy, in which it is entrusted to one group or class of the nation considered the best fitted and most capable of carrying out governmental functions; and democracy, in which governmental power is retained by the people and either exercised directly by the people themselves or indirectly by elected representatives gathered together in legislative assemblies. Opinions differ as to which of these three forms is the best. It has been said, not inaptly, that monarchy is the most efficient, aristocracy the wisest and democracy the justest system of government.

Aristotle points out that each of the systems has its defects. Monarchy is apt to degenerate into tyranny, Aristocracy into oligarchy or the selfish rule of the few over the many and democracy into ochlocracy or the wild, unregulated sway of the mob with slight consideration of those not of their class. Aristotle himself thought a combination of aristocracy and democracy, a sort of mixed system in which the two elements would restrain each other from excesses or misuse of power, the best form.

As far as the American people is concerned, these differences of opinion have only academic interest. It has made its choice and has opted for democracy. Democracy is the governmental system which the American nation desires for the control and shaping of its national affairs. The question and the problem are "Is government as carried on in the United States of America truly democratic and if not how can it be made to conform to the genuine principles and ideals of democracy?"

In answer to this question it must be said that in principle and theory the United States of America is a true and genuine democracy. Its government is based upon the asumption that all power rests ultimately with the people, that all just governments derive their authority from the consent of the governed, that no class or element of the citizenry enjoys any special rights or privileges above any other class but that all citizens are equal in the sight of the law, and that the citizens possess the absolute and indisputable right to modify, alter or repeal any law or statute which does not meet with their approval and even the Constitution itself, should that course appear necessary or desirable. It is, as it has been aptly and eloquently described by the immortal Abraham Lincoln in his famous Gettysburg address, a government "of the people, by the people and for the people." Such words are fitting only in reference to a pure and true Democracy and such evidently was the conception of American government held by the great martyr President and the Americans of his generation. Such, too, had been the concept of the representatives of the thirteen newly constituted American states in adopting the Constitution for they stated explicitly in the Preamble that their purpose in adopting it was "to secure the blessings of liberty to ourselves and our posterity."

The threefold governmental system of America, legislative, judicial and executive, is, moreover, fundamentally democratic. The laws are made by the chosen representatives of the people, they are interpreted by the Judges whom the people, in accordance with the legally adopted method, have placed in their august positions and are carried out and enforced by the executive officials, all of whom, from the President down, are, according to the legal concept of their status, merely the servants of the people. A purer and truer democratic system than this is hardly conceivable.

It must, however, be admitted that this genuinely democratic concept, which is at the base of the American system of government, is not always carried into actual practice in the laws adopted and the governmental institutions established.

MANNER OF SELECTION OF SENATE IS UNDEMOCRATIC

This undemocratic trend is already recognizable in the Constitution itself. The manner of selecting the Senate is an illustration of this. Section third of the Constitution provides that the Senate of the United States shall be composed of two Senators from each State, chosen by the legislature thereof. This is a highly undemocratic arrangement. The Congress of the United States is composed of two houses, the House of Representatives and the Senate, but only the former is representative of the people while the latter represents the states as corporate entities or, to speak more accurately, the legislatures of the states. It is a moot question among the students of statecraft whether a bicameral or unicameral system of legislation, that is to say a Congress or Parliament consisting of two houses or chambers or of only one, is preferable but whichever system is adopted, true democracy requires that the members thereof be elected by popular vote. The Senators, selected by the legislatures, are not truly representative of the people, for the legislatures once in office are to all intents and purposes independent bodies which may be not only irresponsive to the popular will but even directly antagonistic thereto and the men whom they select as Senators may be, and not infrequently have been, such as the people would never have chosen. The Senate may thus become a check and hindrance of the popular will as expressed in the House of Representatives. The seventeenth Amendment to the Constitution, proposed in Congress, May 16th, 1912, and ratified by the consent of the necessary number of states, April 8th, 1913, did away with this wrong through ordaining that the Senators shall be elected by the people of the States. This change, important and beneficial in itself, did not and could not, however, remove the wrong inherent in the whole concept of the Senate as established by the Constitution. The Senate is intended to give equal representation and power to all the states, large or small, by assigning to each an equal number, two, of Senators. This arrangement is fundamentally unjust and undemocratic. We can well understand how it came to be adopted. The thirteen British colonies in North America, which the successful issue of the Revolutionary War had freed from all allegiance to and dependence upon the mother country, felt themselves free and independent states and were jealous of their status as such. Before entering a new union and becoming members of a new nation they desired assurance that they would not be submerged and that their separate identity and position of influence would be preserved. This assurance they found in the creation of an Upper House or Senate which should be representative not of the people as such but of the States and in which all States, without regard to geographical extent, number of inhabitants or resources, should have an equal voice and equal power. But while this motive is perfectly intelligible and, to a certain extent, excusable, it does not alter the fact that this arrangement is intrinsically unfair and productive of the greatest inequalities and injustices, in a word, absolutely undemocratic. Why shall, for instance, a petty Western

State, whose population hardly equals that of a single ward in New York City, have the same power in the Senate as the great Empire State with inhabitants exceeding twelve million in number? Where is the democracy of such an arrangement? Since the consent of the Senate is essential in matters of legislation the Senators of a group of second rate states containing an insignificant minority of population can defeat the will of the majority of the people. Admitting that the bicameral system is desirable the number of members of the Senate should vary according to the population of the States they represent and no State should have more Senators than it is entitled to in accordance with the number of its inhabitants.

THE ELECTORAL COLLEGE METHOD OF CHOOSING THE PRESIDENT IS UNDEMOCRATIC

The method of electing the President, as prescribed in the Constitution, is another example of undemocratic tendencies in that fundamental instrument. Article II of the Constitution prescribes that the President of the United States shall be elected by an Electoral College, whose members shall be appointed by the States, in such manner as the legislatures thereof may direct and which shall be equal in number to the whole number of senators and representatives.* This Electoral College is to have the right and the duty to elect both the President and the Vice-President and its members are to have no restriction upon their liberty of choice except that the persons chosen shall not both be residents of the same state. The undemocratic character of this method is at once evident. The people are to have no voice in the selection of their highest officials, which shall be completely in the hands of a limited number of individuals. The people need not even know who are the candidates from whom their Chief Magistrates are to be chosen. The fact that such a method could be agreed upon is a clear indication that despite the democratic spirit which

* This article was afterwards modified by the Twelfth Amendment but not in its fundamental provisions.

dictated the character of most of the Constitution, there must have been among many, perhaps most, of the members of the Constitutional Convention, lurking aristocratic viewpoints which manifested themselves in a strong distrust of the people. The undemocratic character of this arrangement was too great to be long endured. Though never formally abolished it was speedily nullified by the method at present prevailing, in accordance with which, while electors are chosen in the states in the manner prescribed in the Constitution they are not at liberty to make their own choice but are under the tacit obligation to vote for certain candidates for President and Vice-President nominated by the political party to which they, the electors, belong. Thus, by what may be called an unwritten or informal amendment, the most grossly undemocratic feature of the constitutional provision was removed and the people have a say in the selection of the men who are to stand at their head for four years.

But even the method at present prevailing is far from being unobjectionable. It is by no means truly democratic. Since the electors are chosen by states and equal the senators and representatives in number, it is perfectly possible, and has occurred, that a majority of presidential electors may be elected by a minority of voters. Under such circumstances a President is not truly representative of the people. Since the President is the chief and leader of the whole nation, the office of President should only be occupied by one who has received the votes of the majority of the citizens. The method of choosing the President and Vice-President of the United States should transcend state lines and divisions and should be based upon the elementary postulate of democracy that the chief of the whole people shall be the choice of the majority of the people. Certain undemocratic institutions and conditions which prevailed for a long time were finally abolished and no longer exist. Their historic importance, however, warrants their being considered here.

SLAVERY WAS IN ABSOLUTE CONTRADICTION TO THE SPIRIT
OF DEMOCRACY

Undoubtedly the greatest contradiction to the spirit of democracy was the institution of slavery. It seems incredible that a nation whose struggle for existence had been ushered in by the Declaration of Independence in which occurs the noble sentence "We hold these truths to be self-evident: That all men are created equal; that they are endowed by their Creator with certain unalienable rights; that among these are life, liberty and the pursuit of happiness"; should have tolerated for a moment the complete negation of these principles manifested in slavery, through which one set of men can own other men as their chattels and these latter are as completely deprived of the power of self-determination, and of all human rights and privileges, as though they were dumb brutes or inanimate objects. Incomprehensible as this contradiction seems, it is, nevertheless, a fact, founded, of course, upon the historical conditions of the time. The Constitution nowhere alludes directly to slavery but recognizes tacitly its existence by providing in Article I, Section 2 that "Representatives . . . shall be apportioned among the several states . . . according to their respective numbers, which shall be determined by adding to the whole number of free persons, . . . three fifths of all other persons" and in Section 9 that "The migration or importation of such persons as any of the states now existing shall think proper to admit, shall not be prohibited by the Congress prior to the year one thousand eight hundred and eight." One sees at once that these provisions represent a compromise, that there were delegates to the Convention who recognized the wrongfulness of slavery and the tragic inconsistency of its existence in a free republic but that the slave holding states would not surrender their favorite institution and that the opponents of slavery, in order not to imperil the projected Union, were obliged to yield. The Thirteenth, Fourteenth and Fifteenth Amendments to the Constitution have effectively and permanently removed the stain of slavery from the escutcheon of American democracy but before that happy result was attained almost a century of bitter strife and dissension, culminating in four terrible years of fratricidal warfare, had to elapse and its evil effects have not yet disappeared— and may never completely disappear—from the land.

LAME DUCK SESSIONS OF CONGRESS WERE UNDEMOCRATIC

A number of conditions formerly existing in the governmental methods of the United States were in contradiction to true democracy. Take, for instance, the so-called "lame duck" sessions of Congress. The term "lame duck" is a colloquialism for members of Congress who have been defeated for a second term. Simple logic would require that since these men have lost the sympathy and support of their constituents, who have refused to reëlect them, they should no longer have the power to make laws binding the people who have rejected them. But by a strange inconsistency in the American political system, these "lame ducks" were permitted to return for a period to the halls of legislation and continued to govern their unwilling fellow citizens. That their activity in these unwanted sessions might be influenced by other motives than those of the public welfare was, of course, more than possible. The evil of these "lame duck" sessions of Congress was early recognized but for a long time no remedy was forthcoming. Under the system originally prevailing members of Congress were elected in the November elections but the new Congress did not convene until December of the following year, thirteen months after having been elected. In the meanwhile a session of the old Congress took place, from December of the year of election until the following March, when the terms of the members expired. This was the "lame duck" session, with all its possibilities of evil. To Senator George W. Norris of Nebraska, belongs most of the credit for doing away with this undemocratic and senseless abuse. Seven times he introduced into the Senate a resolution calling for the abolition of the "lame duck" session of Congress. This required an additional amendment to the Constitution providing that the newly elected Congress shall meet on January 2nd of the year succeeding the election. It also required that the terms of the President and Vice-President shall begin in January instead of March 4th as was hitherto the practice. His efforts were finally crowned with success and "lame duck" sessions became a thing of the past.

THE SYSTEM OF POLITICAL PARTIES IS INADEQUATE AND UNDEMOCRATIC

The system of political parties prevailing in the United States is inadequate as a means of expressing the popular will and undemocratic in that it is not necessarily at all a true or correct expression of that will but may be directly contrary thereto. We may premise by assuming that parties are essential to the working of a republic. Differences of opinion among the citizens are inevitable, both as regards the general theory of governmental policies and as regards the merits or demerits of individual pieces of legislation and it may be taken for granted that the only way by which citizens may hope to carry out their views is to organize into parties and to use their united powers to bring about the adoption as a part of the law of the land of the policies and principles which they favor. This implies that all groups holding views or concepts of public policy in which they differ from other groups shall organize as parties in order to use their power and influence to bring about the adoption of their views by the country. This party organization must, if motives and principles are right, be done as a matter of conviction, without regard to the question whether the prospects of success are favorable or unfavorable. It further implies that all members shall meet upon a basis of equality and liberty of action, influenced solely by the viewpoint which is common to all and that no one member or group of members shall be empowered to dictate the policies or methods of the party or the incumbents of public office. Theoretically American political parties are organized in accordance with these principles, actually they pay little or no attention to them, have other objects in view and are guided by totally different considerations. The real aim of the political parties is victory, that their candidates shall be successful in the elections, and the ultimate goal of their striving is the patronage, the rich "plums" in the shape of fat salaried offices and the other emoluments and opportunities for gain which victory puts into their control, in accordance with the principle "to the victor belong the spoils." The genuine underlying motive of party activity in the United States is, therefore, neither ethical nor patriotic, nor even political in any true sense of the word, but purely selfish and mercenary. It was well expressed a few years ago by a prominent politician in New York City, a man very high in the councils of his party, when he said: "I am working for my pocket all the time." The natural and inevitable result of this mental attitude is deep seated and widespread corruption, unrestrained extravagance in the expenditure of public money, waste and squandering of the national resources and, as a consequence, a tremendous and quite unnecessary increase in the cost of government and the burden of taxation afflicting the people.* The whole system of organization of the parties shows conclusively that victory is the one object of their existence. They are organized with rigid military efficiency, with higher and lower officials called "leaders" and with a commander-in-chief known as the "boss." The party organization works with such machinelike force and sureness that it is popularly dubbed "the machine" and sometimes "the steam roller," because of the deadly intensity and mercilessness with which it crushes all opposition. The "boss" is a veritable dictator, practically an absolute monarch, within the ranks of the party organization and over the vast, inarticulate mass of devoted adherents outside. Public officials belonging to the party and who owe ther nomination and election or appointment to it are obliged to regard themselves primarily as its henchmen and only

* There are, of course, individual exceptions among political leaders to this description, high minded and truly patriotic men whose motive is a sincere desire to serve the people, but the description is correct as regards the average type of politician.

secondarily as the servants of the people and woe betide any overscrupulous or conscientious legislator or other official who would dare to set up his will against that of the boss and the little group that is near to him. His fate, exclusion from the party and from public office and preferment, is swift and certain. An illustration of what can happen to an overconscientious public official is given by the experience of former Governor William Sulzer of New York. Governor Sulzer, who had been a loyal Democrat, owed his elevation to the post of Governor, it appears, largely or perhaps mainly to the influence of Tammany Hall. As a consequence he was expected to accept obediently the dictation of the boss of Tammany in regard to his appointments and action on legislation. But Governor Sulzer had other ideas. He set his duty to the people above his party loyalty or obligation to the Tammany boss. He refused to submit to any such control of his official actions and declared that he would follow only the dictates of his own conscience. The consequences of this noble and praiseworthy stand were that charges, for which there was possibly some basis but which would certainly never have been brought had he remained a faithful servant of the boss, were trumped up against him, he was formally impeached and tried by the legislature and deposed from his high office. Today he is living in comparative obscurity in New York City and his political career is, in all probability, definitely and completely ended. A system under which such shameful happenings are possible is the very reverse and antithesis of democracy. It is a vile tyranny of the most repugnant and disgraceful sort. That such a system can exist and be firmly established among a people loving liberty and possessed of the intelligence and energy requisite for self-rule, that such a people can submit to the odious tyranny of the "boss" and even get to look upon it as quite the right and proper thing is one of the strange and inexplicable anomalies of the American political system.

THE EXISTENCE OF ONLY TWO PARTIES IS REALLY ABSURD

Perhaps the most absurd feature of the whole system of political parties in America is the fact that, in the last analysis, there are really no parties at all. Ostensibly there are two major parties, the Republican and the Democratic, and two or three minor parties. But the minor parties have always played such an utterly insignificant part in American politics as to be completely negligible and the two major parties are not separated by sharply defined and clearly distinguishable differing principles. Such differences undoubtedly existed in the past. The questions of slavery and emancipation, state rights and federal centralization, protective tariff versus free trade or tariff for revenue only were such. But no such clearly cut issues separate the parties today. Republicans of today are not necessarily in favor of a protective tariff and contemporary Democrats are not necessarily Free Traders, representatives of both points of view are found in both camps; there are Prohibitionists and anti-Prohibitionists among the Republicans and among the Democrats; the Progressive Republicans of the West are to all intents and purposes Socialists, the Democrats of the East and North are inclined to liberalism while the Democrats of the South are, to put it mildly, Conservative rather than Democratic.

The main effort of the politicians of both parties appears to be "pussyfooting," that is, to avoid committing themselves too clearly and definitely to any particular policy for fear of alienating the voters who hold the opposite view. The result is a state of confusion and uncertainty as regards the political doctrines and purposes of the parties which cannot fail to have a most bewildering effect upon the minds of the voters and to render intelligent and purposeful exercise of the franchise a matter of extreme difficulty, if not impossibility. The reason for this confusion is undoubtedly to be found in the illogical and unreasonable basis upon which these political parties are erected, that, instead of being organizations formed for the ideal purpose of carrying out certain concepts of statecraft, they are at bottom merely instrumentalities for the promotion of private ambitions and the gaining of place and power.

PARTY LOYALTY IS AN ABSURD THING

The matter is further complicated by the fact that, despite the utterly sordid and repellent character of party conditions there is still among the voters much of what is called "party loyalty." Hundreds of thousands, perhaps millions, of Americans feel a sentiment of loyalty and devotion to the party of their allegiance akin to patriotism. The South is fervently and solidly Democratic, large sections of the North are, or were, equally fervid in their Republicanism. Voters with such sentiments will vote for the candidates of their party, no matter how unworthy or undeserving they may be. Such party loyalty is absurd and very injurious to the welfare of the country. One should, as a good citizen, be devoted in loyalty to one's country. But there is no sensible reason for loyalty to a party. A party is fundamentally nothing more than an instrument for carrying out certain political concepts and ideals. As long as it serves this purpose it is deserving of support, when it ceases to do so it should be rejected and cast aside without hesitation or compunction.

There is no sound and valid reason why the people of the Southern states should feel it their duty to uphold the Democratic party with loyalty so unshakable that a nomination on the ticket of that party should be equivalent to election and there is equally little reason why the people of the State of Maine, or any other of the Northern states, should be so intensely and immovably Republican that the election of a candidate of the Democratic party becomes almost unthinkable. Such loyalty to party is mere fanaticism, unworthy of free citizens and extremely injurious to the cause of popular government. Free citizens should be absolutely independent in political matters and should not ally themselves with any party or vote for its candidates unless they have thoroughly examined the platform of that party and find themselves in agreement with its declarations and satisfied themselves that its nominees are men of honor and integrity who may be relied upon to defend the interests of their constituents and carry out their wishes. Above all, Americans in the living present should not permit their political views and actions to be determined by the hostilities and hatreds of a past age. The reason for the sharp division of North and South into Republican and Democrat is, of course, to be found in the unhappy history of the Civil War when a Republican North forced an unwilling South to remain in the Union and abolished its favorite institution of slavery and made the slaves the political equals of their former masters. But that sad and deplorable time lies now far in the past, the Americans of both sections of the country are again a band of brothers and the political divisions between the two elements should pass away with the passing of the former enmities and animosities and the political allegiances of Americans, whether of North or South or East or West, should be decided only by their sincere belief as to what is most promotive of the welfare of the entire land.

TRUE ADHERENCE TO POLITICAL CONVICTIONS WOULD BRING ABOUT THE EXISTENCE OF MANY PARTIES

Such adherence to genuine political convictions is of course incompatible with the existence of practically only two parties with membership based on traditional loyalties instead of principle. It would mean the calling into being of many parties, whose members would be in complete agreement in regard to every article of their political faith. Some of these parties would undoubtedly be quite small, mere groups or fractions with a handful of representatives in Congress. It might happen sometimes that no one party would have an absolute majority in Congress and it might become necessary to administer the affairs of the country by a coalition.* But what of it? Such a division into

* That is a not infrequent condition in Europe. England was governed during the years (1930-1931) by a coalition of Laborites and Liberals. In Germany Chancellor Heinrich Bruning presided

numerous parties, large and small, would have the great merit of presenting, at least, a true, even if somewhat kaleidoscopic, picture of the national thought on political matters. The present conditions in the two major parties certainly do not present any such clear and true picture even of the thought of their own members. The sight of numerous Senators and Representatives voting, for the sake of party regularity, contrary to their real convictions, especially of those whose attitude in the Prohibition question is described as "drinking wet and voting dry," and the frantic efforts of the leaders of both parties to bring about some sort of external and superficial harmony among their discordant and ill-mated camp followers, would be indeed amusing if it were not in reality so tragic. Nothing better could happen to America than for both of these caricatures of parties to go out of existence, to be succeeded by other parties, based upon real conviction and genuine doctrines, even if differing, as to the best methods of promoting the national welfare. From the honest battle of opinions clear and definite results would emerge and there can be no doubt that the sound common sense of the people would find the right policies for securing the general happiness, the greatest good for the greatest number.

PEOPLE SHOULD HAVE MORE INFLUENCE OVER LEGISLATION AND LEGISLATORS

Another grave defect in the governmental system of America, through which its character as a democracy is seriously impaired, is the fact that the people have little influence over the legislators or power to procure the legislation which they wish. Legislators are theoretically the representatives of their constituents and supposed to vote and exercise their legislative power in accordance with the wishes of the people who elected them. As a matter of fact

over a government formed by the coalition of seven or eight parties without which no majority would have been possible. A similar condition prevailed in the United States Senate, where one Senator, Henrik Shipstead, a Farmer-Laborite, held the balance of power.

the generality of congressmen and assemblymen appear to
be far more concerned with the promotion of their own interests than with the welfare of the people and only to
think of these latter when to neglect them would imperil
their careers. When an election is impending the candidates
eloquently proclaim their love for the people and their devotion to the principles of pure democracy but no sooner
is it over and the victors safely ensconced in their new
offices and positions than they forget all their preëlection
promises and hardly seem to be aware that there is a
people. All this is undoubtedly in accordance with human
nature which is after all fundamentally selfish and more
concerned with its own well being than with anything else
but it is certainly in direct contradiction to democratic principles and very injurious to the state. Legislators and indeed all public officials need to be subject to the control
of the people and to realize that they must not put their
personal desires and views above those of their constituents,
that they are the servants, not the masters, of the people.*
Modern political science has devised three excellent expedients for exercising this popular control over the actions
of legislators and making them more responsive to, and
considerate of, the wishes and views of the people. They
are, briefly stated, the referendum, the initiative and the
recall. By the referendum is meant that proposed legislation shall be submitted to the voters, either by action of
the legislature or at their own request, who shall decide
whether they wish it or not; by the initiative is meant
that the voters shall have the right to demand or themselves
to adopt laws which they wish; by the recall is meant that
the people shall be empowered, after the expiration of a
certain time, to remove from office any public official whose
conduct, in the opinion of the voters, has not been proper
or beneficial to the interests of the state. These powers,

* This does not mean that legislators and officials are to be mere
automatons, without will or mind of their own, but it does mean that
they must be in complete sympathy with the people they represent
and, if not, they should not accept election or appointment at
their hands.

judiciously exercised, are well adapted to safeguard the interests of the people, to put "the fear of God" into the hearts of public officials and to teach them prudence and circumspection in their official acts. The referendum is an invaluable means of determining whether existing laws or proposed new laws are really desired by the people or not. Whenever a law is vehemently opposed by a considerable section of the nation, the only right and proper thing to do is to permit the people to express their will at the ballot box, in other words, to submit it to a referendum. That will definitely settle the question whether the people desire that law or not and will remove the matter from the domain of strife and controversy.* True democracy is inconceivable without some such method of ascertaining and asserting the popular will.

The initiative is an even more potent instrument for effectuating the popular sovereignty. It enables the people not merely to control, to accept or reject, legislation but also to initiate and enact of its own accord such law or laws as it may desire.

This may seem to many a difficult or practically impossible matter, that a numerous and unorganized population shall, so to speak, take over the function of the legislature. As a matter of fact, it is really a very simple proceeding. A certain number of voters, fifty or a hundred thousand, sign and address a petition to the legislature or some other agreed upon branch of the government, stating that they desire the enactment of a certain statute, the text of which is given in the petition. The legislature, or other governmental branch, then arranges in the regular way for an election. If a majority of the voters vote in favor of the proposal, it becomes a law, if not, it is defeated. By this simple but direct and effective method the people are enabled to obtain any desired legislation without the hu-

---

* The recent referendum in Finland is a striking demonstration of the value of this method of ascertaining the popular will. Prohibition had been a hotly disputed issue for many years, just as in the United States. The referendum defeated Prohibition by an overwhelming majority and settled that question in Finland permanently.

miliating necessity of begging for it from their own elected representatives, a self-abasement which is often without result. The initiative is indispensable to true democracy.

The recall is the capstone on the edifice of popular sovereignty. It compels the chosen representatives of the people to have the interests of their electors at heart, to use the powers entrusted to them for the benefit of the people and in accordance with their wishes, in short, it is a most effective device for keeping legislators and other public officials faithful to their duties and mindful of their obligations. It is a sovereign remedy against official forgetfulness.

If the defects and abuses described in this chapter are done away with and if the three above mentioned devices for enforcing the popular will are generally adopted, the democracy of the United States will be such in the truest and fullest sense of the word and the government will indeed be "a government of the people, by the people and for the people."

CHAPTER ELEVENTH

THE PROBLEM OF EDUCATION

FROM the earliest beginnings of American history the importance of education for the welfare of the people has been recognized. Hardly had the first settlers reached these shores and while they were still struggling with the primeval forest and wilderness in an effort to establish their homes and find sustenance for themselves and their families, than they took steps to provide for the education of the coming generation. The Pilgrim Fathers landed at Plymouth Rock in 1620 and fifteen years later, in 1635, a Latin school of the English type was established in Boston and in the following year Harvard College was founded at Cambridge, Massachusetts. In 1642 and 1647 the colony enacted laws establishing schools and ordering children to be taught reading and religion.

Education was cared for in various ways and degrees and provided for from various sources, sometimes public and sometimes private, in all the English colonies in America and continued to progress during the entire colonial period. The attention given to higher education was quite remarkable for a country still in the early formative stage of its development and not yet out of its swaddling clothes. Nine American colleges were organized during the colonial period of American history. They were, in addition to Harvard, William and Mary in 1693, Yale in 1701, Princeton in 1746, Pennsylvania in 1753-55, Kings (Columbia) in 1754, Brown in 1764, Rutgers in 1766 and Dartmouth in 1769. Interest in higher culture and science was evidently very keen in colonial America and was apparently not at all discouraged by the necessarily somewhat rude and primitive conditions of life in a pioneering country and age.

The advent of American independence gave a tremendous impulse to education in all its forms and branches. The great public school system was called into being, mainly by public funds and designed to provide all children, even those of the poorest and humblest citizens, with an adequate knowledge of the essential elements of culture, sufficient to fit them for citizenship and for finding their place in the life of the community. Hundreds of institutions of higher learning, colleges, universities and professional schools were also established, mainly by private individuals or corporations and with private funds. The view, also, of the purpose of education, as given in the public schools and higher institutions of learning, underwent a radical change. The establishment of schools in colonial days had been prompted mainly, if not entirely, by religious motives. The colonies, being settlements of Europeans, naturally reflected the European point of view prevailing at the time. In the Europe of that period religion reigned supreme and all public matters were subordinate to and controlled by religious considerations. Those considerations, therefore, gave form and color to the educational movements of colonial America.* With the establishment of the American Republic, however, and the acceptance by the new nation of the principle of the separation of church and state, it was recognized that formal religious instruction could no longer with propriety be imparted by the public schools. Since then the task of the public schools has been conceived

---

* The first schools in Virginia, for instance, were missionary ventures of the Church of England. In 1616 the king ordered the Bishop of London to collect money for a college to be founded in Virginia, largely for the purpose of educating the children of the native Indians in Christianity. The early schools in New England were established chiefly under the direction and guidance of clergymen. The prime mover in the establishment of the Latin Grammar School of Boston was the Reverend John Cotton. In 1637 Rev. John Fiske settled at Salem and conducted the school there. The first teacher of the school at Thompson's Island, off the coast of Massachusetts, was the Reverend Thomas Waterhouse. In 1641 the general court directed the elders of the church to prepare a "catechism for the instruction of youth in the grounds of religion," thus officially sanctioning religious instruction in the public schools.

as that of preparing the pupils to be capable of intelligently
performing the duties of citizenship and taking a worthy
and useful place in life, while leaving direct instruction in
religion to the churches and specific religious schools. Like
the American government in general, the American public
school is non-religious but not anti-religious. While not
itself imparting specific religious instruction it looks kindly
and sympathetically upon manifestations of religious sentiment on the part of the pupils and encourages such sentiment through the closing of the schools or the granting of
leaves of absence on religious holidays without loss of
standing to pupils.*

In the approximately one hundred and fifty years which
have elapsed since the establishment of the American Republic the educational system has grown to tremendous proportions. The statistics given in the most recent census
report, that of 1930, testify most eloquently to the high
appreciation which the American people have of education
and to their generous support of all agencies for its dissemination. In 1930 there were in the United States 23,550
public high schools, 3,500 private high schools, 140 teachers
colleges, 66 state normal high schools, 47 county normal
schools, 26 city normal schools, 52 private normal schools,
106 colleges and universities under public control, 546 colleges and universities under private control and 286 Junior
colleges. Students in American universities and colleges
in 1927-28 numbered 919,381 (563,244 men and 356,137
women). Summer school enrollment in universities and colleges in 1927 was 239,570, in teacher training institutions
144,285 and in extension courses 270,000. For the school
year 1927-28 it is estimated that there was a population
of school age (5 to 17 inclusive) of 30,887,167, of whom
25,989,508 were enrolled in the public elementary and sec-

* Such, at least, is the theory. As a matter of fact, pupils or
teachers, belonging to minority faiths, often suffer loss of salary or
standing through observing the holy days of their faith, while the
holy days of the majority religion are officially recognized through
the complete closing of the schools. The closing of the schools on
both Saturdays and Sundays is, however, a generous act and a real
boon to pupils of all denominations.

ondary schools and institutions of higher learning and 3,421,107 in the private schools, making a total of 29,410,-615. In addition there were 179,756 students in private commercial and business schools, 187,828 in private trade and industrial schools, and 77,768 in nurses training schools. There were in both public and private schools 1,010,232 teachers (209,398 men, 799,816 women) whose average annual salary was $1,277.

The value of public elementary and high school property in 1927 was $5,486,938,599, of private high school property $635,848,000, including endowments of $75,376,000 and of universities and colleges $2,413,748,981 including endowments of $1,150,112,250. Private elementary school property was valued at about $400,000,000. The expenditure for public school education in 1927-28 was $2,184,336,638, a cost per capita for those in average daily attendance of $86.77.

This munificent generosity on the part of the American people in support of their educational system is based, as has already been pointed out, on the desire that the citizenry of the nation shall consist of cultured, intelligent and moral persons, such as alone are fitted to receive the precious gifts of liberty and self-government and on the assumption that education alone is the instrument which can render them capable of properly appreciating and administering these high privileges and responsibilities. Have the hopes and expectations placed by the American people in their educational system, particularly in the public school system, been fulfilled? Have the huge sums expended for the maintenance of the public schools been a wise investment and have the results achieved in culture, in character and capacity on the part of the broad masses of the people been commensurate to the tremendous outlay supplied in order to obtain them?

In asking these questions there is no reference to the technical efficiency of the schools and colleges and no desire on the part of the writer to deny or belittle the work which the educational institutions of America have done and are doing in the imparting of knowledge and the preparation

of students for trades and professions. An investigation
into the achievements of American universities and technical and professional schools would undoubtedly show that,
while they may be deficient in some respects and inferior
to some highly specialized academies of Europe, they compare, on the whole, very favorably with similar institutions
anywhere in the world.* The higher schools, however, do
not constitute a national problem. The national problem is
concerned only with the education given by the public
schools, whether it accomplishes the task assigned to it,
that of training cultured, ethically behaving and efficient
citizens, capable of taking their place in the life and the
government of a free nation.

It is, of course, difficult, if not impossible, to reach a
general judgment upon the workings of a system so vast
and affecting so tremendous a number of persons, as the
American educational system. Conditions, no doubt, vary
greatly in different parts of this great country and perfection cannot be expected from any human institution. But
this much may, in all moderation and without any desire
to indulge in carping criticism or fault finding or to belittle the efforts of the thousands of earnest men and women
who are devoting their lives to the education of America's
youth, be said, that the results of these efforts are, in several respects, painfully disappointing and fall far short of
fulfilling the expectations which may reasonably be attached to them. Neither can it be denied that such a feeling
of disappointment prevails in broad circles of the American
people and that while the public school system is still gen-
erously supported and looked upon as an integral part of

---

* All indications justify the conclusion that technical education in
America stands upon a very high plane. In engineering accomplish-
ments, such as the erection of mighty edifices and the construction
of railroads, bridges and tunnels, and in the organization of vast
industrial and commercial enterprises, America stands unrivaled. In
art, music and literature America also stands worthily at the side
of the other civilized nations. The high esteem with which American engineers and technicians are regarded is shown by the great
number who have been engaged by the Soviet government to aid in
the carrying out of the Five Year Plan.

American national policy, it is not with the enthusiasm and confidence which characterized the earlier periods of American history.

What is it that the American people ask and expect of the public schools? Their demands are moderate enough. They ask that the public schools shall (1) thoroughly train and instruct all their pupils in the three R's, reading, writing and arithmetic, (2) impart to them a correct and adequate knowledge of the English language, the language of the land, so that they shall speak and write it, if not elegantly, at least correctly and decently, (3) familiarize them with the history and governmental principles of America, so as to instill into their hearts the sentiment of patriotism, (4) teach them ethics, impress upon their youthful minds the beauty of righteous and virtuous conduct, (5) teach them cleanliness, politeness, respectful manners and respectable behavior, (6) prepare them for some useful trade or vocation through which they will be able, in later years, to earn their livelihood. These are surely not extravagant or exaggerated demands. They merely ask that the public schools shall train a generation of normal human beings with the indispensable qualities of such, with adequate intellectual, ethical, social and economic abilities to live worthily in a civilized community. Surely American citizens should not fall below this standard.

It is a matter of general complaint that a large proportion of the graduates of the public schools do not measure up to these requirements. Many of the youths and maidens, public school graduates all of them, who apply for commercial or other positions, are sadly lacking in the indispensable knowledge of the elements, they read haltingly and inaccurately, their handwriting is frequently awkward and inexact and not seldom an illegible scrawl * and their arithmetical ability is so slight that they cannot be relied upon even to do the comparatively easy calculations which

---

* Of course, in this age of the typewriter, handwriting has no longer the importance which it had in former times. But only a small proportion of public school graduates have any knowledge of mechanical writing.

are required in every business. Very many of the graduates of the public schools have an entirely inadequate knowledge of the English language. Their training in the public school has not given them the power of cultured and refined diction and has not familiarized them with the rarer terms and expressions of the language so that they hesitate and stumble whenever, in the course of reading, they encounter a word which is outside of the limits of their extremely circumscribed vocabulary. Their ordinary speech is a vulgar *argot*, replete with the lowest form of slang expressions derived from the current lingo of the rudest elements of the populace, even of the so-called "underworld" or criminal classes, and so different from normal English as to be almost unintelligible to those unaccustomed to these linguistic perversions.* Along with this language degeneracy there has gone an almost unbelievable rudening and vulgarization of manners. The American of the older generation was a person of genuinely refined, one might say, delicate deportment. Courtesy, polite demeanor in public and in private, and kindly consideration and attention to all, especially to women, children and dependents, were characteristic even of the humbler classes of society. Children were trained to be and were deferential to their elders and superiors and especially retiring and unobtrusive in the presence of adults. The saying "children should be seen but not heard" aptly describes the sort of conduct which children were expected to observe. The generation now growing up in this country certainly does not conform to this concept. This criticism is not the mere superficial re-

* To give only a few of these slang terms in ordinary use, a male person is referred to as a "guy," a woman is a "dame" or a "skirt," a child is a "kid," a dollar is a "buck," inconsequential talk is "applesauce" or "bull," "to take for a ride" is a euphemism for removing a person to a remote place in order to slay him and "to put him on the spot" means instantaneous and summary murder. "Bootlegger," "Hi-jacker" and "Speakeasy" are slang terms which Prohibition has made familiar to all. The writer has observed this substitution of slang for normal English mainly in New York City but his information is that it prevails among the younger people, male and female alike, in practically all parts of the country.

action of senescent minds baselessly opining that "the former days were better than these" (Ecclesiastes VII, 10)
but is a matter of common observation. Any one riding in
the trolley cars or other public conveyances shortly after
three o'clock in the afternoon when the public schools
have dismissed their pupils and these latter are using the
public means of transportation on their way home cannot
avoid noticing the fact. These representatives of America's
studious youth frequently display an utter lack of good
manners. They force their way into the cars, pushing and
jostling older people, men and women alike, without the
slightest consideration of the comfort of others or any
semblance of an excuse or apology for—apparently without
any consciousness of—the annoyance they cause. Sometimes they even form a so-called "flying wedge" which goes
ahead with the force of a battering ram, ruthlessly tossing
aside whoever has the misfortune to obstruct its progress
and evidently finding great amusement in the excitement and
indignation they create. When they have found their places
in the vehicle, they do not permit any one to forget that
they are there. Their strident voices fill the air with noises
and clamor, stupid jokes, senseless laughter, vulgar inani-
ties of various sorts, all of them unworthy of well bred and
well behaved persons and expressed in a barbarous, slangy
jargon. If the conductor or motorman or any of the passengers attempt to rebuke them or point out the impropriety
of their conduct, these efforts are greeted with open contempt and sneering derision. As a result they are usually
permitted to indulge unhindered in their wild misconduct
and all the adults in the car, passengers and officials, endure
in silence the unbridled pranks of their youthful torturers,
with manifest annoyance but without audible protest or
complaint.

The lack of refinement and good manners on the part of
many of the rising American generation shows itself in
many ways. One of the most conspicuous of these is the
changed attitude of men,—of young men in particular—
towards the female sex and the changed attitude of the
women, especially the younger women, themselves. It may

be that the great deference shown by the Americans of
former generations to the female sex and the extreme deli-
cacy and intense modesty formerly characteristic of American women had in them something of exaggeration, that
simpler and more natural relations between the sexes would
have been better, but they certainly were preferable to the
laxity and utter absence of any standard of propriety which
mark so many of the younger element of both sexes today.
Unrestrained intercourse of youths and maidens at all hours
of the day or night, journeys together unchaperoned into
lonely and remote places, "petting parties" and "necking"
and open, unshrinking conversation on the intimate facts of
life certainly do not make for an exalted type of human
demeanor. A picture which appeared some time ago in
the well known humorous paper *Life* aptly illustrated this
changed standard of manners. A number of women were
represented outstretched upon chairs and sofas in the most
unconventional attitudes and convulsed with laughter.
What was the cause of their hilarity? A gentleman (?)
present had used a profane expression and a friend, a gentleman of the old school, had rebuked him, saying, "Hush,
there are ladies present." The ladies (?) were convulsed
with laughter at the thought that any one could be so old-
fashioned as to imagine that such a trifle as profane language could offend them. Merely a jest, but, alas, only
too sadly accurate in its representation of actually existing
conditions.

Far more serious than the deterioration of manners and
vastly more dangerous to the welfare of the nation is the
moral degeneracy which has come upon so many of the
youth of America. A striking phenomenon in the extraordinary increase of crime in recent years is the dispropor-
tionately large share therein taken by young persons, mere
youths in their late teens and early twenties. This sad fact
has been noticed and deplored by many thoughtful observers. The Wickersham Commission, appointed by President Hoover to investigate the causes of the widespread
disregard of law prevalent in the country and to recommend measures for its better enforcement, commented upon

the extremely youthful age of many law violators. Commissioner Edward L. Mulrooney, head of the Police Department of New York City (1932), in an official report, stated that a great change had taken place in the character of the criminals with whom the police are called on to deal, that whereas formerly they were mostly hardened offenders of mature age, at present the great majority consists of mere striplings, hardly out of their children's shoes, and yet capable of committing the most daring and desperate crimes. The New York *Times*, in its issue of April 3rd, 1932, reported a typical incident of this kind. Four youths, one of 16, two of 18 and one of 19 years of age, were tried for and convicted of the murder of a butcher in Harlem. One was sentenced to death in the electric chair and two to long terms of imprisonment. The jury was unable to agree on the guilt of the fourth defendant and he was held for a second trial. Various explanations are given for this terrifying increase in youthful criminality. By some the blame is laid upon the Great War which with its sanctioning of actions ordinarily severely condemned and punished, such as the taking of human life and the seizing of private property, brought confusion into the moral sentiments of the growing youth. Others attribute it to Prohibition which, through forcing an undesired and unwelcome law upon the people, brought about contempt for all law. Others again say the fault is to be found in the scientific ideas of the modern age, which through undermining traditional concepts of the dignity of the human race and the bindingness of ethical precepts, destroyed faith in the validity of religious and moral teachings and deprived youth of all incentive to the leading of righteous and virtuous lives. Many, again, are inclined to attribute to the "movies" a large share in the development of youthful crime in America. The interesting and indeed astounding invention of pictures that move and speak has brought every aspect of human life nearer and more clearly to the attention of the people than ever before. These new and vivid spectacles are particularly attractive, indeed fascinating, to juveniles and adolescents. A large part of the scenes depicted show crimes, particularly those of daring and violence. It is claimed by many that the power of suggestion and the hero worship natural to youth lead many immature persons to emulate the bold and reckless deeds which they have seen portrayed on the screen. There is undoubtedly much truth in all these explanations.

The present writer does not think it is necessary to go into these fundamental causes of general modern unrest in order to find the reason for the great growth of youthful crime.* To him it seems that the cause is much simpler and more direct. Defective educational methods, he believes, are mainly responsible for this deplorable condition. In other words, the public school must bear much, if not most, of the blame. The tremendous increase in criminality among the youth of America is a clear indication that the public school has failed in one of its most important functions. The function of the public school is not merely intellectual but ethical and spiritual as well. Its purpose is not merely to equip its pupils with a certain amount of mental attainments but, in an even higher degree, to guide and influence their moral natures in such manner that they shall grow up to be honest and honorable men and women. There is something wrong with the public schools when so many of their graduates derive no ethical benefit from the education they have received and repay the state for the expense it has gone to in their behalf by becoming robbers and murderers. This is rather a harsh indictment of the public school system but there can be no doubt that it is ill and if we would cure a patient it is necessary to make

* Candor compels the admission that this view of the increase of crime among the young is not unanimously agreed to. Dr. Carleton Simon, former Special Deputy Commissioner of New York City, as reported in the *New York Times* of May 8th, 1932, strongly dissents therefrom and even claims that youthful criminality in New York State has considerably decreased since 1879. But in a clash of opinion such as this, it would seem that more reliance should be placed upon the mature judgment and experience of Police Commissioner Mulrooney and the view of the Wickersham Commission which devoted many months of study and investigation to this and similar questions.

a correct diagnosis of his ailment. In the opinion of the writer the public schools fail to exercise the proper influence upon the manners and morals of their pupils because they make little attempt to do so, except in a haphazard and sporadic manner. The efforts of the public schools are directed almost exclusively to developing the intellect of the pupils, to filling their minds with the various kinds of knowledge prescribed by the school curriculum. The success of a teacher is measured by the success of his or her classes in passing the prescribed examinations. If the class is able to pass these examinations with flying colors, the teacher is deemed a paragon of pedagogical ability and worthy of the highest commendation; if, on the other hand, the class shows little grasp of the subjects taught and no intellectual keenness, the fault is *eo ipso* assumed to be that of the teacher who, if not exactly deserving of expulsion from the teaching profession, is certainly not considered a worthy member thereof. But the question is never, or very rarely, asked "Has the influence of this teacher been beneficial to these pupils in a moral and social way, have they acquired higher standards of honor, honesty and decency, have they learned to use a pure and refined speech, are they characterized by personal and physical cleanness, courtesy and good manners?

Under these circumstances, with the teachers forced to employ practically all their time and strength in the purely intellectual side of education and to devote many of their supposedly free hours to the correction of reams of papers and the preparation of superfluous and quite unnecessary graphs, it is no wonder that they have neither time nor strength left for the moral and social improvement of their pupils.

Indeed many teachers hardly seem to realize that they have any duty in regard to the ethical side of education but consider, perhaps rightly, that when they have taught the prescribed curriculum they have accomplished their task. The few who have some realization of this part of their educational task and occasionally attempt to fulfill it can do but little because of the pressure of their routine work.

What shall be done in order to impart to the pupils a sense of honor, consciousness of moral duty, courteous manners and refinement of speech? * The writer believes that human beings need to be instructed in the rules of proper moral and ethical conduct just as well as in the other subjects of human knowledge and that they should be directly and systematically taught in the same manner that the subjects which make up the present curriculum are. In other words, morals and manners should form a part of the regular school curriculum and instructors, qualified and competent to teach these subjects, should be regularly appointed members of the teaching staff in the same manner and with the same status as those whose task it is to teach English, history or mathematics.** This is not a strange or revolutionary or even new doctrine. It goes back to remote antiquity, at least as far as the people from whom the modern world has derived most of its spiritual and ethical concepts, the Jews, are concerned. Education in ancient Israel was a judicious combination of the secular-practical and the spiritual-ethical with the greater stress laid upon the latter. The Mosaic Law enjoined that its precepts, directly or indirectly ethical in their purpose, should be carefully and thoroughly taught to the children. "And thou

* It may be thought that too much stress is laid in this treatise upon the matter of refined speech and manners but there can be no doubt, in the opinion of the writer, that there is a close connection between rudeness of speech and rudeness of conduct and but a short distance from violation of the dictates of propriety and good manners to the violation of ethical and juridical precepts.

** In connection with this the report of Dr. William J. O'Shea, former Superintendent of Public Schools of New York, for the year 1931 is interesting. In it Dr. O'Shea gives expression to the view that "Character development is important as a primary aim of the public schools. Knowledge is valuable and reasoning essential but final worth is found only in the human being as a moral personality manifesting good will and extending helpfulness toward his fellows." It is certainly pleasing to find the head of the educational system of New York agreeing so thoroughly with the author of this work but even Dr. O'Shea will hardly claim that the public schools have accomplished any noteworthy results in the way of ethical training.

shalt teach them diligently to thy children and thou shalt speak of them when thou sittest in thy house and when thou walkest on the way and when thou liest down and when thou risest up" (Deuteronomy VI, 7). The wise Solomon laid stress upon the ethical training of the young. "Train up a lad in the way he should go; even when he is old he will not depart from it" (Proverbs XXII, 6). The reference to ethical instruction here is unmistakable: "the way he should go" evidently means moral conduct and the wise king impresses upon his readers that thorough ethical instruction, given in early youth, will permanently determine a man's behavior. The Talmudic sages advise that education be all-embracing, including in its scope man's physical, spiritual-ethical, social and hygienic requirements. "A father is in duty bound to have his son taught Torah, (the spiritual and ethical doctrines of Judaism) a trade, to swim and, some say, to ride a horse" (Kiddushin 29, a). The idea that morality can be taught the same as any other mental or physical accomplishment is in strict accordance with modern psychology which teaches that human actions are mainly the result of habit and ideology. Create certain habitual tendencies in a child, impress certain concepts and convictions, so-called ideology, upon his mind and his conduct will almost certainly be in accordance with those habits and that ideology. Childhood is impressionable in the highest degree, youth and adolescence almost equally so. The character of human beings is, therefore, usually determined by the influences which press upon them early and in accordance with the concepts which they form in the preparatory stage of life, of that which is admirable, desirable and worthy of emulation. A boy, born and reared in the slums, in an environment where the outstanding figures of the underworld are looked up to with feelings of admiration and high esteem, where their daring exploits and death defying crimes are told of in terms of warmest praise, will naturally come to look upon their careers as heroic and glorious and to desire such a career for himself. Another boy, perhaps fundamentally in no wise different, but reared in a loving and reverent home by God-fearing and right-

eous parents, taught to abominate sin and wickedness as
he abominates dirt and rude manners, with the highest
ideals of honor and purity impressed upon him as the only
really worth while ambition in life, will with equal natural-
ness tend to become a fine and noble human type.

It is, therefore, practically certain that direct moral instruction, begun in early years and continued during all
or the greater part of the time of school attendance will
have a great effect upon the mentality of the overwhelming
majority of the pupils and will imbue them with a distinctly ethical ideology, which will be reflected in their
conduct. A particularly skillful and tactful type of teacher
is indispensable for success in this work. A gloomy, frown-
ing, pedantic sort of pedagogue, a "kill-joy," whose manner
is repellent to youth and whose method of instruction
causes ethical conduct to appear as the unpleasant and disagreeable aspect of life, can easily produce the very opposite
of the effect intended. But a pleasant, friendly and kindly
instructor, manifestly of high intelligence but not overbear-
ingly and domineeringly so, one who understands the psychology of childhood and adolescence and is able to show,
in a manner convincing to youthful minds, not only the intrinsic beauty and desirability of honorable and righteous
lives but also the utter futility and hopelessness of careers
of crime, cannot fail to make a deep impression upon his
young hearers and to determine most, if not all, of them
to accept the ethical precepts, thus beautifully presented,
as the guiding principles of their own lives. A particularly
able and convincing type of teacher is required because, under present day conditions, his task is not merely to expound
the positive ethical doctrines but also to antagonize and
to refute the negative influences, the modern anti-moral
theories and anarchistic concepts which reject all received
standards of human duty and paint them, in a manner both
confusing and alluring to youthful minds, as mere "in-
hibitions." The instruction in ethics must be quite detailed
and definite, considering all dubious situations, temptations
and moral difficulties by which modern men are likely to
be confronted and giving clear and distinct admonitions and

directions for every such case, so that there shall be no
doubt or uncertainty in the mind of the pupil as to his
moral duty in any given circumstances and the proper conduct to observe in every emergency. Ethical instruction of
this sort would be of the highest value to those receiving
it and would undoubtedly raise the general level of American conduct.*

Another excellent method of raising the ethical quality
of public school pupils to a higher level and which might
be used to great advantage in connection with the general
public school work, would be to encourage the growth of
the group spirit along ethical lines. It has long been recognized that the sentiment of a common duty or obligation
resting equally upon all members of a certain group and
which all are expected to fulfill, because of their membership therein, with equal loyalty and sincerity, the mental
attitude which is designated by psychologists as "mass
psychology" and in French by the term *Esprit de Corps*,
is a force of extraordinary intensity and potency. A person belonging to any particular group or class, and who is
willing and glad to belong to it, hardly needs to be told that
it is his duty and obligation to adhere to the principles and
ideals of his group. He feels instinctively that such is
incumbent upon him and is usually enthusiastically—and
sometimes fanatically—determined to show his loyalty and
devotion by complete and unquestioning compliance with
the laws and customs of his class. He may even go as far

* In the issue of June 14th, 1932, of the *New York Sun*, a report
of an announcement by Doctor Eugene A. Colligan appeared
stating that an experimental course in character and citizenship to determine the effectiveness of formal instruction in character and citizenship is to be introduced into thirteen elementary
schools of New York City. The reason for the course is given in
the words "while knowledge may glitter, only character counts.
Experience has shown that though we may know the better we frequently do the worse." The writer is gratified to observe that this
recognition has begun to penetrate the educational system but
must express his opinion that the plan, as outlined in the mentioned
article, is only rudimentary. The idea of putting the ethical instruction in charge of the regular class teacher is quite impracticable.
Only specially qualified teachers can hope to accomplish real results.

as to find herein a glorious ambition and to defy all risks and dangers in order to gain the plaudits and encomiums of his fellows through especially effective service to the cause to which they are all attached. This statement is as true concerning actions and undertakings condemned by the general consensus of human opinion as immoral and criminal as it is of principles and practices universally respected as honorable, virtuous and noble. The readiness of gangsters and other members of the underworld to commit the most horrible and revolting crimes in the interest of their class is undoubtedly due to this group spirit. But just as the group spirit works for crime and evil thus also may it be potent for righteousness and ethical well doing.

THE BOY SCOUT MOVEMENT AN EXAMPLE OF ETHICAL INFLUENCE OF THE GROUP SPIRIT

A convincing demonstration of the manner in which the group spirit may be utilized for the promotion of ethical and socially beneficial conduct is given by the splendid youth organization known as the Boy Scouts of America. This organization, arranged upon military lines and with military discipline, strives—and apparently with great success—to instill into the hearts of the youth enrolled in its ranks the noblest ethical and altruistic principles. It emphasizes the thought that conformity to such principles is essential to the concept of a true Scout. Before a boy is accepted as a Scout he must promise: On my honor I will do my best:

(1) To do my duty to God and my country and to obey the Scout Law;

(2) To help other people at all times;

(3) To keep myself physically strong, mentally awake and morally straight.

The Scout Law is a concise but clear and impressive statement of the finest ethical and spiritual rules of conduct. It well merits being given here in its entirety.

THE SCOUT LAW *

1. A Scout is Trustworthy. A Scout's honor is to be trusted. If he were to violate his honor by telling a lie, or by cheating, or by not doing exactly a given task, when trusted on his honor, he may be directed to hand over his Scout Badge.

2. A Scout is Loyal. He is loyal to all to whom loyalty is due; his Scout Leader, his home, and parents and country.

3. A Scout is Helpful. He must be prepared at any time to save life, help injured persons and share the home duties. He must do at least one Good Turn to somebody every day.

4. A Scout is Friendly. He is a friend to all and a brother to every other Scout.

5. A Scout is Courteous. He is polite to all, especially to women, children, old people, and the weak and helpless. He must not take pay for being helpful or courteous.

6. A Scout is Kind. He is a friend to animals. He will not kill nor hurt any living creature needlessly, but will strive to save and protect all harmless life.

7. A Scout is Obedient. He obeys his parents, Scoutmaster, Patrol Leader, and all other duly constituted authorities.

8. A Scout is Cheerful. He smiles whenever he can. His obedience to orders is prompt and cheery. He never shirks nor grumbles at hardships.

9. A Scout is Thrifty. He does not wantonly destroy property. He works faithfully, wastes nothing, and makes the best uses of his opportunities. He saves his money so that he may pay his own way, be generous to those in need, and helpful to worthy objects. He may work for pay but must not receive tips for courtesies or Good Turns.

10. A Scout is Brave. He has the courage to face danger in spite of fear and to stand up for the right against the coaxings of friends or the jeers or threats of enemies, and defeat does not down him.

* Taken from "Scouting and the Jewish Boy," published by the Jewish Committee on Scouting.

11. A Scout is Clean. He keeps clean in body and thought, stands for clean speech, clean sport, clean habits, and travels with a clean crowd.

12. A Scout is Reverent. He is reverent towards God. He is faithful in his religious duties and respects the convictions of others in matters of custom and religion.

There can be no doubt that the above pronouncements of the Scout Law constitute an ideal code of ethical conduct for boy and man.* The striking feature of it is that it lays great stress on actual doing of good. It preaches not only abstention from evil but the constant direct performance of kind and helpful deeds. Those who thoroughly absorb its spirit become typical ideal medieval knights *"Sans peur et sans reproche."* According to well authenticated reports it is very successful in its work and does actually communicate its spirit to the several million lads under its guidance. It is thus rendering an invaluable service to America.

The writer cannot see any valid reason why the wonderful work done for a few million of the youths of America by a single organization cannot be done by the Public Schools for the far greater numbers not enrolled in their ranks. The Public Schools are intrinsically just as capable of utilizing the group spirit and directing it into proper ethical channels as is the Boy Scout organization and their influence would affect American boyhood as a whole and lay the foundations for a vastly improved American citizenry in the next generation. It may well be that the introduction of direct ethical instruction and of a great Boy Scout system would add not inconsiderably to the cost of the public schools but the expense would be well justified. The cost of the elaborate—and, alas, far from efficient— machinery for the curbing of crime, the huge police forces and the numerous great prisons and penitentiaries and their staffs of prison officials, wardens, turnkeys, guards and others, is so tremendous that any influence which would

* There is also a Girls' Scouts organization which applies the same principles to the training of the youth of the female sex.

diminish the tendency to crime and thus render much of this vast crime-fighting apparatus superfluous, would mean a great saving to the community and would be directly beneficial in terms of dollars and cents.

THE PUBLIC SCHOOLS DO NOT EXERCISE SPIRITUAL INFLUENCE

Another respect in which the public school is deficient is its lack of spiritual influence over its pupils. This cannot be exactly considered the fault of the public school but is largely, if not entirely, the result of the American system of the separation of church and state. The founders of the republic, for reasons which seemed to them amply sufficient and of which the majority of Americans still undoubtedly approve, decided not to permit any direct ecclesiastical connection with or influence upon the government or the institutions of the state. But while there were just and weighty reasons for this course there can be no doubt that it also meant a grave and serious hampering of the development of a fine, ethically high national character. Religion in its better aspect, when filled with sublime spiritual aspirations, deep love for humanity and free from bigotry and fanaticism, is a magnificent power for good. An education which is devoid of this fine spiritual influence, which is purely intellectual and practical, tends to make its recipient coldly scholastic, hard hearted and materialistic. Neither can it be denied that, though the American system is supposed to be non-religious but not anti-religious, the rigid exclusion of all religious influence from the public schools is, in a measure, an act of hostility to religion, through which a very large proportion of the pupils are estranged from the faiths in which they were born and completely deprived of the religious element in life.

Religion is presumed to be a private matter, with which the state is not concerned, which can and must be dealt with only by the home and the church. That is an excellent viewpoint in itself and would be eminently satisfactory if home and church were, as a matter of fact, capable of coping and did actually cope efficiently with the problem of the religious education of the young. Notoriously the very reverse is the case. Home and church are not capable of dealing efficiently with the problem of religious training under the conditions prevailing in the United States. The religious education imparted by church and home is, as a rule, superficial and inadequate and the number of pupils reached by it is a mere fragment of the total school population. The inevitable result is that a large proportion, probably the majority, of the children educated in the public schools, grow up without religious training and deprived of the ennobling and spiritualizing influences which flow therefrom.

But how can this spiritual influence be wielded by the public school in a commonwealth in which church and state are separated and may not intrude upon each other's domain? The writer believes that under the system of an absolute divorce of the civic and religious aspects of human life no really adequate solution of the problem is possible. A state which completely banishes religion from its official scope necessarily puts a certain stigma, whether intentionally or unintentionally, upon religion as a system which must be guarded against and not permitted to enter the domain of governmental activity. It creates thus a certain prejudice against religion in the minds of multitudes of people and leads them to withdraw from all forms of religious manifestation. Undoubtedly religion is itself largely responsible for this condition, through the stupid and unrighteous acts of many of its highest representatives, but that undeniable fact does not render this condition any the less regrettable. Incidentally it may be noted that the separation of church and state is not an indispensable requisite either of justice or democracy. The old French republic was a true democracy, according complete equality to all citizens, but it recognized and supported four religions, Catholicism, Protestantism, Judaism and Mohammedanism, as religions of the state. In pre-war Hungary three religions, Catholicism, Protestantism and Judaism were officially "received"—as the phrase in that land expressed it—as religions of the state and were represented in the government. Provision was also made for the instruction, under governmental supervision, of the children of the adherents of these cults in the tenets of their respective religions. These arrangements worked very satisfactorily, involved little or no injustice to any element and were heartily approved of by all. The writer can see no valid reason why this system should not be applicable to and produce equally satisfactory results in America. However the probability of such official recognition and supervision of religion in the United States is so slight that it may be left entirely out of consideration.

The question, therefore, remains, "What can be done by the Public School, under the prevailing system of strict separation of church and state, to foster the religious spirit?" Nothing, apparently, except to observe a general attitude of benevolence and sympathy towards all manifestations of religious sentiment and of scrupulous fairness to all pupils of whatever denomination and the utmost consideration for the religious customs and practices of all. No pupil should be caused to feel that he or she belongs to an unpopular group. To arouse such a feeling is to strike a direct blow at the particular religious group to which that pupil belongs.

This is obviously wrong and in contradiction to the supposed neutrality of the state in religious matters. It cannot fail to have, and actually does have, a discouraging influence upon the religious loyalty of tens of thousands of boys and girls. Every trace of such discrimination should be completely eliminated if the public school is to be really neutral and free from religious bias. The Jewish holy days should be placed upon a basis of absolute parity with those of Christianity and neither teachers nor pupils should be penalized for observing them. No examinations should be held on Jewish holy days, no school celebrations should take place on Christmas or Friday evenings and no Jewish pupils should be asked or expected to participate in such exercises. A spirit of absolute impartiality in all religious matters should prevail. Such an attitude would do much to encourage religious loyalty on the part of all pupils and to give them the spiritual impulse which they so sorely need.

VOCATIONAL TRAINING IS ALL IMPORTANT

Another important aid in improving the ethical and spiritual qualities of pupils is so self-evident and indisputable that it need only be briefly referred to. That is the training of all boys and girls in some trade or vocation by which they may be able to support themselves.* It is an axiomatic truth that inability to satisfy one's material needs is a direct cause of crime. The Bible tells us "For a piece of bread a man will transgress" (Proverbs XXVIII, 21) and the pithy English saying "Satan always finds some work for idle hands to do" has this thought also as one of its significations. A large contingent—perhaps the largest—to the army of criminals is supplied by those who have never learned any trade or profession and are unable to obtain the means of life in any lawful manner.

Of course it must be admitted that, under present-day conditions, the knowledge of a trade or vocation is no longer a guarantee that its possessor will be able to earn a livelihood. In these days of terrible technological unemployment the Talmudic adage "though a famine should last seven years it would not enter the home of an artisan" (Sanhedrin 29, a) is certainly no longer strictly accurate. But, under all circumstances, the position of the one who has learned to render some useful service to society is immeasurably safer and more hopeful than that of the person who is utterly devoid of skill or ability in any vocation whatsoever. The former, even if unemployed, may reasonably expect that at some time or in some place his ability will be needed, in plain words, that he may "get a job," the latter has no recourse except to the rudest form of unskilled, poorly paid labor or to crime. Consideration for

---

* Reference has already been made (page 182) to the desirability of including vocational training in the work of the public school.

the well being of the community requires that all its members should possess the knowledge of some vocation which, in normal times and under normal conditions, can furnish them with a livelihood. This knowledge, as far as the broad masses of the population are concerned, can only be supplied by the public schools. Vocational training should, therefore, be made an indispensable part of the public school curriculum, binding upon all pupils except those who purpose to attend special vocational or technical schools. Such vocational training, besides affording better prospects of economic security to the graduates of the public schools, would also tend to strengthen their ethical sentiments and to increase their social and political trustworthiness through the emphasizing of the conservative views which are the natural result of an assured economic position.*

CORPORAL PUNISHMENT 'SHOULD BE AT LEAST A LATENT RESOURCE OF EDUCATORS

There remains yet one/topic to be considered before concluding this investigation of the educational problem in America. That is the question of the desirability or undesirability of corporal punishment as a means of improving school discipline and of perhaps securing other desirable results.

The first reaction to this suggestion is undeniably an unfavorable one. The employment of physical violence by teachers or other school officials upon helpless pupils is unquestionably repugnant to the finer humanitarian sentiments which are characteristic of modern civilization,

---

* The National Education Association, in its convention at Atlantic City, beginning June 30th, 1932, as reported in the *New York Times* of the same date, announced that it had codified all its most important resolutions adopted during the past seventy years in a permanent platform. One of the outstanding planks of this platform is a demand that vocational training be made a part of the regular school system for both youths and adults. The present writer is evidently, therefore, in agreement with the leading educators of the country in insisting upon vocational training in the public schools.

especially in America. Without going into all the details of
arguments which are urged against corporal punishment,
the main course of reasoning is that the infliction of physical pain and suffering is not a legitimate part of education,
that school officials have no right to such control over the
persons of pupils as to morally justify beating and castiga-
tion, that the childish offences of which pupils can be guilty
are not so severe as to require repression by physical means
and that beating is a relic of barbarism, unworthy of the
present age of enlightenment and humanity and which tends
to defeat the very ends of education by arousing sullen
resentment in the minds of pupils who have suffered physical punishment against state authority and all who represent it. Moral suasion, appeals to the reason and sense of
honor of pupils and, above all, the arousing of their interest
in their class work, it is claimed, are the only ethically justified means of maintaining discipline and proper standards
of conduct in schools and any system of education which
cannot attain satisfactory results by their use and must
resort to the brutal method of physical punishment, has
merely demonstrated its inefficiency and incapacity to properly carry out its task.

There is unquestionably much truth and correctness in
this reasoning. The ideal school or school class is the one
in which there is no disciplinary problem, in which the sense
of honor of the pupils is so high that they would not be
guilty of insubordination or disorder and whose interest in their studies is so great that the thought of
unruly conduct does not enter their minds. There are
undoubtedly some classes of this type and happy is
the teacher whose good fortune places him or her in
charge of such a class where no time or strength need be
wasted on the mere maintenance of order and decent
conduct but where the teacher may concentrate on making the instruction interesting and efficient in the highest
degree.

But no one will claim that such ideal conditions are characteristic of the average class. The classes in which disciplinary efforts are unnecessary, are few and far between

while, on the other hand, there are many classes, especially those whose pupils are drawn from the slums of the great cities and who are in close association with and under the influence of the ideology of the underworld, where the whole atmosphere is one of antagonism to and defiance of the teacher and where the maintenance of discipline and good behavior is a task of the utmost difficulty. To think of controlling the unruly and rebellious dispositions of these ruffians of the schoolroom by kind words and pleasant smiles alone without any reserve force behind them would be about as sensible as to try to subdue the criminal elements of the great cities by abolishing the police and substituting for them the psalm singing battalions of the Salvation Army. After all, a class or a school is only a replica in miniature of the society or community from which it is drawn and just as governments, despite the advance of civilization and the increased prevalence of kindly and merciful ideas, find it impossible to dispense with armed force and punitive measures in order to subdue the law-defying elements of the populace and to preserve the safety of life and property, thus also school officials cannot relinquish the right to corporal punishment if they wish to hold in check the so-called "toughs," the hardened, authority-flouting rowdies who are the bane of the great majority of American schools.

To preserve discipline without any physical means of punishing the unruly and the insubordinate is a task transcending the powers of all but a few exceptional teachers. That the efficiency of the instruction is seriously impaired by this constant battle with the powers of disorder, needs no special statement. But the harmful effects are much more far-reaching. There results a general lowering of the standard of demeanor. Courtesy and refinement in the intercourse of the pupils with each other cannot develop properly where so much rudeness and violence are of constant occurrence. Worse yet a general contempt for authority is aroused in the minds of many pupils through their observation of the weakness of the teacher, who is to them the representative of state power, and his or her inability to control the insubordinate elements in the class. This is the ideology from which the later gangsters and criminals are bred.

The conclusion is, therefore, inescapable that complete reliance in education cannot be placed upon moral suasion and the gentle methods of appeals to the better nature of pupils, to their reason and honor. The power to resort to force, to punish corporally must also exist. This is the general opinion of the teachers themselves and they, surely, are better qualified to judge than educational theorists, led astray by modern fads and afraid of being considered reactionary.

This coercive power need not necessarily be in the hands of the teachers. It might be entrusted to special punitive officials, to whom teachers could report the cases of pupils guilty of flagrant insubordination and who would be empowered to inflict suitable penalties. Most teachers would undoubtedly prefer not to exercise this function themselves. It must always be exceptional and only resorted to in cases of urgent necessity and should never be so severe as to actually endanger the health of the pupil. The pupils must understand that the feeling of the teachers and school authorities towards them is one of kindness and friendship and that only disorderly and insubordinate pupils need fear physical punishment and pain. But the power to inflict corporal punishment must exist if the disciplinary problem is ever to be banished from the school. It would probably need to be actually used only very rarely as the mere knowledge that such punishment could be inflicted would have a sobering effect upon pupils inclined to unruliness and would improve their conduct a hundredfold. Corporal punishment, therefore, instead of being completely excluded from educational methods, should be recognized as a potent force, which, when intelligently and judiciously used, can greatly lighten the task of the teacher and add to the educational and moral effectiveness of public school work. Proper consideration of the principles propounded in this chapter and their actual application to the educational

methods of the public school system would, in the opinion
of the writer, free that system from most of the defects
now inherent in it and make it a far mightier engine than
it at present is, for the development of a socially capable,
intelligent and ethically-minded American citizenry.

CHAPTER TWELFTH

THE PROBLEM OF IMMIGRATION

In the first period of the settlement of America by Europeans there was no thought that there would ever be a problem of immigration, no apprehension that the time would ever come when there would be opposition to the free entrance into America of any decent and honest human being who desired to establish his home upon its hospitable soil. The continent was so vast and, except for the small number of aborigines, so uninhabited and empty and its resources were so overflowingly rich and abundant that there seemed to be practically no limit to the population that it was capable of supporting. Indeed there was an absolute need for new inhabitants. Vast numbers of willing workers were required to cut down the primeval forests, to build roads and houses, to till the soil and to provide the commerce and industry which are indispensable to every civilized society but especially to one that is young and engrossed in the task of growth and development. Such conditions bring about an appreciation of the value of human beings. Every one is needed, every one can perform some useful task in the upbuilding of the new community. It is a time such as that of which the prophet said "I will make a man more precious than gold, a human being more valuable than the fine gold of Ophir" (Isaiah XIII, 13). Small wonder that, under such circumstances, the prevailing sentiment is that of hospitality, that new arrivals are not looked upon with suspicion and fear, but, on the contrary, are desired and accorded a glad and cordial welcome. Such an attitude is most natural since every new settler adds to the strength of the community and increases the value of real estate and the profitableness of every agricultural, commercial and industrial enterprise.

This hospitable attitude was characteristic of early
America and, with the exception of a few sporadic outbursts
of antagonism to particular immigrant elements, lasted for
nearly four centuries, from the first settlement of the continent to the early seventies of the nineteenth century.*
Two powerful motives combined during the early period of
American national history to increase this desire to welcome new additions to the already existing population, the
consciousness of the possession of a vast country, whose
power and wealth would be greatly augmented through the
accession of new multitudes and the new spirit engendered
by the wonderfully successful uprising against Great Britain and the adoption of a liberal democratic form of government for the newly established nation. The latter motive
caused the leading spirits of America to consider their nation the chief champion of liberty and the rights of man
everywhere on earth and to declare this land the haven
of refuge for all the victims of tyranny and oppression
in every form, political and religious. This spirit was
typical of America during the greater part of the nineteenth
century and was proclaimed again and again with unmistakable clearness and emphasis in the public pronouncements of statesmen and the eloquent addresses of orators
at Fourth of July celebrations and other occasions of patriotic assemblage.**

* The American or Know-Nothing movement, which existed from
about 1853 to 1856, is the first important instance of an anti-foreign
or anti-immigration tendency in American life. It was intense
while it lasted, even resorting to anti-foreign riots and other acts of
violence, but was not able to influence the immigration policy of the
United States nor to deter the inflow of immigrants.

** How sincere this spirit was even as late as 1892, when the restrictionist movement was already very strong, can be seen from a
special consular report on "European Emigration" by F. L. Dingley,
in which the author expresses himself as follows: "Our country has
always been justly proud that it is an asylum for the oppressed, the
theater of unlimited catholicity, but our capacity to assimilate all
those whom Europe has pinched, dwarfed and persecuted is being
severely taxed, although Americans would regretfully see the time
when the law of self-preservation should even temporarily suspend
the law of human brotherhood and silence the benedictions of uni-

The downtrodden and oppressed of the Old World heard the joyful message and responded gladly to it. Not only patriotic leaders of unsuccessful rebellions, obliged through the failure of their efforts to flee their native lands, such as Lajos or Louis Kossuth of Hungary and Carl Schurz of Germany, sought and found a safe refuge and cordial welcome and great honor in this country but the masses of humble folk were also deeply stirred by the glad tidings and began, in ever increasing numbers, to wend their way westward seeking new homes in the glorious land where not only hitherto unknown abundance of bread and material comfort but also political and religious liberty would be their happy portion.

The emigration to the United States of America during the nineteenth century is one of the most noteworthy events of recorded history. It was a stupendous outpouring of humanity, a veritable *"Völkerwanderung"* but undoubtedly on a far greater scale than the tribal migrations of the ancient world. Out of all nations and regions the hosts came, at first mainly from the countries of Northern and Western Europe, later from the South and East of that continent. Shortly after the discovery of gold in California in 1849, Asiatic immigrants, mainly Chinese, began to pour in.*

At first this inpouring was viewed with perfect equanimity and indeed in a friendly and hospitable way. This was in accordance with the spirit of the Declaration of Independence which had considered it one of the greatest misdeeds of the King of England that he had sought "to prevent the population of these states by refusing to pass laws to encourage the migrations of foreigners hither." In this spirit Congress in 1864 enacted a law for the encourage-

versal asylum." These words express well the original spirit of American national hospitality though facing the probability of its abrogation.

* No reference is made in this connection to the entrance of African Negroes into this country, inasmuch as these Negroes were in no sense of the word "immigrants" but captives brought hither against their will. Their presence in the country is, therefore, in no way a part of the problem of immigration.

ment of immigration.* This was all in accordance with a
fundamental principle of American state policy, a principle so exalted in its lofty concept of the intrinsic dignity
of humanity and its genuine spirit of liberty that in these
days we look at it dubiously and unbelievingly, the principle that it is an inherent right of man to choose his
domicile and to change his place of abode from place to
place and from land to land in accordance with his own
wish and for his own reasons. This principle has been so
well and clearly expressed by Mr. Justice Field on September 21st, 1874, in the case of Ah Fong versus the United
States that the writer will quote here its essential part in
full. Ah Fong was a Chinese woman to whom admission
to the State of California had been refused on the ground
that she was being imported for immoral purposes and
whose case was appealed to the Supreme Court of the
United States. Mr. Justice Field, among other pronouncements, expresses himself as follows: "By the fifth article
of the treaty between the United States and China, adopted
July 28th, 1868, the United States and the Emperor of
China recognize an inherent right of man to change his
home and allegiance and also the mutual advantage of the
free migration of their citizens and subjects from one
country to another for purposes of curiosity, of trade or as
permanent residents." Such was the truly broad, liberal
and humane doctrine of man's inherent freedom of motion
and action professed by the United States of America at
that time and to which the ancient empire of China gave
its assent. Small wonder, indeed, that the hearts of men
everywhere throbbed with joyous emotion, that the name
America became a symbol for redemption and happiness and

* The enthusiastic response of mankind to America's invitation
can be seen from the statistics of immigration. In 1820, the first
year that the number of immigrants was recorded, they numbered
8,385, in 1838 they were 38,914, in 1856, 200,436, in 1872, 422,790, in
1892, 644,352. In the years before the World War European immigrants were arriving at the rate of about a million annually. The
total immigration up to 1920 amounted to approximately thirty-
four million.

that the thronging multitudes poured in, eager to share in the prosperity and liberty of this blessed land.

No one can truthfully deny that this immigration was, on the whole, highly advantageous and beneficial to all concerned. America conferred a priceless boon upon millions of unhappy and unfortunate human beings, lifted them out of the Slough of Despond into lives of comfort and well being but the immigrants repaid a thousandfold all that had been done for them. By their unfailing industry, by their hard labor in the sweat of their brows they turned the waste places into gardens, built roads through the trackless deserts, tilled the soil and brought forth enormous crops, labored in mines and factories and in every other kind of productive activity, in short, by their tireless zeal and energy they developed the latent resources of America and changed it from a primeval wilderness, the abode of savage beasts and still more savage men, into a smiling land of unparalleled wealth and prosperity, the home of the mightiest and happiest nation the world has ever known.* Nor have they failed to show their devotion to their adopted fatherland in the supreme test which tries men's souls, the test of warfare. In every war in which the United States has been involved, the armies of the Republic have contained great numbers of foreign-born soldiers who acquitted themselves most bravely. In the recent World War the rosters of some of the regiments sounded like a catalogue of European nomenclature.

Neither can it truthfully be said that the incorporation of this vast mass of mainly non-Anglo-Saxon elements into

* Here is the proper place for the writer, himself the son of Jewish immigrants, to acknowledge the great debt of gratitude which the Jewish people owe to America. America, by opening its gates to the persecuted and afflicted of Israel, did perhaps no more for them than for other peoples and races but the effect was tremendously greater. America saved the life of the Jewish people. When in 1881 massacres of Jews raged in Russia, hundreds of thousands found refuge here. The Jews of America were thus enabled to become almost the only source of help to the greatly endangered communities of Eastern Europe after the recent World War. Needless to say that American Jews are deeply grateful and enthusiastically loyal and devoted to the welfare of the land.

the American nation has had any injurious effect upon the American national character. The American people is as truly American today as at any previous period of its history in everything which constitutes the characteristics of its England-derived nationality. The English language is still its national tongue, the English culture, albeit somewhat modified by its American environment, is still the heritage of the people of all the forty-eight states. In no essential point has American nationalism been altered from the form which it had assumed when the War of the Revolution changed the British colonies in America into an American nation. This most remarkable fact is due to the whole-hearted sincerity with which the various immigrant groups entered into the scheme of American nationality, to the almost pathetic eagerness with which they sought to identify themselves thoroughly and completely with the new land of their allegiance. There has been absolutely nothing on this side of the Atlantic like the national conflicts and rivalries which have confused and harassed the political life of European nations, nothing comparable to the determined insistence of European minorities throughout the generations upon their right to their own separate languages, schools and cultural and political institutions. The first immigrant generation in America seeks, it is true, in a sort of half-hearted way, to preserve its ancestral tongue and culture, but this is mainly due to a purely sentimental attachment to the traditions of their ancestors together with a natural inability on the part of many to acquire at once the language and culture of their new environment. The second generation, however, and all following generations are completely Americanized. The language and culture of the land are theirs, their point of view is also that of their native land and but few of them take any interest in European affairs. It has often been commented upon, sometimes wonderingly, sometimes with pleased approval, that young Americans of the most diverse ethnic origins are almost indistinguishable, they are very much like each other and very different from their parents. As far as the descendants of the immigrants are concerned, the "melting pot" has unquestionably been a huge success. There are many millions of people in the United States of undeniably non-English descent, whose mother tongue is nevertheless English and who have no connection whatsoever with the countries from which their ancestors came. They are to all intents and purposes as completely American as those of purest Anglo-Saxon origin. There has also been a tremendous amount of mingling and fusion of the various elements so that the predominating majority of the white population of the United States can no longer be considered as of any one single European stock but as an amalgamated people, descended from all the races of Europe. The extent of this intermixture is strikingly shown by a contemplation of the racial origin of the Presidential and Vice-Presidential candidates in the recent Presidential campaign (1932). Of the four candidates three, at least, have non-Anglo-Saxon blood in their veins. Herbert Hoover is of German-Swiss and Franklin D. Roosevelt of Dutch descent while the Republican candidate for the Vice-Presidentship, Curtis, is of American Indian origin, a member of the Kaw tribe of Kansas. Yet who ever thinks of these men as other than Americans in the fullest sense of the term? The fusion of the Caucasian elements of the nation is so complete that governmental documents ignore, as regards them, all distinctions of origin and refer to the racial divisions of the population simply as "white" and "colored."

This remarkable assimilation and amalgamation of the immigrant elements with the native population did not suffice, however, to preserve undeviating the sentiment of friendliness to immigration. The nineteenth century was still young when voices began to be raised in protest against the admission of such great numbers of aliens. About the middle of the century, in the early fifties, came the Know Nothing movement which, with its intense agitation against foreigners, created great excitement for several years. This movement, like the sporadic protests which had preceded it, failed to have any effect upon the immigration policy of the United States. The traditions of liberty and the broad concept of the rights of man were too deeply grounded in the national consciousness of the American people to be easily overthrown. How deeply grounded these sentiments were was shown in the course of the terrible Civil War by the emancipation of the slaves and by the magnanimous grant to them of the full rights of citizenship after the end of that fratricidal struggle. It required a long and persistent effort on the part of the enemies of immigration before public sentiment would brook any interference with the time honored concept of America as the haven of refuge for the oppressed and persecuted of all nations, in which all men could find a welcome and an opportunity.

In the seventies the anti-immigrant agitation became so intense that its ultimate success could be plainly foreseen. It was directed against certain aspects of European immigration but mainly against the immigration of the Chinese. As regards the first mentioned agitation it was amply justified. Many European municipalities and communities had taken advantage of the freedom of admission prevailing in America to rid themselves of the scum of their population, their paupers, their diseased, their mentally affected and their criminals. Instead of bearing themselves the burden of these excrescences of the community, they would provide them with traveling expenses and a little extra money and send them to America where, under existing laws, they could not be excluded. The resentment of the American people against such abuse of their hospitality was, naturally, very intense and found expression in strong and vehement protests.

The agitation against the immigration of Chinese was even more intense and was undoubtedly racial in character. Other reasons were alleged, such as that the Chinese laborers were able and willing to work, because of their lower standard of living, for a lower wage than the white laborer and would thus deprive the native American workingman of his employment and also that they were addicted to certain forms of vice and crime. There was, of course, some truth in these charges but they were evidently not the basic cause for the anti-Chinese agitation. European workingmen are also accustomed to a lower standard of living than Americans and are able to subsist on lower wages; neither is the white race by any means free from vice and crime, nevertheless there was at that time absolutely no opposition to the immigration of Caucasians *per se*. The real reason for the antagonism to the Chinese was, therefore, evidently racial. The Caucasian inhabitants of the United States were strongly opposed to the growth of a numerous Mongolian element in their land. This antagonism was intensified by the fact that the Chinese are undoubtedly capable of underbidding the white laborer and that the population of China is so enormous that, should free immigration be permitted, the Chinese immigrants could easily outnumber the white population of America.

The anti-Chinese agitation began naturally in California whither most of the Chinese had directed their steps. San Francisco, the chief city of the state, was also the center of the agitation. In connection with it a certain Dennis Kearney, a born folk-orator and mob leader, attracted nation-wide attention by the fierce vehemence of his harangues, delivered on the sand lots of San Francisco, and his success in rousing the mob to furious hatred of the Chinese. Whether or not there was justification for this bitter opposition to the immigration of Chinese, and other Asiatics, is not now under discussion but it was certainly in contradiction to the doctrines of the rights of man then ostensibly forming a part of the American political system.

From now on the progress of anti-immigration legislation was rapid. On May 6th, 1882, Congress adopted a law prohibiting the immigration into the United States of Chinese laborers, on August 3rd of the same year it prohibited the immigration of all convicts, lunatics, idiots and persons liable to become public charges and in 1885 it added the prohibition of the immigration of all contract laborers, except certain preferred classes such as clergymen and instructors in colleges and seminaries. These prohibitions were subsequently made more rigid, culminating with the adoption in 1929 of a quota system based upon the un-American principle of national origins and under which the

number of permitted immigrants is restricted to about
165,000 annually. Under the pressure of the prevailing depression this has been up to the present so administered as
to exclude practically all immigrants. Large numbers of
aliens and persons of foreign origin and a not inconsiderable
number of native Americans are leaving the land so that at
present the, for America abnormal and unprecedented, condition exists that, instead of being a land into which hordes
of immigrants pour, it has become a land from which alike
the stranger and the native emigrate.

Under these circumstances it might be said that there is
no problem of immigration in America. Paraphrasing the
anti-Semitic gibe that the only country which has no Jewish
problem is one which has no Jews, we might say that since
America has no immigrants it has also no immigration
problem. That would be, however, a very superficial judgment. It must be remembered that the present suspension
of immigration, due to the paralysis of commerce and industry and the consequent unemployment now prevailing
is, in all probability, only temporary. Soon or later, in
the opinion of most economists, prosperity will return,
America will again be the land of opportunity, there will
be an insistent demand for more workers and hosts of
would-be immigrants will knock at its gates demanding
admission. It will then be incumbent upon the American
people to decide whether the traditional American spirit of
hospitality shall be restored or whether the Chinese wall
of exclusion now surrounding this country shall be rigidly
maintained.

Viewing the question in a broader way it must furthermore be considered that there is great room for doubt
whether the problem has been properly settled, whether the
solution now attained is either morally justifiable or for the
best interests of the country. Problems have proverbially
a way of remaining unsettled until they are settled properly. Objections are felt by many earnest thinkers to the
whole theory of the exclusion of immigrants and to various
details of the existing laws.

It is self-evident that the forcible exclusion of a human

being from a land in which he wishes to make his home
and his forcible restriction to one circumscribed region of
the earth, or a few such regions, are in crass contradiction
to the concept of mankind as a band of brothers with equal
rights and privileges and, therefore, to the fundamental
doctrine of human liberty. It is in direct contradiction
to the statement in the Declaration of Independence that
"all men are created equal and with an equal right to
life, liberty and the pursuit of happiness," it is flatly
opposed to the formerly fundamental principle of American
polity, so well stated by Mr. Justice Field in his famous
Ah Fong decision, that a man has "an inherent right to
change his home and his allegiance" and that he may
"migrate from one country to another for purposes of curiosity, of trade or of permanent residence." What can be
apparently more axiomatic than that a man has a right to
select his place of abode, to leave his old home and go to
a new place if he thinks it is to his advantage? The Talmud
counsels men to act thus. It says: "let him who is unhappy in one place, seek his happiness in another place"
(Baba Metzia, 75, b). But how can one follow this excellent advice if, when attempting to do so, he is driven
back by grim watchmen at the frontier of the new land
he would enter. Deprive men of this liberty of motion,
of this right of self-determination and you turn the world
into a huge dungeon and all its inhabitants into wretched,
helpless prisoners. What could be more contradictory to
the concept of human liberty of which America is supposed
to be a foremost exponent? With keen sarcasm the opponents of immigration restriction point to the statue of "Liberty enlightening the World" standing so proudly in New
York harbor, and ask, "What kind of liberty does America
represent when honest and industrious persons, who would
gladly join in upholding its sublime ideals, are not even
accorded the liberty of stepping upon its shore?"

The argument herewith presented for unrestricted liberty
of migration is undoubtedly very forceful and, considered
from the standpoint of the abstract doctrine of human
liberty and the inherent rights of man, absolutely unan-

swerable. Nevertheless it is emphatically rejected by most of the foremost leaders of American thought, men earnestly devoted to America and its ideals; in fact, the writer does not know of a single American statesman or political thinker who upholds it in its entirety, with all that it implies. The argument of the opponents runs as follows: Absolute liberty is a beautiful ideal but it is only a dream, iridescent and gloriously radiant, but still only a dream, a figment of the imagination incapable of realization. This applies to many aspects of human life where the inherent rights of one man come into conflict with the inherent rights of another and are restricted thereby. Should absolute liberty prevail among men, instead of producing well being and happiness it would bring about a state of universal hostility and antagonism, would lead to a "war of all against all." It is desirable and it should be the effort of all liberal governments to attain as closely to the ideal of liberty as possible but this effort should always be guided and controlled by considerations of practicality and feasibility. These considerations apply to the migrations and changes of domicile of men just as they do to every other domain of their activity. Their inherent rights are restricted and limited by the inherent rights of others. That is the hard and cold fact which may not be overlooked.

The first duty of a government is to its own people, to those already domiciled in the territory over which it exercises sway. No nation can forego its control over its own country, can afford to open wide its gates to whosoever would enter, without let or hindrance. To do so would mean to relinquish its sovereign rights. And it has an undoubted right to say what kind of people it wants, to fix the requirements for those who would join it. A country is the national home of the people who inhabit it and just as people who occupy a personal or family home have the right to say whom they will admit within their four walls, thus also has an entire nation the right to declare whom it will permit to enter its land either for temporary or permanent residence or to become citizens. It has no right to hamper or molest any element of its own population for all born in the land or lawfully admitted to its citizenship are members of the nation and entitled to the equal protection of the law but over against the outsider or alien it has perfect liberty of action.

During a long period of years the American people exercised the virtue of hospitality in an extraordinary degree. It welcomed all mankind to its land and accepted the newcomers into the full rights of citizenship without distinction of race or religion and with no other obligation or requirement than that of loyalty and willingness to abide by the law. It did this because it was actuated by a love of humanity and believed in the doctrine of human liberty and equality and also because the great dimensions and fertility of its land and its limited population enabled it to provide homes and sustenance for many millions of new inhabitants. But now the point of saturation has been reached, the once small people has grown to be the third most numerous nation in the world; prosperity and abundance are by no means general; the welfare of the native population must be the first concern of the government and so the time has come to call a halt to the flood of immigration and either to restrict it to such proportions as are consistent with the interests of the nation or to forbid it altogether. This does not mean a surrender of the American principles of liberty and humanity but simply recognition of the realities of the situation which prevent the complete realization of the abstract ideals. "Charity begins at home" and, therefore, America must care for its own before endeavoring to promote the welfare of the rest of the world.

The writer believes that he has stated fairly and impartially the two opposing views on the question of immigration, the view of the liberalist and that of the restrictionist. The liberal view certainly appeals more to our abstract sentiment of right and humanity but the restrictionist arguments strike us with the sledge hammer blows of hard facts and impregnable realities, the incontrovertible rights and prerogatives of nations and governments to control their own lands and defend their own interests. No one can successfully deny the postulate that nations do possess such rights and powers, that they are sovereign in their own territories and that it is not only their right but also their moral duty to restrain the incoming of extraneous elements into their lands if it be really productive of harm and injury to the indigenous population. The restrictionists, therefore, have to this extent, the better of the argument. They have it especially by the logic of facts for the restrictionist argument has won over the American people as a whole, in particular their law-givers. One cannot argue with facts. But they have not won the argument completely. After all moral sentiments are not mere figments of the imagination, justice, righteousness, mercy, kindness, sympathy, brotherhood, liberty, equality and humanity are not mere mouthings without actuality or validity, they are exalted principles of human conduct which should have a most potent influence upon the actions of nations as well as of individuals. The term "civilization" too, though of extremely dubious significance, does imply a certain moral obligation.* A nation may have the legal right, according to the principles of international law, to close its gates to every alien, with reason or without reason, but, if it makes any pretension to civilization or enlightenment, it has no moral right to do so. A civilized nation must respect the finer ethical principles and itself be guided by them, must uphold the inner dignity and personal worth of human beings as such and in its treatment of the alien be actuated by these considerations as far as is consistent with the interests of its own nationals. If, therefore, aliens seek

---

* A story told of Baron Hayashi, one time Japanese minister to Great Britain, illustrates aptly this dubious signification of the term "civilization." After the conclusion of the Russo-Japanese War, a great meeting took place in London at which Baron Hayashi was a speaker. In the course of his remarks he said: "We Japanese are no strangers to you Europeans. You have known us for a long time but you never considered us a civilized people. You knew that we could do beautiful work in metals and in silk, that we were expert gardeners and accomplished in various arts but still you thought us barbarians or, at best, semi-civilized. But now that we have fought a great war, defeated the Russians and slain a few hundred thousand of them, you consider us highly civilized."

admission into its territory and there is no real ground to apprehend that their advent will bring harm to the land or if there be some urgent and imperative reason why these aliens desire to leave their native land and seek refuge in another country, then no truly civilized or enlightened nation should, for a moment, think of refusing entry to the stranger who comes, under such circumstances, as a humble suppliant for admission.

These principles should guide the conduct of the United States, as a truly civilized and enlightened nation, over against the intending immigrant, who would fain make his home on its soil. It should exercise its power of supreme control firmly and in such manner as to protect the interests of its established population but judiciously and in a spirit of humanity and mercy. The immigration law should not be hard and inflexible, excluding without distinction all outside of a certain limited quota, but should be elastic, making allowance for certain categories or individuals whose coming would be either (A) manifestly not injurious to the country or (B) clearly beneficial or (C) appealing specially to traditional American sympathy for the downtrodden and oppressed.

Some concrete illustrations of the application of these principles might be given as follows:

Under Caption A. (1) Suppose that a family of sound, healthy, decent people, possessed of some wealth should desire to come to America, say from Holland or Sweden or, for that matter, from any other European country, with the purpose of buying land and tilling it and becoming American citizens, would there be any sensible reason for excluding them or subjecting them to the vexations and delays of the quota? Such people would be highly desirable and admissible under both Captions A and B. (2) Suppose that a person, poor and humble, but industrious and of good character, should be desirous of coming to America but would be willing to go to a remote, thinly populated section, to support himself and his family by the toil of his hands, what reason would there be to exclude him? Such a person renders a real service to the country. He helps the building up of the land and creates new values. He is also of aid in lessening the loneliness of the rural districts. It is absurd to apply one law of immigration to great, congested municipalities and to wild, unpopulated regions. It may be undesirable to permit immigration into Greater New York—though even this may be disputed—but by no logical exercise of the reasoning faculties can it be considered undesirable to permit immigration to Oklahoma, South Dakota or Alaska. There is room for many millions of people in those and similar thinly populated regions and their presence would add to the prosperity of the entire United States. Under Caption B. Suppose a skilled artisan, possessing the knowledge of some art at present unknown in this country or a manufacturer desiring to manufacture here some article at present not produced in America, should desire to come here to take up his vocation, why should he be subjected to the quota? The presence of such persons is a direct benefit to the country, increasing employment and business. Instances of this kind might be greatly multiplied but those given suffice to illustrate the principle. Under Caption C. The fame of America as a haven of refuge for the oppressed and persecuted has always been a wonderful moral asset. It would be a great moral calamity to completely lose that prestige. To exchange the reputation of being a land to which the unhappy victims of political and ecclesiastical tyranny can turn with hope and confidence to find in it deliverance from persecution and surcease of sorrow for the ill repute of being the home of a hard-hearted, unfeeling people that cares nought for the sufferings of the unjustly oppressed and spurns from its gates those who come to it imploring refuge would be indeed a spiritual disaster of the first order. Such a disaster should not happen to America, should indeed be out of the question for the American people are by nature warm-hearted and kindly and sympathize sincerely with those who suffer for conscience' sake and there is abundance of room in this broad land to provide homes for all such. Those, therefore, who must flee from their native lands because their political or religious views or racial descent are not favored by the powers that be, should not knock at the gates of this country in vain but should find a ready entry and a cordial welcome.

The adoption of an elastic system of immigration control, such as here outlined, would, in the opinion of the writer, solve America's immigration problem by excluding the criminal and morally and physically unfit, preventing the flooding of the land by an excessively numerous throng of immigrants not in themselves undesirable but exceeding the absorptive capacity of the land, while at the same time, providing for the admission of a reasonable number of select and especially suitable newcomers and upholding the hallowed tradition of America as the sanctuary of liberty and the refuge of the oppressed. It is not easy to harmonize these apparently contradictory principles but by a judicious combination of loyalty to the ideals of American liberality and proper consideration of the practical demands of the time it can be successfully accomplished.

CHAPTER THIRTEENTH

THE PROBLEM OF WORLD POLICY

THE world policy or attitude towards foreign nations of the United States, as originally adopted, may be described as one of "splendid isolation" or "friendly aloofness." This was in accordance with the admonitions of its immortal first President, George Washington, who, in his classic Farewell Address, had solemnly enjoined upon his countrymen to avoid entangling alliances and, while friendly to all nations, to be unduly partial to none. But it was also largely, if not mainly, due to the fortunate geographical, political and economic conditions under which the American Republic was ushered upon the stage of the world and continued to exist during its early history.

Its fortunate situation, separated by thousands of miles of ocean from the powerful nations of the Occident and the Orient, and with only two weak neighbors, Canada and Mexico, on the north and the south, freed it almost completely from the fear of military attack. Its rich and productive soil, extending through a variety of climates and yielding in abundance all the necessaries of a comfortable existence, made it independent for its sustenance of all other countries, except as regards the condiments and luxuries demanded by a pampered taste. Its rapidly growing population, with its multifarious needs, was able to absorb all that America's industry could produce and made it quite unnecessary to seek foreign markets. It was only natural, therefore, that the American ideology became one of self-centredness and that the American population, although almost entirely of European origin, quickly lost touch with the countries of its ancestry and looked upon itself as a new and distinct people, with different interests and a different destiny. To the American people applied with remarkable accuracy the words with which Balaam described ancient Israel, "Behold, It is a people that dwelleth alone and doth not account itself among the nations" (Numbers XXIII, 9). This sentiment of self-sufficiency and self-centredness persisted throughout the nineteenth century and part of the twentieth. Gibbons, in his "Introduction to World Politics," speaking of the Chicago exposition of 1893, shows strikingly how this American concept of aloofness and unrelatedness to the world was revealed even in that great undertaking of ostensibly international significance. "The Chicago exposition," he says, "was a world's fair in name only. Although we asked the world to celebrate with us, the invitation was really given for the purpose of demonstrating our self-sufficiency. We were not seeking political alliances or economic understandings; we had no surplus of food products or manufactured articles for which to find markets; and American capital was not looking for investment abroad." * The home market furnished by an empire of over three million square miles and its energetic and prosperous population, with an unusually high standard of living and exceptional consumptive power was amply sufficient for all America's needs.

These conditions were radically different from those prevailing in Europe and are a satisfactory explanation for the difference between the European and the American points of view in matters of world policy. Over-population and inadequacy of resources with which to support the teeming multitudes drove the nations of ancient Europe and Asia early to a policy of conquest and colonization. They were obliged to seek new territories in which their supernumerary population could find homes and the means of subsistence.** Such conditions had brought about the

* Herbert Adams Gibbons, "Introduction to World Politics," p. 328.
** Judged by present day standards, the countries of the ancient world can hardly be considered overpopulated. The primitive methods of agriculture then existing and the undeveloped state of industry, however, made it extremely difficult to procure sufficient food for large populations and famines were of periodical occurrence.

Voelkerwanderungen, the great migrations of the peoples in the early centuries and even after the nations of Europe had been organized in regular governments and the boundaries of the countries had been more or less definitely fixed, conditions were not radically altered and continued to exercise their propulsive force.

These conditions are responsible for world politics and the various methods and proceedings by which it is carried out. These methods include war and negotiations and agreements of various kinds. Sometimes two or more nations will engage in a bitter struggle for the possession of a certain country or region, sometimes a warlike, powerful nation will seize the land of a primitive or weak people unable to defend it; sometimes several nations will agree peaceably to divide among themselves the territory of another nation or to apportion among themselves "spheres of influence" or "concessions" of various sorts. The principle at the bottom of these various methods is very simple and is always the same, to get possession of something belonging to some one else by whatever means happens to be most convenient.* World Politics is the name for the science which teaches and the system which employs these devices for the promotion of national interests.

After the discovery of America a great era of colonizing activity, based upon the seizure of new territory, began. This was carried on mainly by the nations of Northern and Western Europe, who had easy access to the sea, the English, Dutch, French, Spanish and Portuguese. The scope of this chapter does not make a detailed description of their conquests and annexations necessary. Suffice it to say that they were by no means limited to America but

---

* The moral justification of these procedures is a matter for the discussion of the casuists. The usual defense is that "necessity knows no law" except the *Jus majoris fortis*, the law of the greater force. Sometimes it is defended by the alleged right of a superior civilization to displace an inferior one. The people of supposed inferior civilization would hardly admit the correctness of this argument. The truth is that the use of violence by nations to promote their interests is one of the cases where theory and practice clash and concerning which no argument is of any avail.

extended to every part of the world. England, especially, built up a vast colonial empire, so great, it is said, that "the sun never sets upon the British Empire and the beating of British drums accompanies the sun around the world."

In all of this world colonization the United States at first took no part whatever. Its gaze was concentrated upon America alone and it had but slight interest, indeed hardly a thought of a political nature, for the rest of the world. On this side of the Atlantic, however, it succeeded in building up, in the course of the nineteenth century, mainly by peaceful measures, through purchase from France, Spain and Russia, but partly by war with the native Indian tribes and Mexico, a magnificent empire. At the end of the Revolutionary War the territory of the United States was limited to a comparatively narrow strip along the shore of the Atlantic Ocean; a hundred years later it stretched from the Atlantic to the Pacific, embracing all the land between Canada on the north and Mexico on the south and including the great dominion of Alaska, almost an empire in itself. The steps by which this tremendous accession of territory was gained need not be recounted here; they are a matter of general historical knowledge. What interests us here is the fact that the United States developed early a definite and well considered world policy of its own. Essentially, that is as far as object and some of the means employed are concerned, it did not differ from the world policies of the other nations. Nevertheless it was different in certain important regards; instead of being general it was limited to one part of the world, America, and it was carried out without resorting to alliances, *"quid pro quo"* arrangements—unless the mere payment of comparatively small sums of money for absolute possession of vast territories can be considered such—and without restrictive agreements of any sort. It was a wise and very practical policy and showed that the young nation had already attained a high degree of political maturity.

Less than a fourth of the nineteenth century had elapsed when the United States took a step which proved that it was already imperial minded, that it realized to what commanding position in the Western Hemisphere destiny had called it and that it had the courage to assume the responsibilities which that preëminence placed upon it. On December 2nd, 1823, President Monroe issued the pronouncement henceforth known as the Monroe Doctrine. It stated in plain and direct words that the American continents were no longer to be considered fit subjects for colonization by any European power and that any attempt to extend the European system to any portion of the American hemisphere would be regarded as the manifestation of an unfriendly disposition towards the United States. The effect of this emphatic declaration, stating in diplomatic but unmistakable terms that the United States would resist by force of arms any attempt by a European power to take possession of any part of America, was tremendous. It was certainly audacious for it meant that the United States took to itself the hegemony of all America but its success was complete. The European powers yielded unwilling compliance but they had too high a respect for American prowess, which had been so brilliantly manifested in the two wars with England, to risk testing it.

The Monroe Doctrine was issued primarily in the interest of the United States but it was of especial benefit to the Latin American states. It was in effect a guarantee of their independence and freed them from all fear of foreign domination. It had also the effect of making America more American and removing it completely from the sphere of European political influence. It may well be considered one of the greatest political pronouncements in the history of the world.

The issuance of the Monroe Doctrine stamped the United States as an exclusively American power with no concern and hence no possessions outside of the American continent. The huge task of settling and developing its own vast territorial expanse absorbed all its energies for the greater part of the nineteenth century and kept its thoughts concentrated upon its own great homeland. But a change was to come over the spirit of its dream. Great as is the American continent it was not great enough to absorb the sum total of American energy and American enterprise. The productivity of American industry began to exceed the absorptive capacity even of the great American consuming public and foreign markets became a necessity. American capital in vast quantities began to seek investment in foreign countries and thus it became desirable, or even indispensable, that America should have political influence in various other regions of the world. The United States began to evolve from a self-centred, strictly American nation into a world power, with possessions and dependencies and business interests in many parts of the outside world and deeply concerned, therefore, with the outside world's affairs.

The change began to take place after the Chicago Exposition of 1893. Up to that time the United States maintained successfully and undeviatingly its traditional attitude of voluntary aloofness, of perfect contentment with its own continent and its own economic opportunities. That exposition had been conceived, as already pointed out, not so much in the spirit of international interdependence as to demonstrate American self-sufficiency. But only a few brief years elapsed and the new trend became plainly visible. American commercial enterprise began to spread throughout the world and new non-continental territorial possessions came under the American flag. In 1898 the United States took possession of the pearl of the Pacific, Hawaii, and in the same year, through the successful issue of the Spanish-American war, it became owner of Puerto Rico, the Philippine Islands and the island of Guam. In 1899 through an arrangement with the German Empire it acquired possession of a part of the Samoan Islands. In 1903 it purchased from the Republic of Panama the Canal Zone and five islands in the bay of Panama and leased from Cuba coaling and naval stations at Guantanamo and Bahia Honda. In 1914 it leased from Nicaragua the Corn Islands and a naval base on the mainland and in 1916 it purchased the Danish West Indies which it then renamed the Virgin Islands.

The acquisition of these extra-continental possessions

certainly constituted a departure from the earlier American
standpoint and involved the United States in questions
which the earlier American policy would have sedulously
avoided. Thus the results of the Spanish-American war,
giving America possession of Puerto Rico and the Philip-
pines, forced it to intervene in Cuba and the affairs of the
Far East, notably China. But these developments were at
least natural, the logical results of the working out of
American history. The new possessions were mainly in the
vicinity of the American continent and it could be considered as an extension of the Monroe Doctrine for the
United States to take possession of them rather than to
permit them to be acquired by a European power. The
Philippine Islands, though situated in the Far East, came
into the possession of the United States as a result of its
war with Spain which had been caused by the latter's mis-
government of Cuba, a specific American question.

But when the United States permitted itself to be drawn
into the World War it certainly departed radically
and fundamentally from its traditional foreign policy.
There would be no purpose in discussing here the causes
which led to that titanic conflict of the European powers
or the question as to which nation or nations bore the greatest share of responsibility for bringing that frightful
calamity upon the human race. The Peace Treaty signed
at Versailles is based upon the presumption that Germany
is the guilty party and that, therefore, it must bear the
burden of reparation of the damage done and of indemnify-
ing the nations against whom it waged war for their pe-
cuniary losses resulting from its wanton attack.

Students of history are by no means agreed that this
assumption is correct. Some of the most important and
best informed hold that the guilt was about equally divided.
Europe had for several decades preceding the great outburst
of 1914 been divided into two hostile camps, on the one
side the Tripartite Alliance composed of Germany, Austria-
Hungary and Italy, on the other the Triple Entente, consisting of England, France and Russia. These nations were
—with the exception of England, which, however, possessed

the mightiest navy in the world—armed to the teeth. They all had the system of compulsory military service and every able bodied man was instantly available for warlike purposes at the call of his government. The relations between the two groups were those of mutual hatred and suspicion. There was a tacit assumption on both sides that war was inevitable and only a spark was needed to kindle the conflagration. That spark was given on June 28th, 1914, at Sarajevo, capital of Bosnia, by the assassination of the Austrian Archduke Franz Ferdinand and his wife by Gavril Prinzip, a fanatical member of the Norodny Obrana, a revolutionary society of Serbians of Austrian nationality. The long anticipated war could no longer be restrained. After diplomatic negotiations and preliminaries, which need not be narrated here, it burst forth in all its fury and intensity.

All this was, of course, a matter of purely European concern with which America was in no wise concerned. In its beginning the World War differed not at all from the many previous European conflicts in which the United States had never dreamed of participating. Like them it turned upon questions of inner-European importance and was motivated by inner-European national ambitions and aspirations, rivalries and hatreds. That the great republic situated on the other side of the Atlantic and separated by approximately four thousand miles of land and sea from the scene of the conflict would ultimately participate and bring about the decision was something which probably no one anticipated. All the probabilities spoke against it. Not only were the interests of the United States in no wise involved in the conflict but it was clearly in the interest of the United States, with a population drawn from all European nations, not to take sides in such a contest, for, no matter what side it would espouse it would be sure to offend some important element of its citizenry. Strict neutrality coupled with an offer of its good offices for the purpose of bringing about a cessation of hostilities was the only attitude which the United States could logically be expected to assume. That it could be induced to relinquish this wise and natural attitude, an attitude sanctified by its traditions of almost a century and in accordance with its established foreign policy as enjoined by its great First President, remains one of the puzzles of history.

There was no reason in the issues of the war itself to justify American interference. They were matters which did not concern America in the least. But from the beginning of the conflict the sympathies of the American people were more on the side of the Allies than of the Central Powers and as the conflict continued this pro-Allies sympathy grew stronger and intenser, particularly in the circles nearest to the government and most influential in shaping the course of public affairs. For this tendency there were several causes. One of the most important of these was undoubtedly the ineptitude of German diplomacy. The German nation had splendid representatives in most of the fields of human endeavor. Its soldiers, its artisans, its scientists, its industrialists were among the most capable and efficient in their respective vocations. But its diplomats were conspicuously poor with next to none of the skill and finesse which marked the diplomats of England and France. They not only failed to grasp some of the greater problems involved in the war but even seemed hardly to understand the elements of their vocation. They were not only unable to swing the sympathies of the American people towards the German side but could not even prevent the development of an intense anti-German sentiment in America which had much to do with finally driving America into the war on the side of the Allies.

It must, of course, be admitted that the task of the German diplomats was one of unusual difficulty. Germany was hampered by difficulties from which the Allies were free. Unlike Great Britain it had no place on the American continent under its political control. It was, therefore, forced to violate the neutrality of the United States and other nations in order to carry on its propaganda and espionage service. The cables to America were in control of its enemies. In order to keep in touch with its agents without being subject to the surveillance of its enemies, Germany was obliged to resort to underhand practices. The British control of the ocean made it impossible for Germany to purchase war supplies in the United States while the Allies did so on a huge scale. This also tended to draw the sympathy of the American people to the side of the Allies.* These conditions made the task of German diplomacy a difficult one indeed. But, admitting all these special difficulties, German diplomacy showed itself conspicuously devoid of competency and was, undoubtedly, largely responsible for Germany's final defeat.

Another and very potent cause of anti-German feeling in America was the irritation and bitter resentment produced by the German submarine campaign against the shipping of the Allies and of those neutrals who were considered as giving aid to the Allies. Among these neutrals the United States was the most important because it was the chief source of supply from which the Allies drew immense quantities of munitions of war and all kinds of other needed articles.** The Germans were undoubtedly guilty of improper interference with neutral commerce if we hold to the view that the relations of neutral nations with nations at war should be perfectly free and not interfered with by the armed forces of either belligerent. But this view is very slightly upheld by the world powers and perhaps least of all by Great Britain. In the early stages of the war British violation of American neutral rights through the arbitrary Orders in Council declaring a complete blockade of Germany was much greater than that of Germany and elicited sharp protests on the part of the United States against Great Britain's interference with American sea borne commerce and mails. But gradually the American protests against British actions became milder and merely theoreti-

* Gibbons, "Introduction to World Politics," pp. 358-359.
** The sinking of the British liner *Lusitania* in 1915 was one of the chief causes of anti-German feeling in America. Nearly a thousand American citizens went to their death in that awful tragedy and German pleas that their action was justified because the *Lusitania* was a vessel of their enemies and loaded with munitions, thus making it technically a war vessel, could not stem the tide of American horror and indignation. The execution of the English nurse, Edith Cavell, also aroused feelings of intense resentment.

cal while the notes to Germany became constantly sterner and more insistent.*   On April 14th, 1916, the United States demanded of Germany strict punishment of the submarine commanders responsible for attacks on the American vessel *Sussex* and other American vessels, full indemnity and guarantees that the incidents would not be repeated. On May 4th Germany replied that it had exercised great restraint in the use of submarines but could not give up this weapon of defense against Great Britain. It promised, however, to instruct the submarine commanders to give warning before sinking vessels and to make every effort to save life. At the same time it urged that the United States insist that Great Britain cease its interference with sea borne traffic. On May 8th the United States acknowledged the receipt of this communication but stated that it "could not discuss the suggestion that the safety of American citizens should depend on the action of other governments." On January 31st, 1917, Germany withdrew its promise and announced an unrestricted blockade of its enemies' coasts. On February 3rd President Wilson gave German Ambassador Bernstorff his passports and on April 6th the United States declared war against Germany.**

In entering the war the United States declined to com-

* There were other causes for the intense anti-German feeling in America but they need not be considered in detail. Under the combined influence of all these courses America decided to depart from its traditional policy and to enter the European war.

** Anti-German feeling all over the world, which had begun to decrease since the war and promised to disappear altogether, has been greatly intensified by the actions of the Hitler *régime* at present (1933) in full control in Germany. This fanatically reactionary government, with its policy of ruthless extermination of all liberal thought and its brutal medieval persecution of the Jews, deserves and is finding the utmost condemnation of all enlightened persons. But it can hardly be said to represent the sentiment of the majority of the German people. The phenomenal rise of the Nazi movement was due to a number of unfortunate historical causes. But even in the election which brought it triumph it did not attain an actual majority. Certainly at the time of the war the ideology upon which Naziism is based either did not exist or was of negligible influence in German national life.

pletely depart from its traditional policy of aloofness and become one of the Allied Powers. It declared itself merely an "Associate." The European and American armies fighting the Central Powers were officially designated "the Allied and Associated Forces." In accordance with the same concept of America's relation to the war General John J. Pershing, the American Commander-in-Chief, refused to permit his men to be divided among the French and English and insisted on maintaining his forces intact, as a separate, independent American army. This policy of separateness was essentially a legal technicality, a distinction without a difference. As far as the actual conduct of the war was concerned the American army formed an integral part of the Allied forces opposing the Germans. But from the American point of view it was a useful and desirable thing. It showed clearly that, although America, for its own reasons and purposes, had entered the war on the side of the Allies, it had not completely merged and amalgamated itself with them. After the war this stood the United States in good stead, enabling it to remain outside of various European agreements and entanglements which, at the best, would not have been in its interest and, at the worst, might have saddled upon it intolerable burdens and responsibilities.

In itself the participation of America in the World War forms one of the most glorious episodes in American history. It turned the scale of war which, up to the intervention of America, had favored the Germans, to the side of the Allies. To America must be conceded the credit of having brought victory to the Allied cause. Without the aid of the American troops, in addition to the tremendous American assistance in munitions, other supplies and money, the Allies could not conceivably have conquered the trained and mighty armies of Germany, led by the most skillful military leaders in Europe. They, the Allies, were in desperate straits when America decided to intervene. The following extract from an appeal by Lloyd George pictures graphically the hopeless condition of the Allied cause over against the tremendous German offensive and the salvation which America's aid brought them.* "We are at the crisis of the war. Attacked by an immense superiority of German troops our army has been forced to retire. This battle, the greatest and most momentous in the history of the world, is just beginning. The French and English are buoyed up by the knowledge that the great Republic of the West will neglect no effort to hasten its troops and ships to Europe. It is impossible to exaggerate the importance of getting American reinforcements across the Atlantic in the shortest space of time." These words need no interpretation. They express in unmistakable terms the alarm and apprehension in Allied circles that without the speedy aid of America their cause was lost. The same intense apprehension of impending disaster combined with dogged resolution not to yield as long as resistance was possible, is visible also in the words of Sir Douglas Haig, Commander-in-Chief of the British army, in his order to his troops of April 12th, 1918. "There is no other course open to us but to fight it out. With our backs to the wall and believing in the justice of our cause, each one of us must fight on to the end."

Such utterances, completely devoid of the usual boastfulness and bombast of the *miles gloriosus;* couched, on the contrary, in the simple appealing phraseology of those in mortal dread, prove convincingly that the Allies were in a position of the utmost peril, from which only the vigorous help of their newly found American "associates" could rescue them. And that is exactly what the Americans did. They saved the Allies from crushing, humiliating defeat, they turned a lost war into one completely victorious. In accomplishing this the American soldiers displayed the most magnificent courage and wrought deeds of almost unbelievable prowess. In the Argonne where the Allies had encountered only failure the Americans, by dint of furious fighting and unyielding persistency, won a splendid victory. The Hindenburg line, which the Allied armies had found absolutely impregnable, yielded to the sledge hammer blows

* Message from Lloyd George to the English Ambassador to the United States, quoted in an address by Oreste Poggiolini at Florence, Italy, April 6th, 1918.

of the American warriors. The American marines, in particular, displayed such reckless daring and joy of battle that the Germans, in bewilderment, called them "Teufelshunde," a term, the English rendition of which "Devil dogs" does not express its full significance. Every American heart must beat higher and swell with pride and exultation at the thought of the heroic deeds and the overwhelming achievements of America's embattled youth on the gory battle-fields of Europe, amid the horrors of modern warfare. The pride and wonderment grow apace when one reflects that this heroic host consisted of men practically untaught in the military art, drawn from peaceful pursuits, from the counting house, the factory and the farm and sent, after a few months of necessarily superficial training, across the sea to face the thoroughly trained soldiers of the, at that time, greatest military nation of Europe. There can be no doubt that the American armies turned the tide of warfare and decided it in favor of the Allies. If therefore this decisive importance is glossed over or if the attempt is made, as it is made by certain Allied writers, to poohpooh or belittle the part which the soldiers of America took in deciding the titanic conflict, it can only be attributed to petty jealousy or ill will or a deliberate attempt to obscure the facts.

But while the American heart swells with pride at the thought of the glorious achievements of American warriors on the battlefields of Europe, that same heart cannot feel equal satisfaction when it ponders on the questions: "Was our participation in the European war justified? Was it necessary? Did it serve a useful purpose?" Today when more than fifteen years have elapsed since the close of the war, when the war psychosis has given way to normal mentality and it is possible to consider all these questions calmly and dispassionately and without danger of being deemed unpatriotic, the writer feels that they must be answered in the negative. American participation in the European war was not called for because we were in no way directly concerned with the issues of the conflict. We came into the war indirectly because Germany had allegedly violated the rights of, and committed outrages against American citizens.

Admitting the truth of these allegations they did not necessarily constitute a *casus belli*. It was perfectly possible for the United States to make allowance for the excited mentality of a nation engaged in a life and death struggle and either to take no action in regard to these alleged violations of American rights except to warn its citizens to keep away from the zone of danger or to seek a remedy through the ordinary processes of diplomacy. That is what we did in the case of England's violations of American rights and there was no logical reason why the same method of procedure could not have been applied to Germany. At this very time gross outrages had been committed in Mexico against American citizens. Many had been murdered or otherwise grossly abused. But the United States did not declare war against Mexico. Instead President Wilson issued a proclamation warning American citizens from going to Mexico during the duration of the disturbed conditions as he could not guarantee their safety. The moral of this action of our government in its application to Germany is obvious. Similar action in the case of Germany would have eliminated all danger of war.

The Great War did not, in the opinion of the writer, serve any useful purpose, or if, perchance, some minor benefits resulted, they were purchased far too dearly at the cost of the frightful injuries and sufferings which it inflicted upon the human race. It brought no real benefit either to the nations of Europe or to the American people. The total of casualties and financial losses which it caused reached a stupendous, almost unimaginable height. In the more than four years of conflict a total of 65,038,801 men were brought into the struggle. Of these 8,538,315 were killed and 21,219,452 were wounded. The cost of carrying on the titanic struggle is estimated by statisticians at $300,000,-000,000.* Can any sane person sincerely claim that the results attained justified such wholesale slaughter of the choicest specimens of youthful humanity, mainly of the white race, and such unparalleled destruction of the wealth of the world. Of this enormous total America's share was

* Statement of the United Press of August 2nd, 1932.

very great, mainly in financial sacrifices because, thanks to its late entrance into the war, its human losses were not so extreme. Even so 176,000 Americans perished on the battle-fields of Europe and several hundred thousand were in-jured, a large proportion of them permanently maimed or crippled or incurably diseased. These latter are, of course, entitled to pensions, the annual cost of which amounts to about $1,000,000,000. In April, 1917, before the United States entered the war, its entire national debt amounted to $980,000,000 and was rapidly decreasing. From April, 1917, to November, 1918, the Government appropriated for war purposes $57,000,000,000 of which it actually spent $36,000,000,000. The national debt in 1932 amounted to $20,000,000,000.* Foreign nations owe us for cash loans advanced to them in connection with the war, approxi-mately $12,000,000,000 the prospects for the recovery of which amount it would be optimistic to call poor.

Great as these losses were, America suffered an even greater loss in the sacrifice of the position of aloofness and independence in world politics which it had previously enjoyed. The advantages of that position, which George Washington, in his great wisdom, had clearly foreseen, were simply incalculable. Through it America was free from all the embarrassments and troubles which come from en-tanglement in world affairs, it could enjoy the friendship and esteem of all nations equally since it was friendly to all and hostile to none and, for the same reason, it could profit by the trade and commerce of all and was able to offer its good offices for the settlement of controversies and hostili-ties arising between the nations without being itself involved or dragged into actual participation. All these advantages it lost when it forsook its position of political aloofness and became an active participant in a European war, deciding the issue in favor of one group of nations against another. By that act it bound itself, more or less, to the European system of world politics and what that may involve no man can foretell.

* Statement of Mr. Peter O. Knight, attorney and financier of Tampa, Florida, in the New York *Sun* of July 20th, 1932.

What did America gain in return for its immense sacrifice of the lives of its youth and its wealth? Love of truth compels the answer "Absolutely nothing." While the European victor nations, most especially France, appropriated great slices of German territory and all of its colonies, the United States did not increase its national domain by one square inch of German soil. The Allies exacted huge indemnities from vanquished Germany of which the United States did not receive, or even demand, one penny. Nor can it even be claimed that the United States received the gratitude and appreciation of all the nations whom it had saved from certain defeat. Certainly discrimination against American products, amounting, in some cases, to virtual exclusion from the market such as France and, in lesser degree others of the former Allies, have recently decreed, does not look like gratitude and appreciation. Still less does the manifest reluctance of the victor nations, particularly France, to repay the loans advanced to them by the United States in the time of their highest need, bear that appearance.

But all this is today a matter of the past. What has happened cannot be undone. The question of living interest and importance is "What shall America's future world policy be? Shall the United States acknowledge and accept as a definitely established fact that it has entered upon a new period in its history, that it has joined the family of the nations of the Old World and is henceforth to be an active participant in general world politics, with a special leaning towards the nations formerly united in the Entente, or shall it strive to return to its former state of aloofness and to avoid, as far as the altered conditions will permit, all involvements and entanglements with foreign nations as contradictory to traditional American policy?

There are two schools of thought on this subject among contemporary American political leaders. For the sake of brevity only the points of difference between the opposing views shall be stated here, omitting all detailed historic description and reference to personalities. The one school might be described as the group of the Europe-minded.

They hold that America should enter completely into the European system of nations and participate fully in all conferences, discussions and understandings of these nations in reference to world politics. They urge strenuously that America join the League of Nations and the International Court of Justice, the merits of both of which they praise in the highest terms. The other school of thought take the directly opposite view. They declare that the entrance of America into the Great War did not at all signify that the American people had definitely renounced its historic attitude in regard to foreign relations, that while America found it necessary to join the Allies in waging war upon Germany, it did not thereby obligate itself to any further close connection with them and that now America must return to its traditional policy of abstinence from concerning itself with the affairs of nations outside of the American hemisphere. They are the Upholders of American Traditionalism.

The second view has unquestionably the sympathy of the overwhelming majority of the American people, who believe that European quarrels and troubles should not be permitted to becloud the happy life of their separate continent and who object with particular strenuousness to the participation of American troops in European wars. This view is reflected in the attitude of Congress, which refuses to permit America to be drawn into any closer political relation with Europe and has repeatedly rejected all proposals for American membership in the League of Nations or the International Court of Justice. This course, it seems to the writer, is the correct one for the United States to pursue. Our one time associates in the greatest of wars must not be permitted to think that henceforth the man power and the wealth of America are at their disposal whenever their ambitions and their necessities render them desirable. To pull the chestnuts out of the fire for others and burn one's own fingers in the process, is not a pleasant or profitable rôle and America should never again be willing to play it. This does not mean that America should assume an attitude of hostility or enmity to any other nation or that, if opportunities for legitimate profit exist in other countries, its citizens may not take advantage of them. The traditional policy of America, while inculcating avoidance of entangling alliances, enjoins friendship with all mankind and there is also no reason why American energy and skill shall not find lucrative employment anywhere on earth. The power of America should also be energetically employed in defense of the rights of American citizens in foreign countries whenever those rights are unjustly and improperly interfered with. The name "American citizen" should be one which secures respect and courteous treatment for its bearer everywhere on earth. But, apart from protecting the rights of its own nationals, America should rigidly abstain from mixing in the affairs of other nations, except for the purpose of averting war and promoting peace and harmony. America's power, whether military or diplomatic, should never again be employed to promote the interests of one foreign nation or group of foreign nations against another such nation or group of nations. In such matters a policy of strict and absolute neutrality should be undeviatingly observed. As regards the nations of the Western Hemisphere the United States should scrupulously respect their sovereignty and independence and observe strict neutrality should wars unfortunately arise between them. It should give them no reason to suspect it of desiring to assume the hegemony of the entire Western Hemisphere and reduce them to the position of vassal states. It should do even more. It should show especial unselfish interest and solicitude for the welfare of the American states and endeavor to bring to their perfect realization the ideals of Pan-Americanism, so that unfriendly rivalry and war shall be forever banished from both Americas and all their nations shall constitute a harmonious and mutually helpful brother band. Summing up, the world policy of the United States should be based on the principle of friendship for all nations but partiality for none. It should gladly endeavor to promote peace and harmony among all nations and should never take up arms except in defense of its own sovereign rights, if they are clearly invaded and a peaceful solution is impossible. Prudence requires that the United States maintain an adequate army and navy but they should be used only for defense purposes and never in an aggressive war. Towards the nations of the Eastern Hemisphere it should observe in general an attitude of aloofness, in particular rigidly abstaining from all interference in their internal affairs, but towards the American nations its attitude should be that of neighborly interest and helpfulness, to the end that they be all united in mutual trustfulness and harmony, assisting and benefiting each other and perfectly free from the fear of antagonisms, hostilities and wars, such as have stained with blood and tears the history of the Old World.

An American world policy, such as here outlined, would tend to bring the United States and with it all of the nations of the New World, to the realization of its ideal purpose of providing a home in which all the inhabitants can dwell in liberty, peace, safety and happiness. Its influence would spread throughout the world, and tend to bring these happy conditions everywhere and thus become a source of well being and blessing to the entire human race.

CHAPTER FOURTEENTH

THE NEW DEAL

On March 4th, 1933, Franklin Delano Roosevelt became President of the United States of America. He at once launched vigorous action against the prevailing economic dangers which threatened to undermine the American economic and political edifice. His efforts in this direction are known as NRA (initials of National Recovery Administration) or The New Deal. They represent a determined and systematic attempt to remove, as far as it is possible under the existing economic system, the extraordinary depression which has weighed so heavily during the past five years on the economic life of America and to bring back normal and customary prosperity. It is an attempt worthy of the warmest support and coöperation of the American people.

Prohibition was styled by Herbert Hoover, "a noble experiment." Opinions may and do differ as to whether that phenomenal failure deserved such an encomium. But there is no room for doubt that the New Deal does deserve that laudatory description in the fullest sense of the words. It is a wonderful, a magnificent experiment. It is a sincere and intrepid attempt to overcome, through broad and intensive use of the powers of government the dark forces which so gravely threaten the economic well being of America, to take arms against a sea of troubles and by opposing end them.

When President Roosevelt was installed in his high office the condition of the country can only be described as one of economic demoralization. The economic machinery had practically ceased functioning. Thousands of banks all over the country had failed and brought about the virtual paralysis of the banking system, the stocks of the best industrial and commercial enterprises had sunk to unprecedented low levels, real estate was practically valueless, the farmers and planters were loudly lamenting that the prices of their products were lower than the costs of production and the number of the unemployed had reached the staggering total of twelve to thirteen million, with their families about a third of the entire population. The stoutest heart might well have quailed over against a situation of such gravity, bristling with problems of such stupendous difficulty. President Roosevelt showed no signs of trepidation nor even of uncertainty and hesitation. On the contrary he grappled at once with the frightful difficulties by which he was confronted and with an energy and directness and fertility of resource which amazed his countrymen and aroused the admiring attention of all the world.

He turned his attention first to the perilous banking situation. On March 5th, one day after his inauguration, he caused a Bank Holiday to be declared. By executive order every bank in the United States was closed for a period of four days. The object of this drastic action was to prevent further demoralization of the banking system and to restore public confidence through the weeding out of the unsound institutions and the reopening of the sound ones under government license. This policy proved conspicuously successful. The number of bank failures, which had averaged four or five daily before the bank holiday, was reduced under the licensing method to about one tenth of the previous amount. In order to strengthen the capital structure of the banks deemed worthy to continue, the Reconstruction Finance Corporation, RFC, organized shortly thereafter, invested about a billion dollars in the preferred stock, debentures and capital notes of some 5700 of these institutions. With a view to still greater protection to depositors the Federal Deposit Insurance Corporation was organized under the provisions of the Glass-Steagall banking act. This insures $2,500 of every individual deposit in all participating banks. The number of depositors benefited by this protection reaches the enormous total of

54,000,000, some 97 per cent of all depositors in the country. In order to assist depositors whose money is in closed banks a special agency within the RFC advances on the securities of these banks up to 50 per cent of the amount of the deposits. About $600,000,000 has been used in this way to aid depositors.

The success of this banking relief is convincingly shown by the fact that of the 16,000 banks closed during the banking holiday less than 1600 are still unlicensed and of the $32,000,000,000 of deposits less than $1,000,000,000 remain frozen in unlicensed banks. The New Deal contemplates other improvements in the banking system which will greatly increase its soundness and safety but the above mentioned are sufficient to show the wisdom and usefulness of the plan.

Little more than four weeks later an even more radical action, the devaluation of the dollar, was begun. On April 19th, Secretary Woodin announced that the United States had gone off the gold standard. This was followed by an immediate decline in the value of the dollar in international exchange. This decline was accelerated by huge purchases of gold by the government at almost double the rate hitherto prevailing. All citizens were ordered to deliver all gold in their possession, with the exception of an insignificant amount, to the treasury and to receive paper money in return. Violent fluctuations in the value of the dollar resulted, producing considerable uneasiness in financial and commercial circles, which ceased when the dollar was stabilized at its present value of slightly less than sixty cents.

The object of the devaluation of the dollar was to increase the price of commodities in the domestic market while making American exporters more capable of competition in the world market. Both of these results would, of course, be beneficial to the economic condition of America and seem to have been, in some measure, attained. This devaluation policy does not work evenly. Americans obliged to live abroad suffer by the lower purchasing power of their American dollars. But it is clear that this lowered value deters many Americans from traveling or residing abroad and thus tends to keep in America the huge sums formerly spent by American tourists and residents in foreign countries, thus giving a decided impetus to American resorts and transportation companies and American business in general. It also discourages foreign exports to America which again tends to increase American production and employment. It seems undeniable, therefore, that the devaluation of the dollar is economically beneficial to America.

The New Deal has endeavored and is endeavoring strenuously to combat unemployment and need among the American people. The NRA, as applied to commercial and industrial enterprises, is the most conspicuous example of this praiseworthy effort. It pursues mainly the following objects:—

1. To eliminate ruinous competition and increase the profitability of industry and business by the adoption of uniform codes regulating the conduct of the various enterprises in the most advantageous manner.

2. To increase the number of persons employed by decreasing the number of working days and hours in the week, the five day week of forty hours or less being the ideal.

3. To insure adequate remuneration for, and prevent the exploitation of, employees by establishing a minimum wage in each vocation. Public works of various kinds have been undertaken to provide gainful occupation for the host of unhappy unemployed. The CCC (Civilian Conservation Corps) is the most interesting and perhaps the most beneficial of these undertakings. More than 300,000 young men have been put to work in the national forests, improving them in various ways and increasing their value as a national asset. For this they receive good fare and an adequate wage and lead wholesome, physically and mentally beneficial lives, a striking contrast to their previous misery and wretchedness.

These young men belong mainly to destitute families to whom they have sent from their wages an estimated total of $50,000,000.* Three great agencies have been created by the government for the purpose of dealing with the problems of unemployment and industrial and agricultural depression, the Civil Works Administration, CWA, the Public Works Administration, PWA, and the Agricultural Adjustment Administration, AAA. All three have been munificently endowed and have made generous use of their funds in order to accomplish the tasks assigned to them. The CWA has as its purpose to provide work relief to some 4,000,000 unemployed and is doing so with the aid of a fund of $400,000,000.

The PWA has the double responsibility of relieving unemployment and of stimulating industry through aiding promising projects of various kinds. The tremendous sum of $3,300,000,000 was placed at its disposal all of which it has used for aiding more than 15,000 approved projects.

The AAA has the difficult task of improving agricultural conditions concerning which the complaints have been loudest and most vehement. It has been very successful in the South where its work in increasing the profitability of the cotton and tobacco crops has been thoroughly satisfactory. It has not yet worked so well in the normal agriculture of the rest of the country. Nevertheless, the farmers' income increased a billion dollars, rising to $6,000,000,000 in 1933. The aim is to raise it to $12,000,000,000 and keep it there.

The recognition of Soviet Russia by the United States which took place in November, 1933, undoubtedly was inspired by the same motive as all the other actions of the

* In *American Forests,* organ of The American Forestry Association, issues of 1933 and 1934, appears a number of interesting articles and editorials in reference to the work of the CCC and letters from youths employed in the national forests. The letters are particularly impressive, indeed pathetic. They describe in touching words the joy of the writers and their gratitude to the government for having rescued them from conditions of tragic suffering and given them pleasant work and sustenance and thus banished radical and subversive thoughts from their minds and imbued them with new love for and patriotic devotion to their country.

New Deal, to bring economic benefit to the American people.

It is not to be supposed that President Roosevelt is any more in sympathy with Russian Communism or Anti-Religionism than his predecessors in the presidential office, but he evidently felt that the American manufacturer and exporter should be given the full opportunity to reap the benefits of trade with that enormous and potentially so wealthy country. It is yet too early to say whether these expectations will be fully realized but it seems certain that American recognition of Russia will result in a substantial increase in trade between the two countries.

Great work has also been done since the incoming of the Roosevelt Administration in the direct relief of poverty and distress.

The Federal Emergency Relief Administration, FERA, coöperates with private agencies and with state and city governments in the relief of the destitute. It has contributed about $500,000,000 for this worthy purpose and purchased $300,000,000 worth of food products for distribution to the needy.

The Home Owners Loan Corporation, HOLC, refinances the mortgages on the homes of distressed home owners unable to meet the interest on the mortgages in such manner as to enable the owner to retain his home. The Farm Credit Administration, FCA, does the same for distressed farmers.

One of the most interesting and promising forms of relief work is the establishment of subsistence farms. A number of rural colonies or settlements have been established for distressed city inhabitants. Each family in these colonies is provided with a small cottage and a few acres of land and the necessary implements for farming on a small scale. The families can obtain all needed food from their land and local industries will supply what is needed additionally for a comfortable livelihood. This is a venture laden with possibilities of great development.

All in all the record of the NRA or the New Deal in the year which has elapsed since its inauguration to the

time of this writing is a most inspiring one. There is
nothing like it in all the previous history of the country.
It has relieved a tremendous amount of distress, it has
visibly increased business activity all over the land and
best of all it has changed gloom and hopelessness into the
brightness of optimism and courage.

The fact that such a vast amount of the nation's wealth
is required in order to accomplish these results is no argument in its disfavor. If it is right to use billions of dollars
in order to win a war it is certainly right to use similar
amounts to win such glorious victories of peace, to subdue
the demons of starvation and misery. President Roosevelt
and his group of advisors and coadjutors are entitled to the
love of the American people for the real desire to promote
the national welfare shown in these plans and to their
admiration and gratitude for the clarity of vision, the
courage and the unyielding pertinacity with which they
have pursued the ideal of the economic rehabilitation of
America. But, admitting and asserting all this, it nevertheless cannot be claimed that the New Deal is an adequate
and permanent solution of America's economic problem or
the ideal method of dealing with American conditions. It
must first be noted that it is paternalistic in the extreme
and a far cry from the "rugged individualism" formerly
characteristic of America and from the principle that "that
is the best government which governs least." This departure from American traditions may, indeed, be defended
as an unavoidable outgrowth of changed conditions. "Tem-
pora mutantur et nos mutamur in illis." Times change
and policies and methods must be changed in accordance
therewith. Unrestrained and unguided individualism is no
longer adequate in this age of tremendous mechanical development and gigantic commercial and industrial com-
binations. A more serious criticism is that many, if not
most, of the actions undertaken by the NRA are necessarily
temporary and, while involving the country in huge expenses, hold out no prospect of permanent economic betterment. The CWA is scheduled to cease its activities on
May 1st, 1934, and Mayor La Guardia of New York City

is protesting vehemently that the city is in no position to care for the additional host of needy who will be thrust upon it. Other municipalities are in the same position in this regard as New York. The FERA cannot continue indefinitely to pour out hundreds of millions of dollars for relief purposes. Public works cannot be unceasingly undertaken for the sole purpose of employing the unemployed. In the meanwhile the national debt swells to colossal proportions and the interest alone constitutes an almost unendurable strain upon the national resources. The conclusion is inescapable that NRA offers no definite and permanent solution of America's economic problem. Should there be a great intensification of industrial activity, absorbing most of the idle workers, coupled with a general revival of prosperity, an endurable condition might be created enabling the government to dispense with most of its emergency relief work. What the prospects are for such a desirable consummation is hard to say. But even then the problem would not be solved; it would still be latent and liable to raise its ugly head at any unfavorable change in the economic constellation.

Paternalism cannot heal America's economic sickness. Fraternalism remains, in the opinion of the writer, the only system which offers a true and lasting cure for the economic ills of the nation. What that system is and how it would work out, have already been set forth in the chapter on the Economic Problem and need not be again stated in detail. But this much may here be said that Fraternalism is fundamentally sound because it is in accord with natural conditions and because it permits a natural unfolding of individual energy, neither unduly restraining nor artificially stimulating it.

Along that road lies hope for the true and logical harmony of production and distribution which shall finally banish the specter of economic maladjustment, with its accompanying conflicts and sufferings, from America and from all civilized lands.

CHAPTER FIFTEENTH

HITLERISM IN AMERICA

Hitlerism or Naziism * is a foreign disease, a pernicious psychical malady of post-war Germany, which has infected the political power and through it the entire cultural and social life of that once enlightened and highly civilized land. In view of this distinctly foreign origin Americans might think that it is no concern of theirs, that, while they oppose and condemn a system which breeds tyranny and oppression, cruelty and brutality, in Germany as everywhere, they may regard it with a sort of remote, detached interest, somewhat as they do Voodooism in Haiti or cannibalism in Mid-Africa. Such a view would be a very grave error.

Hitlerism is a very real, a very threatening danger to America against which it behooves America to take resolute and energetic steps to defend itself. That is so because Hitlerism is strongly propagandistic and seeks to convert other nations to its perverted concept of statecraft. Voodooism and cannibalism constitute no menace to those who do not sympathize with them because they are content to remain restricted to their present followers and make no effort to gain new adherents.

Naziism is the very reverse. Its leaders are filled with a furious conversionist zeal and strive with fanatical fervor to spread the doctrines which they have, by dint of brute force, made dominant in Germany. The Nazi government maintains a special Bureau of Enlightenment and Propaganda in Berlin, under charge of the notorious Paul Joseph Goebbels. There is also reported to be a "Grand Nazi Council for German propaganda abroad" consisting of thir-

* Hitlerism and Naziism are synonymous terms and will be used indiscriminately in this chapter.

teen members under the presidency of Dr. Alfred Rosen-
berg. There can be no doubt of the existence of worldwide
Nazi propaganda and there are strong indications that
special efforts are being made to win over the public opinion
of America to sympathy with Nazi views, in particular to
its Anti-Semitic theories.*

A brief consideration of the views and practices of Naziism will suffice to show what a frightful calamity for this
country its adoption by the American people, or any considerable portion thereof, would be. The Nazi governmental creed is the direct antithesis of the principles on which
the American republic is based; its adoption would mean
the complete destruction of the political doctrines which
Americans hold sacred and inviolable and under which this
nation has prospered so mightily. The British oppression
of North America which caused Patrick Henry to burst
forth into his famous peroration "I know not what others
may think but, as for me, give me liberty or give me death"
was kindness itself compared to the reign of terror under
which, since the advent of the Hitler régime, Germany
groans. Hitlerism is the outspoken foe of liberty or democracy in any form. For them, both unspeakably precious to all true Americans, it substitutes the principle of
Führerschaft or leadership, that is, the unrestrained sway
of so called leaders, who are really self-constituted or party
chosen dictators, absolute rulers to whom all must submit,
without any power to enforce or even to express a contrary
view. It has divided German citizenship, upon the basis of
an absurd racial theory, into two classes, an upper class
of genuine citizens and a subordinate class of barely tolerated helots, and deprived the lower of the two, those in
whose veins some Jewish blood flows, of all political prefer-

* The *American Hebrew,* a leading Jewish Journal of New York,
has devoted much effort to the investigation of Nazi propaganda
in the United States and has uncovered a mass of startling facts
proving the existence of such propaganda on a vast scale. Con-
gressman Samuel Dickstein has also conducted such investigations
with similar results. These disclosures caused the speedy flight, for
the purpose of avoiding arrest, of Heinz Spanknoebel, apparently,
up to the time of his flight, the chief Nazi agitator in America.

ment and almost completely of the opportunity to earn a living. How repugnant to American principles of equality and equal opportunities for all citizens this is needs no direct statement. To whatever domain of German life we turn our eyes we can see the heavy hand of Naziism blighting and stifling all free manifestation and genuine progress.

From the universities it has driven forth hundreds of the best scholars and scientists, some because they were "Non-Aryans," a euphemism for Jews, some because they held liberal views, unwelcome to the powers that be.

Dozens of the finest littérateurs have been forced to flee the country. All labor unions have been abolished, their funds confiscated and their members reduced to a condition of virtual slavery. Women have been driven from the high position in society to which the progress and liberality of the nineteenth century had raised them and bluntly informed that the only purpose of their existence is expressed in the three words "Kinder, Küche, Kirche," "children, kitchen and church." The mailed fist of Naziism has not even paused before the sacred portals of the houses of God.

In simpler words Naziism has not hesitated to invade the holiest domain of man's life, his religious sentiments. With the Catholics, it has, evidently through fear of their great power, made a sort of tolerable concordat or agreement but, nevertheless, worries and annoys them in various ways.

The Protestants it has sought to force under domination of a Reichsbishop and to deprive their faith of its historic character which it considers too Jewish and to introduce in its stead the so called German church, a sort of revival of primitive Germanic paganism. This attempt has been bravely resisted by several hundred Protestant clergymen and, for a time at least, foiled. As for the Jews Naziism does not recognize them at all as a religion but only as a racial group. Nevertheless it has dealt their religious life a staggering blow through the prohibition of their ritual method of slaughter, thus forcing conscientious Jews to the choice of either violating the precepts of their faith or de-

priving themselves of flesh food. Liberty of speech is, of
course, dead. The press is gagged and cannot utter a word
except in accordance with governmental policy. All of
these crimes against basic human rights are committed in
the name of *Gleichschaltung,* that is, coördination of all
the forces of the nation in the service of the state, as
Naziism conceives it. And in the meanwhile, the heads-
man's ax clangs horribly and the concentration camps are
chokingly full of the best brain and brawn of the land.*
This simple, and by no means exhaustive, presentation of
Nazi views and practices is amply sufficient to show how
utterly repugnant the characteristic doctrines of Naziism
are to the principles which the American concept of the
state holds fundamental and indispensable. Whether the
Nazi state calls itself authoritarian or totalitarian, whether
it professes as its fundamental political principle leadership
or coördination is all one to the American way of thinking
which holds all these doctrines in utter abomination.

America stands for liberty and democracy and is in no
mood to be carried away by theories reminiscent of the ages
of barbarism even though they cloak in pseudo-scientific

* American indignation and condemnation of the Hitlerite policies
has been strong and outspoken from the very beginning of the Nazi
régime. Probably the strongest and most striking expression thereof
was "The Case of Civilization against Hitlerism" at Madison Square
Garden on March 7th, 1934. Twenty-two leading Americans, representing various views and elements of the community, addressed an
audience of more than twenty thousand persons and condemned
in ringing words the crimes of Hitlerism. Alfred E. Smith, F. H.
La Guardia, Millord E. Tydings, Bernard S. Deutsch and John
Haynes Holmes voiced the horror of American public opinion.
Raymond H. Moley spoke for the liberals, Matthew Woll for
labor, Harry W. Chase for the scholarly world, Seth Wakeman for
the International League for Academic Freedom, Stephen S. Wise
for the Jews, Arthur J. Brown for the Protestant churches, Michael
Williams for the Catholics, Roger N. Baldwin for Civil liberty,
L. F. Barker for the physicians, Stanley High for literature, Abraham
Kahan for the Socialists, Gustavus Kirby for sport and Edward J.
Neary for the American Legion. Dr. Hans Luther, the German
Ambassador, was invited to defend the Hitler régime but did not
attend. The unanimous verdict, with one exception, a woman
Hitlerite, was "guilty."

phrases their systematic design for the enslavement of the people.

For the protection of its cherished institutions and as a matter of self-defense, America is in duty bound to keep Nazi propaganda from its shores and to suppress and uproot the Nazistic agitation which has already found lodgment within its borders. Mental contagion is strikingly similar to physical contagion and fully as dangerous and just as governments have the right and the duty to exclude noxious plants and animals and disease bearing substances of all kinds from their lands thus have they the same right and duty to ward off the intellectual and spiritual contamination produced by the propaganda of brutally reactionary, hate inspiring and liberty destroying systems.* That Naziism deserves to be described as such a system is patent to any liberal thinker.

Professor Raymond Moley characterized it aptly when he said "I hate this thing because it is the enemy of my country, my faith and my right to be free."

Of course whatever legislation is adopted in America to curb Nazi propaganda must be such as is in harmony with the principles of Americanism and does not violate the right of free speech. But it seems clear that propaganda which seeks to calumniate, humiliate and degrade one portion of the population and to cause it to be hated and despised by the other elements and which upholds and inculcates illiberal and reactionary doctrines tending to

---

* How contagious ideologies such as that of Naziism can be is shown by the fact that an organization similar to that of the Nazis, and like it violently anti-Semitic, has been formed in America under the name of "The Silver Shirts of America." Its leader is one William Dudley Pelley. All of these movements seem to need inspiration drawn from shirts of some special color, Italian Fascists from black shirts, German Nazis from brown shirts and our American reactionaries from shirts of a silver color. The present period of history might well be called "the shirt age." Incidentally it may be noted that Mussolini, the Italian dictator, is a well meaning man, sincerely desirous of promoting the welfare of his people and free from racial or religious prejudices. But he is strongly anti-democratic and that fact has had most unfortunate consequences.

undermine the foundations of the American republic, has exceeded the legitimate limits of free speech and may properly be suppressed.

It is the duty of all governments, even of the freest, to suppress crime and agitation of this disruptive and destructive sort must certainly be classed as crime.*

But better and more potent than forcible suppression would be the development of a strong sense of brotherhood among all the various elements of the American population and a fuller understanding of American ideals which would render such noxious propaganda harmless and hopeless *ab initio.*

When all Americans, without distinction of ethnic origin or religious adherence, fully realize that they are citizens of the greatest and most wonderful nation that the earth has ever seen, that they are, in fact, members of a mighty and unparalleled organization for the promotion of human happiness and well being and that the intrusion of European antagonisms, prejudices and bigotries can only mar and perhaps destroy these splendid realities and even more splendid possibilities, there will be no room in their hearts or minds for such vicious and inhuman propaganda. Americans of German origin, in particular, should be assured that American opposition to Naziism does not mean antagonism to them as an ethnic group but only to the brutally reactionary governmental system now exercising unrestrained sway in Germany. Movements for the promotion of good will such as the National Conference of Jews and Christians deserve the support and encouragement of all true Americans.

Such universal brotherhood of all Americans, such loyal coherence of all and justice and fairness to all the varied

* In the 1934 session of the New York State Assembly a bill has been introduced by Assemblyman Breitbart making the dissemination of such propaganda a misdemeanor punishable by fine and imprisonment. In the issue of the *American Hebrew* of March 9th, 1934, Mr. Max J. Kohler, in a learned and detailed article, treats from the legal point of view the questions involved in this bill and shows that it is right in principle. From the Democratic platform of 1916 he cites an emphatic denunciation of such propaganda.

elements of American citizenry, constitute America's best defense against Nazi propaganda and will effectually prevent its invasion of the peaceful domains of our blessed country.

CHAPTER SIXTEENTH

CONCLUDING OBSERVATIONS

THE picture of America, which has been presented to the reader in the preceding chapters of this book, is that of a nation with many virtues and many faults, of a country wonderfully rich in possibilities but which has failed, in a number of ways, to utilize them properly and has, consequently, not brought to its population that measure of liberty and happiness which might legitimately have been expected. Do the unfavorable aspects of the picture mean that the American experiment has failed, that the history of America has been merely another example of the defeat of human hopes and aspirations, of the collapse of the sweet dreams which have filled the minds of the idealistic lovers of humanity since time immemorial, only to end in final downfall and despair? If we contrast the actual conditions with the bright imaginings of idealists, especially if we compare the economic conditions prevailing in the present years of depression (1929-1934) with theoretic concepts of American prosperity, we might be inclined to assent to this gloomy verdict and to think that America does not differ in any essential regard from the countries of Europe and has not brought any appreciable amelioration to the suffering exiles of the Old World who sought a refuge from their miseries on its supposedly hospitable and bountiful shores. Such a judgment would, however, in the opinion of the writer, be hasty and superficial. America does represent a distinct advance in the history of the world and its existence has been, and is, a decided benefit and a source of great advantage and blessing not only to its own inhabitants but to mankind in general, so that we may safely say that without America the world would be immeasurably poorer.

We must first realize that perfection does not lie in

257

human things. All human works, all human institutions are afflicted with the blemish of defectiveness, of insufficiency. Perfection is the ideal, the scintillating expectation which, though always hoped for by the noblest minds, is never completely realized. It is adequate ground for satisfaction with any human creation if it be fundamentally good and sound and its faults not overwhelmingly great and numerous. As the Talmudic saying puts it: "Happy is he whose sins can be counted." From this viewpoint America may be deemed happy for its basic and fundamental qualities are excellent and admirable and its defects are not so numerous that they may not be counted.

Furthermore, though perfection is not in human things, the tendency to progress is an intrinsic characteristic of human nature. Mankind has an instinctive desire to attain to that which is better and finer than its present state, to rise from the lower to the higher, to add to its knowledge and its power, to make its life freer, brighter and happier. Ofttimes these advantages can only be acquired at the cost of struggle, strife and sacrifice but, nevertheless, the desire to obtain them is constant throughout human history.* Of all nations America is probably the one most distinguished by desire for progress and advancement in all the domains of human endeavor, political, economic and spiritual. Sometimes this progress has been gained only at a tremendous cost in blood and treasure but America has never shrunk from the sacrifice when convinced that it was right and necessary.** This love of progress, this striving after

* It may be urged over against these views that the desire for progress is not universal, that some races are extremely retrograde and non-progressive. The truth, however, is that the so-called retrograde nations are not really non-progressive. Their opposition to progress is due to the fact that they do not think that that which is put before them as progress is really so or that, in their ignorance, they do not see how they could attain to it. Many nations, formerly considered barbarous, have in recent years adopted most of the characteristic institutions of Occidental civilization.

** The Civil War, for instance, cost America millions of lives and billions of dollars but it left the United States indissolubly united and with the ugly blot of slavery forever removed from its escutcheon.

the better and higher things, gives us the firm confidence and sure hope that America will not remain irrevocably afflicted by the evils and shortcomings which have crept into its political, social and economic systems but will, in course of time, overcome them and approach ever nearer to its glorious ideal of liberty and happiness.

It is not, however, merely hope for the future which inspires us with the conviction that America is a storehouse of blessing and well being to the world. That which it has already accomplished and is still accomplishing is ample justification for looking upon it in that light. The benefits which America has brought to mankind are, indeed, stupendously great. The evils from which the world has mainly suffered during the ages of the past are three, poverty, inter-racial and inter-religious hatreds and deprivation of liberty. All three of these America has lessened and alleviated in great measure. Its contribution to the solution of the problem of poverty is magnificent. Of the approximately one hundred and twenty-five million persons who dwell in the United States the overwhelming majority live, in normal times, in a condition which would be considered affluence in most of the other countries of the world. The American standard of living of the masses is proverbially higher than in other lands and as for the bitter privations and utter wretchedness which are the lot of the submerged millions of Europe, to say nothing of the teeming multitudes of Asia and Africa, they are practically unknown in this blessed land. Best of all, when poverty and suffering rear their ugly heads in America, as in the present unfortunate period of depression, they are not accepted as inevitable, as fixed and permanent conditions which cannot be altered, as they are to a very great extent in the countries of the Old World. On the contrary, they are looked upon as a reproach to the nation, to remove which every effort must be made and billions of dollars of public and private wealth are poured out to relieve suffering, to find jobs for the unemployed and to bring back the normal condition of American prosperity. To provide adequate sustenance for such a vast population is no mean achievement. But America's contribution to human welfare is not limited to its own people. The American people send every year hundreds of millions of dollars to the other countries of the world, more especially to those of Europe, to alleviate the poverty and promote the welfare of their inhabitants. The Rockefeller Foundation which has an annual income of approximately $14,000,000 and which uses its resources for the promotion of health work in all lands, is a typical instance of this universal American benevolence.* Therefore, although the economic system of America is far from perfect and has by no means succeeded in bringing about the ideal condition of an adequate and humanly worthy living for all the people, it is nevertheless unquestionably true that America has performed a gigantic work in promoting the material and economic welfare of a great section of mankind and, to a certain extent, of the entire human race.

The same can be said of America's contribution to the improvement of human relations, to the abolition of racial and religious hatreds and antagonisms, in a word, to the inculcation of a broad spirit of tolerance. As we have seen, America is by no means free from prejudice and bigotry. The Jew, the Negro and the foreigner can tell a tale, in many cases a very sad and pathetic tale, of the unfair and unjust social and economic discriminations under which they suffer and which tend to make their lives grievous trials and burdens. It is impossible to defend such narrow mindedness, to say one word even in palliation of such barbarous and inhumane views, so utterly in contradiction to the fundamental principles of democracy. But it is possible to understand this phenomenon, otherwise

---

* Another outstanding example of this benevolence is the work done by the Jews for the relief of their suffering brethren in Europe, mainly Eastern Europe, and now Germany. It is estimated that since the beginning of the World War American Jews have contributed over a hundred million dollars for this purpose and that but for this aid the majority of Eastern European Jews would have perished of starvation. Other elements of the American population have contributed in a similar way for the relief of their affiliated peoples in Europe and the Near East.

puzzling in a supposed land of liberty and equality, and this understanding, while it will not cause us to forgive, will, at least, lessen our wonder and our amazement. American ethnical and religious antagonisms are a pale reflection of those prevalent in other countries. But they are only a pale reflection, they lack utterly the bitterness and the intensity of the antagonisms and hostilities of the Old World. There is nothing in America to parallel the flaming hatred of Protestant Irish to Catholic Irish and *vice versa*, of Magyars to Slavs, of Poles to Germans and Russians and of European anti-Semites to Jews. In particular America has nothing to parallel the furious enmity of Indian Mohammedans and Hindoos which periodically deluges the streets of Indian cities with blood and paralyzes their normal economic life. American intolerance is furthermore the sentiment of a petty minority. The great majority of Americans are sincerely tolerant, even liberal in their sentiments and movements such as the Ku Klux Klan fail to impress them. There are also organizations, such as the National Conference of Jews and Christians, which have as their object the removal of inherited bigotries and antagonisms and the promotion of tolerant and brotherly relations between all the various racial and religious elements of the population, on the basis of a broad, elementary human understanding. The American government, in particular, and that is a matter of the highest importance, is entirely free from all such prejudices and endeavors to treat all classes with equal consideration. The importance of American racial and religious prejudices—though they are certainly bad enough, Heaven knows—must not be exaggerated and there is reasonable ground to expect in the course of time, if not complete cessation of such prejudices, at least, a great diminution and softening thereof, so that they will no longer play an important part in American life.

As regards the third evil from which men have suffered and still suffer so greatly in so many countries, and from which America should not, under normal conditions, suffer the lack of proper liberty, it is not quite so easy to give optimistic assurances. America is the classic land of liberty. It is a mere truism to say that the concept of human freedom cannot be separated from the concept of Americanism. Were it otherwise Abraham Lincoln could never have uttered, in his unforgettable address on the battlefield of Gettysburg, as a self-evident and undeniable statement, the words "Four score and seven years ago our fathers brought forth on this continent a new nation, conceived in liberty and dedicated to the proposition that all men are created equal." America, therefore, in accordance with the sentiment of this noble utterance, is, by its very nature and essence, consecrated to the task of preserving and maintaining genuine liberty and equality for all who dwell within its borders.* It would be impossible to assert that present-day America is completely loyal to this splendid inherited principle of liberty. Of course, a certain clash and contradiction between the concepts of law and liberty cannot be avoided. Law necessarily restricts and limits the liberty of the individual. At no stage of human development and in no form of human society, whether primitive or advanced, can absolute liberty of action be accorded to the individual. That would mean the war of all against all and the tyranny of the strong over the weak. It would not be liberty in any true sense of the term. Human society needs laws and a government able to enforce them in order to protect men from each other and to maintain peace and order in the community.

But a nation desiring to be free and to avoid oppressing and tyrannizing over its citizens or subjects, will make its laws as few as possible and carefully see to it that they do not infringe upon elementary human rights, such as liberty of speech and personal habits and will be especially zealous in guaranteeing exact and even handed justice to all who appear before the courts, even if they be criminals of the deepest dye or adherent of unpopular and detested

* This sentiment is also expressed by the inscription on the Liberty Bell in Federal Hall, Philadelphia: "And ye shall proclaim liberty throughout the land to all the inhabitants thereof" (Leviticus XXV, 10).

movements. All this is, of course, axiomatic. Various incidents of recent years have, however, created a strong impression in the minds of many that American legislative bodies and judicial tribunals do not always conform scrupulously to this principle. During the World War, under the laws of Sedition and Espionage, constitutional rights were practically abolished, men were cast into jail for exercising their constitutional right of freedom of speech and opposing America's participation in the conflict, or for refusing, as conscientious objectors, to perform military service. America went, in this regard, much further than England. It may be argued that war possesses an abnormal status and that abrogation of usual rights must be permitted in war time if necessary to win the war. As the Latin proverb puts it: *"Inter Armis taceunt leges,"* "When the weapons speak the laws are silent." Be that as it may, there is no excuse in a free country for infringement of liberty in time of peace. And several apparent instances of such infringement have occurred.

The life imprisonment of Thomas Mooney in California for alleged participation in a crime of which there is a widespread conviction that he is innocent and the execution in Massachusetts, under similar circumstances, of Sacco and Vanzetti, are incidents which have deeply grieved many thoughtful Americans and have aroused bitter condemnation and indignant protests all over the world. The condemnation and indignation are intensified by the fact that it is very generally thought that the real reason for the punishment of these men was not because of their supposed connection with the crime of which they were found guilty, but because they were Radicals, members of organizations opposed to the political and economic systems prevailing in the land. According to these views, their punishment was not a judicial but a political act, aimed not so much at the condemned men individually as at all those who hold the same views and having as its aim to deter them from adhering to or propagating such views through terror of the possible consequences.

If these views are correct, no proof is needed that such

action is in utter contradiction to the constitutional right of American citizens to liberty of speech and liberty of opinion in matters political as in all other matters, and constitutes, therefore, the gravest possible infringement of their civil liberty. That it was consummated under observance of the required judicial procedure does not diminish the gravity of the wrong. In certain Southern states public opinion is strongly opposed to trade unionism and the organization of laborers for the protection of the interests of their vocation. Delegates of Northern workingmen's organizations who have come to Southern towns for the purpose of organizing labor unions have been met by committees of local citizens and politely but firmly told to go back home and informed that a refusal to comply might be attended with serious consequences. The State of Tennessee has a statute prohibiting the teachers employed in state schools from teaching the Darwinian theory or that part of it which holds that the human race is descended from a lower form of animal, akin to the ape. Under this statute a certain Thomas A. Scopes, a teacher in a State High School who had taught the Darwinian theory, was found guilty and condemned to jail and the payment of a heavy fine.

The prevention by groups of citizens of the organization of laborers' unions, may be considered mob action for which the state cannot be held responsible but when the state prohibits a teacher employed by it from teaching his scientific conviction that constitutes an infringement of his liberty which may be technically legal but is certainly in contradiction to the fundamental civic rights of the citizen. The effect of all this governmental and popular action is, of course, to intimidate those who hold unpopular views and terrify them into concealing or leaving unexpressed their opinions in which they differ from the majority. That such terrorism constitutes a most serious violation of their civil liberty is self-evident.

The Sunday laws existing in twenty-four of the forty-eight States of the Union and which compel the citizen who observes another day of the week as holy time to abstain from work and business on Sunday infringe gravely on the liberty of the non-Sunday-observing citizen. There is no moral justification for compelling a person who conscientiously abstains from all secular occupation on one day of the week to observe also another day. Twenty-four of the states recognize the wrongfulness of this discrimination and exempt Seventh Day observers from observing the Sunday but the other twenty-four still maintain this unfair and unjust discrimination.

Despite these violations of the spirit of liberty which should of right prevail in America the writer is of the opinion that America is still basically true to its traditions of freedom. Its constitution still stands, its fundamental institutions have not been changed and the supposed deviations and inconsistencies above recorded, and all others of the same kind, are to be considered, not as permanent alterations of America's political system but as mere temporary aberrations and evils which will surely be remedied as time rolls by and the injurious character of their influence on America's precious heritage of liberty is more and more clearly recognized. Nor are there lacking encouraging incidents which testify to the strength of the democratic principle in America. The recent repeal of National Prohibition by the vote of the people of thirty-six states was such an incident. This was a splendid demonstration of the orderly working of constitutional methods and, therefore, a convincing proof of the success of Democracy. In a sense the inconsistencies may be looked upon as the sicknesses of childhood which must be gone through before the strength of maturity and perfect health are attained. As nations go America is still very young, a mere child among the families of earth. One hundred and fifty-eight years are too short a period for the definite development of the national character of so great a nation as that of the United States, especially when that development is complicated by the inclusion of many heterogeneous elements.

The American nation dedicated itself at its foundation to the ideal of true democracy but a large part of its population, including many who stand in high places and who help shape its destinies, have not grown up to that ideal, do not fully realize what true Democracy implies. True Democracy implies that all the people, that all the members of the nation shall have an equal and untrammeled right to express their views in matters political and to exercise their influence in shaping the course of the nation, providing that that expression and the exercise of that influence are carried out by lawful and peaceful methods.

It may very well happen and, indeed, is practically certain to happen, that the views and proposals of one class of the population are extremely disagreeable, even repugnant, to another class. True Democracy will endure them, will recognize the right of those who hold them to their opinions and is content to leave the decision to the vote of the majority of the people. A large part of the American people have not yet been able to swing themselves up to this high concept of Democracy. They are good, sincere and moral people, loyally devoted to their own concepts of what is right and proper and very anxious to have those concepts prevail in the government of the country but they do not quite realize that the democratic principle on which America is founded requires that all views and concepts be entitled to free expression and to whatever measure of influence they may wield. Radicals of every kind, Anarchists, Socialists, Communists and all of that ilk are the pet aversion of these inherently conservative Americans and they are inclined to think almost any method of suppressing these disagreeable agitators justified.

What these good Americans do not realize is that force has never yet succeeded in suppressing an intellectual movement, be it spiritual or material. We can learn from Russia and England the wrong and the right way to deal with this problem. Czaristic Russia exerted all its enormous force to suppress its enemies, the Nihilists, and failed utterly. Today the Nihilists, under their modern name of Bolsheviki, rule the vast former empire of the Czars. England, wiser and with a better understanding of psychology, allows its radicals and malcontents to give full vent to their feelings and to discourse upon their theories to their heart's content. In London, in front of Hyde Park, one may see and hear all sorts of orators holding forth. The stout, stolid Bobby never interferes with them as long as they limit themselves to vocal efforts, to "shooting off their mouths" and refrain from violence. And the result is that England stands impregnable, despite the vaporings of all Radicals. And, in this instance, the example of England is a good one for America to follow.* It is not advisable to refuse those who oppose the government the opportunity to express their objections and thus give them the idea that they are being unjustly and unfairly suppressed. That method of procedure breeds the very sentiments of rebellion and readiness for violence which it is its object to prevent. The policy of non-interference with mere talk, no matter how violent, would, it seems to the writer, be far wiser. It would, in general, afford sufficient opportunity to all agitators to advocate their policies and would take away from them all chance of claiming that they were being deprived of their constitutional right to freedom of

* In the issue of the *New York Times* of August 21st, 1932, appeared a letter signed Arthur Hunter under the heading "Free Oratory in Hyde Park." The writer evidently thoroughly understands his subject and is himself apparently conservative in his views. The portion concerning the treatment of radical speakers is most illuminating in this connection and is essentially as follows: "The policemen do not interfere, whatever is said, but merely keep order.... An amusing incident was told of a Communist who was advocating the destruction of the government. When he urged his audience to go to 10 Downing Street, the official residence of the Prime Minister, to hang him, a policeman stepped forward and called out, "All of you gents as wants to go to Downing Street and 'ang the Prime Minister please take one step forward and the h'others one step to rear." The laughter which followed this announcement resulted in the orator quickly deciding to close his address. The extent to which the government allows free expression of opinion is rather startling at times to us. Last year I saw a procession of tens of thousands of persons passing through the principal streets bearing hundreds of red flags and advocating the inauguration of a Soviet government. There was no disorder and no roughness of any kind by the police. The march ended in Hyde Park where they broke up into groups listening to addresses by their leaders. Having thus given expression of their opinions, they went quietly home." The contrast between the conditions here described and those sometimes prevailing in America is noteworthy.

speech.* The armed forces of the nation, the police and
military, can be trusted to deal swiftly and thoroughly with
any attempt to pass from the domain of talk to that of
overt action.

Despite all these fallings away from the splendid ideals
embodied in the Constitution and the original sentiments
of Americans, the fundamental principles of American liberty remain unshaken. Freedom of speech still exists legally although most leading Americans use it moderately
and conservatively, perhaps a little timidly, and radical
expressions of opinion are rare. Nevertheless prominent
thinkers and educators like Nicholas Murray Butler and
John Dewey, concerning whose patriotism and loyalty to
America there cannot be an atom of doubt, do not hesitate
to criticize existing conditions openly and fearlessly. This
temperate and moderate, yet frank and sincere freedom
of speech may be relied upon to ascertain, in keen and pene-
trating investigation and analysis, the sources of the evils
from which America suffers and to find the remedies which
will heal them.

America has gone through many severe trials during the
century and a half of its existence, some of which have
shaken the republic to its very foundations, but the good
sense and calm courage of its people have enabled it to
surmount them all. Those fine qualities are still characteristic of the American people and will, without a doubt,

* From this point of view the wisdom of the law refusing the use
of the mails to publications advocating "treason, insurrection or
forceful resistance to any law of the United States" is open to grave
doubt. It is so hard to draw the exact line between legitimate opposition to public policy and that which is treasonable, that this law
may very conceivably be utilized by an unpopular administration to
suppress perfectly lawful and proper opposition. This possibility is
clearly indicated in proceedings concerning the refusing of the
mailing of certain issues of *The American Freeman* by the Post
Office Department, reported in the *New York Times* of August 17th,
1932. Mr. William C. O'Brien, representing the Post Office Department, said that the articles in question, "incited to violence." Mr.
Arthur G. Hays, representing the American Civil Liberties Union,
said, "If the government can bar this publication, there isn't any
magazine opposing the government's policy that can get through the
mails."

bring about the right and proper solution of the many difficult problems by which it is confronted, a solution which will not only make for security and material prosperity but will be in accord with the glorious traditions and ideals of American liberty. Lovers of America need not despair, nor even fear. The people of America are not going to sacrifice any of the glorious heritages which have come to them from the past nor any of the splendid possibilities offered by a wonderful present and a still more wonderful future. They will not themselves forge the chains which will make them and their children slaves.

On the contrary, they intend to use the irresistible power which democracy gives them to overcome the errors of the past and to secure for themselves and their descendants a finer, happier and nobler national existence, an existence unmarred by stupid prejudices and bigotries, unscarred by devastating poverty and grim privation, unwarped by narrow-minded and obscurantist perversion of legislative power but all lit up with the light of brotherly kindness, abundant prosperity and happiness and, above all, refulgent with the radiance of true American liberty. American patriots may joyously envision an America of the future more glorious and magnificent than it has ever been, even in the most inspiring periods of the past. "Greater will be the glory of this latter house than of the former, saith the Lord of hosts" (Haggai II, 9). Americanism, overcoming by the invincible power of an aroused people all the obstacles and difficulties which have hitherto hemmed its progress, will come to its full fruition, will rise to hitherto undreamed of heights, and will create upon this still young continent a truly ideal commonwealth which will secure to all its people the priceless possessions of peace, material and spiritual well being and genuine freedom. The signs are many that the American people are now resolved to see that these lofty aspirations associated with the term "American" become a matter, not of mere theory, but of actual fulfillment and realization and that their resolve will be carried out is certain for "The voice of the people is the voice of God."

BIBLIOGRAPHY

BOOKS ON GENERAL AMERICAN CONDITIONS

CHAPTERS FIRST, SECOND AND FOURTH

B. J. Lossing, "The Achievements of Four Centuries," New York, Gay Bros. & Co., 1890.

Sir C. W. Dilke, "Greater Britain," Philadelphia, Lippincott, 1869.

G. Brueckner, "Amerika's Wichtigste Charakteristik," St. Louis, C. Witter, 1857.

J. Baumgarten, "Eine Ethnographische Rundreise," Stuttgart, Rieger, 1882.

L. S. Rowe, "Las Democracias Americanas y sus Deberes," Santiago, Imprenta Universitaria, 1917.

G. Remak, "Die Vereinigten Staaten," Philadelphia, Thomas, Cowperthwait & Co., 1849.

D. Pector, Notes sur L'Americanisme, Paris, J. Maisonneuve, 1900.

A. A. Everett, "America," A general survey of its political situation, Philadelphia, H. C. Cary, 1827.

M. Thomson, "American Empire, Present and Future," New York, 1899.

J. H. Finley, "American Democracy from Washington to Wilson," New York, Macmillan Company, 1919.

J. F. Cooper, "The American Democrat," Introduction by H. L. Mencken, New York, A. A. Knopf, 1931.

Charles Recht, "American Deportation and Exclusion Laws," New York Civil Liberties Bureau, 1919.

J. B. Bryce, "The American Commonwealth," New York, Macmillan & Co., 1914.

Carol Aronovici, "Americanization," St. Paul, Keller Publishing Company, 1919.

Julius Drachsler, "Democracy and Assimilation," New York, The Macmillan Company, 1920.

CHAPTER FIFTH

The Negro in America

P. A. Bruce, "The Plantation Negro as a Freeman," New York, G. P. Putnam's Sons, 1889.

W. H. Fleming, "Slavery and the Race Problem in the South," Boston, Dana, Estes & Co., 1906.

E. G. Murphy, "Problems of the Present South," New York, The Macmillan Company, 1904.

F. Tannenbaum, "Darker Phases of the South," New York and London, G. P. Putnam's Sons, 1924.

M. S. Evans, "Black and White in the Southern States," London, Longmans, Green & Co., 1915.

W. J. Edwards, "Twenty-five Years in the Black Belt," Boston, Cornhill Co., 1918.

A. P. Comstock, "The Problem of the Negro," University of Chicago Press, 1912.

S. Winston, "Studies in Negro Leadership," American Journal of Sociology, Chicago, 1931.

K. Miller, "American Code of Caste," New York, Macmillan Co., 1918.

J. M. Mecklin, "Democracy and Race Friction," New York, Macmillan Co., 1914.

C. E. Locke, "Is the Negro Making Good," Cincinnati, Methodist Book Concern, 1913.

L. B. Moore, "What the Negro has done for Himself," Washington, D. C., R. L. Pendleton, 1910.

B. T. Washington, "The Story of the Negro," New York, Doubleday, Page & Co., 1909.

W. P. Calhoun, "The Caucasian and the Negro in the United States," Columbus, S. C. Bryan Publishing Co., 1902.

CHAPTER SIXTH

The Jew in America

S. Wolf, "The American Jew as Patriot, Soldier and Citizen," Philadelphia, The Levytype Co., 1895.

E. J. James and others, "The Immigrant Jew in America," New York, B. F. Buck & Co., 1906.

B. Drachman, "Anti-Jewish Prejudice in America," article in *The Forum*, July, 1914.

J. D. Krauskopf, "Prejudice, Its Genesis and Exodus," New York, Bloch Publishing Co., 1909.

Addresses in Celebration of the Two Hundred and Fiftieth Anniversary of the Settlement of the Jews in the United States, New York, 1906.

United States, an exhaustive article on the Jews of the United States in Vol. XII, of the Jewish Encyclopedia.

Madison C. Peters, "Justice to the Jew."

Ada Sterling, "The Jew and Civilization," New York, Aetco Publishing Co., 1924.

Z. Vance, "The Scattered Nation."

CHAPTER SEVENTH

The Economic Problem

W. G. Sumner, "Problems in Political Economy," New York, Henry Holt & Co., 1889.

P. Von Struve, "Ueber einige grundlegende Motive im National-Ökonomischen Denken-Internationale Zeitschrift für Philosophie der Kultur, Tübingen, 1911.

F. Stoepel, "Die Freie Gesellschaft," Chemnitz, E. Schmeitzner, 1881.

J. H. Stallard, "The True Basis of Economics," New York, Doubleday and McClure Co., 1899.

L. Southerns, "Physical Economics, Fundamental Principles," London, Labour Publishing Co., 1921.

H. L. Smith, "Economic Aspect of State Socialism," London, 1887.

Henry George, "Progress and Poverty," New York, D. Appleton & Co., 1880.

M. B. F. Major, "The Ethics of Economics," London, S. Sonnenschein & Co., 1908.

Karl Marx, "Zur Kritik der Pölitischen Ökonomie," Stuttgart, K. Kantsky, 1922.

M. W. Meagher, "Alluring Absurdities, Fallacies of Henry George," New York, American News Co., 1889.

T. Von Mossig, "Die Staatenentwickelung als Produkt von Überfluss und Mangel," Vienna, A. Dorn, 1912.

C. C. North, "The Sociological Implications of Ricardo's Economics," University of Chicago Press, 1915.

E. R. A. Seligman, "Economists," New York, 1921.

E. Atkinson, "The Elements of National Prosperity," Boston, 1882.

J. R. Bellerby, "A Contributive Society," London, Educational Services, 1931.

A. Hook, "Unemployment, Its Cause aud Cure," London, Labour Publishing Co., 1924.

H. Grossmann, "Das Akkumulations und Zusammenbruchsgesetz des kapitalistischen Systems," Leipzig, C. L. Hirschfeld, 1929.

E. Goetschal, "Gut, Geld und Kapital," Bern, P. Haupt, 1921.

Irving Fischer, "The Nature of Capital and Income," New York, Macmillan Co., 1912.

R. P. Dutt, "Socialism and the Living Wage," London, The Communist Party of Great Britain, 1928.

E. M. Zurana, "Inquietud Universal, Sus Causas," Madrid, Editorial Rens, 1920.

F. O. Willey, "The Laborer and the Capitalist," New York, Equitable Publishing Co., 1896.

Norman Thomas, "What is Industrial Democracy?", New York, The League for Industrial Democracy, 1925.

Edwin Atkinson, "Labor and Capital Allies, not Enemies," New York, Harper & Bros., 1879.

M. Atkinson, "The New Social Order," Melbourne, Macmillan Co., 1920.

J. De Quivroga Barja, "La Crisis del Capitalismo," Madrid, A. Margo, 1930.

CHAPTER EIGHTH

The Problem of Religion

D. L. Furber, "Religion and Education in a Republic," Boston, Rand, Avery & Co., 1881.

C. E. Fitch, "Civil and Religious Liberty in America," Albany, 1893.

E. F. Abbot, "Free Religion in a Free State," Baltimore, J. P. Des Forges, 1872.

P. Belmont, "Political Equality and Religious Toleration," New York and London, G. P. Putnam's Sons, 1927.

W. Birney, "Function of the Church and State Distinguished," Battle Creek, 1897.

S. H. Cobb, "The Rise of Religious Liberty in America," New York, Macmillan Co., 1902.

A. C. Dieffenbach, "Religious Liberty, The Great American Delusion," New York, W. Morrow & Co., 1927.

J. M. Dohan, "Our State Constitutions and Religious Liberty," *American Catholic Quarterly Review*, Philadelphia, 1915.

L. Hühner, "The Struggle for Religious Liberty in North Carolina," American Jewish Historical Society, 1907.

L. Johnston, "Religious Liberty in the United States," Catholic University *Bulletin*, Washington, D. C., 1903.

J. S. Williams, "Religious Liberty in New York," Columbia University *Quarterly*, New York, 1915.

CHAPTER NINTH

The Problem of Prohibition

S. Crowther, "Prohibition and Prosperity," New York, The John Day Co., 1930.

J. Danielson, "Lincoln's Attitude Towards Prohibition," New York, Barnes Press, 1927.

C. S. Darrow and V. S. Yarros, "The Prohibition Mania," New York, Boni & Liveright, 1927.

E. L. Douglass, "Prohibition and Common Sense," New York, Alcohol Information Committee, 1931.

P. S. Du Pont, "Eighteenth Amendment Not a Remedy for the Drink Evil," Association against the Prohibition Amendment, Washington, D. C., 1929.

F. S. Elder, "The Problem of Liquor Control," Kansas City, Mo., Hyde Park Press, 1930.

H. W. Farman, "Confessions of a Prohibitionist," Hartford, Conn., Federation of Churches, 1923.

H. Feldman, "Prohibition, Its Economic and Industrial Aspects," New York and London, D. Appleton & Co., 1927.

Irving Fisher, "Prohibition at Its Worst," New York, The Macmillan Co., 1926.

M. J. E. Hartmann, "Prohibition and Its Consequences to American Liberty," St. Louis, Model Printing Co., 1923.

W. E. Borah (Senator), "The Constitution and Prohibition," Westerville, O., American Issue Publishing Co., 1926.

F. I. Cadawallader, "The Farce of Prohibition," New York, the Author, 1919.

J. M. Beck, "The Revolt Against Prohibition, An Address in the House of Representatives, February 7th, 1930," New York, Association Against the Prohibition Amendment.

H. Bogusat, "Das Alcohol verbot in den Vereinigton Staaten von Amerika und seine Folgen," Berlin, C. A. Schwetschke & Sohn, 1924.

E. Cole, "Sobriety," Philadelphia, Meroduk Publishing Co., 1925.

J. S. Auerbach, "An Indictment of Prohibition," New York and London, Harper & Bros., 1930.

CHAPTER TENTH

The Problem of Government

"A Syllabus in Government," the University of the State of New York, Albany, New York, 1918.

H. Taylor, "Origin of Government," Oxford, B. H. Blackwell, 1919.

W. C. MacLeod, "The Origin of the State," Philadelphia, 1924.

J. Hart, "Wie der Staat Entstand," Berlin, 1921.

"Soubies et Carette, Les Régimes Politiques au XXe Siecle," Paris, E. Flammarion, 1906.

C. A. Petrie, "The History of Government," London, Methuen & Co., 1929.

J. W. Burgess, "The Sanctity of Law," Boston and New York, Ginn & Co., 1927.

Noah Webster, "Sketches of American Policy," Hartford, Hudson & Goodwin, 1785.

W. J. Bryan, "The Royal Art," New York, F. H. Revell&Co.,1914.

C. F. Dole, "The American Citizen," Boston, Heath & Co., 1900.

H. J. Laski, "Politics," Philadelphia and London, J. B. Lippincott Co., 1931.

CHAPTER ELEVENTH

The Problem of Education

C. G. Pearse, "The Common School as an Instrument of Democracy," *Journal* of the National Education Association of the United States, 1916.

F. B. Pearson, "The Reconstructed School," Yonkers, World Book Co., 1919.

Noah Porter, "The American Colleges and the American Public," New York, C. Scribner's Sons, 1878.

Whitelaw Reid, "American and English Studies," New York, C. Scribner's Sons, 1913.

E. H. Reisner, "The Evolution of the Common School," New York, The Macmillan Co., 1930.

J. Ross, "The Heart of Democracy, the American Public Schools," Sandusky, J. Ross, 1930.

H. O. Rugg, "Culture and Education in America," New York, Harcourt, Brace & Co., 1931.

W. F. Russell, "Education in the United States," New York, Information Service, American Red Cross, 1920.

D. L. Sharp, "Education in a Democracy," Boston and New York, Houghton Mifflin Co., 1922.

J. Swett, "American Public Schools, History and Pedagogics," New York, American Book Co., 1900.

W. H. Taft, "Is a National Standard of Education Practicable," *Journal* of National Education Association of the United States, 1915.

J. J. Tigert, "The Faith of the American People in Public Education," Washington, D. C., Government Printing Office, 1925.

R. L. Wilbur, "A Philosophy of American Education," New York, National Industrial Conference Board, 1931.

F. D. Neill, "Earliest Efforts to Promote Education in English in North America," St. Paul, Minn., Macalester College Contributions, 1892.

CHAPTER TWELFTH

The Problem of Immigration

A. W. Thomas, "Facts in a Nutshell About Immigration, Yellow and White," Washington, D. C., Columbia Publishing Co., 1912.

R. Tritoni, "L'Immigrazione negli Stati Uniti, Politica," Roma, 1931.

Mr. Justice Field, "Power of the State to Exclude Foreigners, etc.," San Francisco, E. Bosqui & Co., 1874.

"Problems of the Immigration Service," Washington, D. C., Government Printing Office, 1929.

"Biological Aspects of Immigration," Washington, D. C., Government Printing Office, 1921.

"Proposed Restriction of Immigration," Washington, D. C., Government Printing Office, 1921.

"Analysis of America's Modern Melting Pot," Washington, D. C., Government Printing Office, 1923.

R. DeCourcy Ward, "Some Thoughts on Immigration Restriction," Boston, Immigration Restriction League, 1922.

J. Chickering, "Immigration Into the United States," Boston, C. C. Little and J. Brown, 1848.

Levi P. Morton, "Immigration, Its National Character and Importance," Address to the House of Representatives, Washington, D. C., Government Printing Office, 1880.

W. C. Herron, "Immigration," Cincinnati, 1892.

R. E. Ireton, "Immigration, a Vital National Issue," New York, Liberal Immigration League, 1908.

"Immigration, with Particular Reference to the Jews," Addresses by M. J. Kohler, Hon. C. Nagel and J. H. Schiff, New York, 1911.

T. A. Hourwich, "Immigration and Crime," Chicago, 1912.

M. J. Kohler, "The Immigration Problem and the Right of Asylum for the Persecuted," Baltimore, 1913.

G. E. Barston, "Shall We Bar the Immigrant?" Barston, Texas, 1914.

S. L. Gulick, "A Comprehensive Immigration Policy and Program," New York, 1915.

W. G. Harding, "Immigration and Americanization," Address at Portland, Oregon, July 4th, 1923, Washington, D. C., Government Printing Office.

Y. Ichihashi, "Japanese Immigration," San Francisco, Japanese Association of America, 1913.

CHAPTER THIRTEENTH

The Problem of World Policy

W. F. Johnson, "America's Foreign Relations," New York, 1916.

J. M. Mathews, "The Conduct of American Foreign Relations," New York, 1922.

J. B. Moore, "Principles of American Diplomacy," New York, 1918.

A. C. Coolidge, "The United States as a World Power," J. H. Latané, "The United States as a World Power," New York, 1907.

A. B. Hart, "The Monroe Doctrine, An Interpretation," Boston, 1916.

A. T. Mahan, "Interest of the United States in the Sea Power," New York, 1902.

L. C. and P. F. Ford, "The Foreign Trade of the United States," New York, 1920.

J. B. Lockey, "Pan-Americanism, Its Beginnings," New York, 1920.

J. H. Latané, "The United States and Latin America," New York, 1920.

P. J. Treat, "Japan and the United States," Boston, 1921.

M. M. Kalaw, "Self-Government in the Philippine Islands," New York, 1919.

F. A. Ogg, "National Progress; 1907-1917" (Vol. XXVII of the *American Nation*, New York, 1918).

W. E. Weyl, "American World Policies," New York, 1917.

J. W. Foster, "A Century of American Diplomacy," Boston, 1900.

H. A. Gibbons, "An Introduction to World Politics," New York, The Century Company, 1922.

W. J. Abbot, "The United States in the Great War."

G. Murray, "Faith, War and Policy," Boston and New York, Houghton Mifflin Company, 1917.

CHAPTER FOURTEENTH

The New Deal

"The A B C of the N R A," Staff of the Brooking Institution, Brooking Institution, Washington, D. C., 1934.

Franklin D. Roosevelt, "Looking Forward," New York, John Day Company, 1933.

United States, National Recovery Administration, Handbook for Speakers, "The President's Emergency Reemployment Program," Washington, D. C., Government Printing Office, 1933.

J. H. Richardson, "President Roosevelt's Recovery Experiment," London Quarterly and *Holborn Review*, London, 1934.

R. W. G. Mackay, "America 1933 and the Industrial Recovery Act," Sydney, Australia, 1933.

Nathan Isaacs and C. F. Taeusch, "The NRA in the Book and in Business," *Harvard Law Review*, 1934.

Charles Gulick, Jr., "Some Economic Aspects of the N I R A," Columbia *Law Review*, Brattleboro, Vt., 1933.

J. G. Frederick, "A Primer of 'New Deal' Economics," New York, *The Business Bourse*, 1934.

CHAPTER FIFTEENTH

Hitlerism in America

Marggrete Wiener, "Vom Nationalsozialistischem Wirtschaftsprogram," Berlin, 1931.

E. W. D. Tennant, "Herr Hitler and His Policy," London, *English Review*, 1933.

Rolf Stuermer, "Was will der National-sozialismus," Berlin, Roesicke, 1930

Johannes Steele, "Hitler as Frankenstein," London, Wishart & Co., 1933.

Fritz Sotke, "Die National-sozialistische Staatsidel," Berlin, 1932.

Dr. Rudolf, "Nationalsozialismus und Rasse," Munich, F. Eher, Nachfolger, 1931.

Hans Phillip, "Der Jud ist Schuld," Vienna, Wiener Volksbuchhandlung, 1932.

Nordicus (Pseudonym), "The Iron Fist in Germany," New York, Mohawk Press, 1932.

Adolf Hitler, "Mein Kampf," Munich, F. Eher, Nachfolger, 1931.

Ludwig Kuhner, "Nazis, Der Blödeste Hokus-pokus der Nachkriegszeit," Aachen, Freie Presse, 1931.

INDEX

Schools, public, should be absolutely non-sectarian, 114-115; task of, 178-179; statistics of, 179 et seq.; force for Americanization, 114; results of, disappointing, 181; demands of people on, 182; public complaints concerning, 182-183; blamed for low ethical condition of youth, 187 et seq.; do not exercise spiritual influence, 196 et seq.

Schurz, Carl, German revolutionist, 207

Science given as an explanation for increase in crime, 186

Science, Christian, classed as Christian sect, 112

Scopes, Thomas A., punished in Tennessee for teaching Darwinism, 264

Scotland, first temperance society, 129

Scott, Howard, proposer of Technocracy, 78

Scouts, Boy, excellent methods of, 193 et seq.; Law of, 193 et seq.

Sedition, attempts to force un-American legislation a species of, 121

See, Holy, accused of controlling Catholic citizens, 119

Seligman, Prof. Edwin R. A., proposes "socialized individualism," 92

Senate, U. S., former manner of selection undemocratic, 20, 161-163

Senators, each state entitled to two without regard to population, 19; elected by popular vote under the Seventeenth Amendment, 20

Separation, of Church and State violated by participation of clergy in politics, 121-123; not indispensable in a Republic, 197

Serajevo, capital of Bosnia, scene of murder of Austrian Archduke, 229

Service, compulsory military, 229; propaganda and espionage, 230

Shintoism, not represented in U. S., 112

"Silver Shirts of America," the, organization similar to the Nazis, 21, 254

Simon, Dr. Carleton, denies increase in youthful criminality, 187

Skibbereen, Temperance Society at, 130

Skill, human, required to provide sustenance for men, 61-62

Slang, low form of speech, 183; examples of, 183

Slave hunters, methods of, 37

Slavery, in U. S., cruel and inhuman, 38; contrary to democracy, 165

Slaves, emancipated in British Colonies, 38; in United States, 38

Slave Trade, African, 37; begun by Portuguese, 37; English 37

Sleeping cars, Pullman, Negroes excluded, 42

Smith, Alfred E., defeated because Catholic, 21; condemns Hitlerism, 253

Socialism, 77 et seq.

Socialists, disliked by Americans, 266

Soil, ultimate right to, vested in Nation, 102

South Africa, modern agricultural methods lessen number of laborers, 65

Southern States, aversion to the Negro in, 35

Soviet, government engages American technicians, 181

Spain, infested by brigands, 72

Spanknoebel, Heinz, Nazi agitator, 251

Speakeasies, reason for, 151

Speech, Freedom of, should not be refused to radicals, 267-268

Spirit, group, can be utilized ethically, 193; power of, 193

Spirituals, Negro, 40

Squandering, of national resources, 73

St. Domingo, 37

State, must protect welfare of its nationals, 102

States, desired to preserve their identity, 162; produces inequalities, 162-163; Latin-American, effect of Monroe Doctrine on, 226

Stowe, Harriet Beecher, depicts slavery conditions in "Uncle Tom's Cabin," 38

Straus, Nathan, highly esteemed Jewish citizen, 51

Street cars, need only one man, 67

Stuyvesant, Peter, Dutch Governor of Nieuw Amsterdam, unfriendly to Jews, 46-47

Suasion, moral, as means of discipline, 201

Submarine Campaign, German, arouses anger against Germany, 232

Subsistence farms, 247

Subway trains, mechanical operation of, displaces men, 66

Sulzer, Governor William, deposed for refusal to obey boss, 169

Sunday laws, infringe on religious liberty, 112-114

Sussex, American vessel attacked by Germans, 232

Tammany Hall, methods of, 169

Tariff, lowering it will not solve the economic problem, 95; protective, not necessarily characteristic of policy of Republican Party, 170

Taxation, unendurable, 73

Tchinovnik, Russian official, 75

Teacher, must antagonize anti-moral tendencies, 191

Technocracy, economic system proposed by Howard Scott, 78

Technological cause of unemployment, 65

Teetotalers, 130

Temperance, American Society for the Promotion of, 129; same as Total Abstinence, 130; movement at first voluntary, 130

Tennessee, State of, prohibits teaching of Darwinism, 264